shadowy heroes

IRISH STUDIES

shadowy heroes
Irish Literature of the 1890s

WAYNE E. HALL

SYRACUSE UNIVERSITY PRESS
1980

Wayne E. Hall received the M.A. and Ph.D. from Indiana University and has studied at the University of Tübingen in Germany as a Fulbright Fellow. He has contributed to *Éire-Ireland* and *Irish Renaissance Annual* and is currently Charles Phelps Taft Postdoctoral Fellow at the University of Cincinnati.

A version of "Edward Martyn (1859–1923): Politics and Drama of Ice," copyright 1980 © by the Irish American Cultural Institute, is reprinted here by kind permission of the Irish American Cultural Institute and the editors of *Éire-Ireland*.

A version of "Esther Waters: An Irish Story" is reprinted here from *Irish Renaissance Annual I* (April 1980), ed. Zack Bowen (Newark, Del.: University of Delaware Press, 1980), by permission.

Library of Congress Cataloging in Publication Data

Hall, Wayne E.
Shadowy Heroes: Irish literature of the 1890s.

(Irish studies series)
Bibliography: p. 227
Includes index.
1. English literature—Irish authors—History and criticism.   2. English literature—
19th century—History and criticism.   3. Ireland in literature.   4. Ireland—History
—1837–1901.   I. Title.   II. Series.
PR8750.H3   820'9'008   80-21383
ISBN 0-8156-2231-7

contents

illustrations

acknowleðgments

A number of generous people and equally generous institutions have helped me in preparing this work, and I am under special obligation to all of them. Thanks very much to the Charles Phelps Taft Foundation of the University of Cincinnati, whose assistance, in the form of a postdoctoral fellowship, enabled me to complete this book; to the American Council of Learned Societies, for a postdoctoral grant to do summer research in Ireland; to Indiana University, for a grant-in-aid for research in Ireland; to Professor Donald Gray, Indiana University, for guiding this through its first version as a dissertation; to Professor Richard Fallis, Syracuse University, for editorial guidance and comments; to Professors Scott Sanders, Henry H. H. Remak, James Naremore, and Alfred David, Indiana University; Hugh Staples and Edgar Slotkin, University of Cincinnati; and Paul F. Casey, University College, Galway, for editorial comments and helpful suggestions; to Malcolm Brown, for writing *The Politics of Irish Literature*; to Fritz Senn, for making Irish studies come alive; to Arlene and to my parents; to Ciaran and Geraldine Nicholson, for Irish hospitality and friendship; and to Heather, for almost everything, but especially for understanding. Finally, this work is dedicated to Andy.

Cincinnati, Ohio   Wayne E. Hall
May 1980

introduction

T he Irish writers of the 1890s seek over and over to create for their literature and nation a hero, to define his values and, most importantly, to determine what he is to do. They frequently cast him as a dark, tragic figure, paralyzed by his own passionate nature or thwarted by external forces that frustrate his intentions and overturn his accomplishments. Material victories prove ephemeral and some-times lead to the complete ruin of the person who has relied on action; but more often, "too good for this world," he gains a moral victory in his loss. The external defeat necessary to define his heroism also confirms the superiority of his inner qualities: simplicity, innocence, disciplined pride, spiritual intuition, and the capacity for transcendent vision. The literary hero, like the Irish artists in their society, cultivates failure and frustration as an essential part of his experience, or else he withdraws completely from action. Because he is often a distinctly Irish hero who bears a name from Celtic legend or who stands for Irish independence, he contributes on one level to a nationalistic and politi-cal consciousness. But insofar as he fails to act or demonstrates the unreliability of action, the Irish hero is an anomaly within a broad national commitment in the 1890s to revolutionary social and political change.

The 1890s proved to be the last full decade in which the Protes-tant Ascendancy possessed anything approaching its once total control over land, power, and privileges in Ireland. In gradual decline ever since the Great Famine, the Ascendancy could no longer resist the demands for change, especially for land reform. The large mass of people had long regarded landlordism as one of the most pernicious causes of Ireland's many problems. In the wake of the Famine, voter hostility began to strip the landed class of its representation within the Irish parliamentary party. Seeking to head off the Home Rule policies

of the party and its leader, Charles Stewart Parnell, Westminster passed down several land bills in the 1880s that steadily chipped away at the large estates, many already encumbered by the economic squeeze of fixed costs and falling revenues. Especially during the years 1879–82, when the Land War brought about a more local and violent assault against landlordism, agrarian discontent also helped clear the way for those principles and practices that, over the next thirty years, transformed many tenants into the owners of the land they tilled.

The writers of the 1890s, faced with the rising prosperity of the lower and middle classes, identified their own interests with those of the old social order and the landed gentry. They saw modern Ireland moving in the wrong direction, away from its cultural traditions and a time when society had been aristocratic, feudal, ritualized, and unified. Members of the Ascendancy, attracted to the same ideals of the past, did not lack for connections to the artistic movement, even as they continued to influence Ireland's political affairs. Captain John Shawe-Taylor, who initiated the Land Conference summons preparing the way for the Wyndham Land Act of 1903, was one of Yeats's heroes and Lady Gregory's nephews. Another nephew, Sir Hugh Lane, later suggested the creation and endowment of a Dublin gallery for modern art. Sir Horace Plunkett, associated with Lady Gregory's circle by the mid-1890s, enlisted the help of George Russell in promoting agricultural cooperation. The practical men of power in Ireland could find much in common with the poetic dreamers.

An aristocratic vision of life began to take shape as the framework most conducive to a great national renaissance of art. Such a heritage promised the writers a continuous cultural tradition, disciplined and full of conviction, based on the validity of excellence. Property, especially land, gave to its holders an awareness of time and place and an organic connection to a whole society. The Big House, permanent and powerful, served as the ritualized center in a stable, hierarchical community that accorded each person a definite status and thus created a strong network of loyalties. Like the tenants, the aristocrats had earned their privileges, for they maintained high standards of conduct, governed the ill-equipped masses, and kept alive the tradition of excellence. Those ages most settled and static, like the Medieval period, seemed closest to the ideal. And if such a culture had never actually existed in Ireland, then literature could create it. Historical limitations gave way before mythic possibilities. The past became subjective, a code of heroic values and precise patterns, not a linear sequence of events and experiences. Sequences progressed

and changed, sometimes dangerously, while history, it was hoped, need not.

The hero in such an age might well be cultured and urbane, his ideals in perfect proportion to those of his society. Yet history did progress, in ways the writers were acutely aware of, and modern Ireland required a new kind of heroism. In England, perhaps, poets could still claim a harmony between the private code of the hero and that of his society, see him as idealized man replacing an ideal Christian savior and representing England's material power besides. Ireland had experienced a different legacy, however, one that had little to do with power or success. Lady Gregory felt that the Irish poet "is in touch with a people . . . whose heroes have been the failures . . . who went out to a battle that was already lost."[1] This melancholia of the lost cause grew out of a national sense of tragedy. Ireland had suffered defeat and domination by a greater military power, and the subsequent occupation of the country drove home even deeper the feeling that a precious heritage was lost. In the wake of such a legacy, therefore, the hero could not serve his society in any useful way except by presenting an ideal image, aloof and lonely, of values translated into a single life. The image did, however, preserve a messianic potential for salvation.

The theme of the lost cause suggested at once passivity and power. British journals often personified "Hibernia" as a beautiful woman threatened by ape-featured terrorists and protected by strong John Bull. The Irish readily adapted this image to their own female figures, Cathleen ni Houlihan or the Shan Van Vocht. Since heroes stood more clear of external reality, not merely acted upon by circumstances but free to act and shape destiny, the heroine seemed more subjective and involved with personal feelings. She herself likely would not succeed, but especially within the context of Catholic beliefs in the Virgin Mary, the heroine suggested other possibilities of rebirth and redemption. Ireland's defeat seemed to give the nation a spiritual power greater in its way than British material might. In an article evoking the influence of "defeated and conquered Judea," Yeats claimed that "the spiritual history of the world has been the history of conquered races."[2] A great movement in Irish art, Yeats felt, could release this spiritual force; if Ireland accepted such a movement, "The Irish race would have become a chosen race."[3]

The Irish Renaissance turned to the Jewish theme as readily as did the popular press. John F. Taylor, lawyer and literary society member, compared Ireland to the Israelites in the court of the Pharaoh, a speech later recalled by both Yeats and Joyce. In late 1899 Taylor

published a series in the *Daily Express* on the Dreyfus case in France, which had been covered by the papers as early as 1894 and which further suggested an Irish-Jewish connection to Taylor. The opposition of an advanced, powerful civilization to a simple, agrarian community provided one of the central structures for the literary movement. Like Egypt, England had created an industrial collective and an attendant materialism that corrupted morals and ideals. The Irish had sustained the communities and, to prove their point, would create new ones, from literary societies in the capital city of the decadent empire to secret cults in remote Irish castles.

Central to this dichotomy was a commitment to Ireland as an essentially agrarian country. Literature needed contact with the soil to maintain its strength, "Antaeus-like," and its appropriate relationship to past and place. Without an authentic and traditional agrarian culture, a literature of the people would remain artificial or sentimental. The landlord-tenant system thus emerged as a key stabilizing element, one that allowed economic customs to perfect themselves and then to lead into aesthetic patterns. Secure, simple, traditional labor would foster efficiency and joy, formal unity and spontaneous grace. A supernatural sense of the land and its regional myths, like racial uniformity, also unified the society by transcending class differences. By contrast, interest in material progress, especially among the middle class, would divide the various sectors. Greater economic freedom would only make the tenants worse off; education should be limited to a select few.

Agrarianism was an organic model based on religion and nature and opposed to the city, a mechanical model of technology based on materialism and industrialism. One could have Progress (rationalism, science, this world), or one could stay with Providence (faith, myth, the mystery of nature). Especially when linked to a social and aesthetic unity that would replace modern disunity, the choice seemed clear. Industry helped science and rationalism render spiritual values intellectual and artificial. Amalgamating all cultures and hence lacking any roots, the city became abstract and imitative, an environment deadly to an artistic movement.

Although hostile, the criticism of industrialism and urban life was frequently sound. The writers condemned labor that had been stripped of tradition and injected with a new, artificial tension. Industry ignored the mystery of life and created the dangerous illusion of power over nature. Functional and pragmatic, it destroyed any sense of the sublime. Modern communications weakened the uniquely local

traditions and contributed to the anxiety of rootlessness. Victorian writers such as Morris, Carlyle, and Ruskin had earlier defended feudalism over industrial modernism and opposed the tendency in nineteenth-century naturalism to deplete any emotional faith in the unity of life. The Irish writers, in turn, combatted the English doctrine of progress by looking toward the traditions of their own country.

Irish Catholicism presented the literary movement with a unique problem, however. The writers themselves, with few exceptions, were not Catholic and saw the Church as allied with utilitarianism in its view of nature as something humanity could exploit for its own use. Catholicism denied the possibility of a transcendent spirit in nature, while the writers celebrated the untouched waste places. The Church stressed the relationship of the individual to society, while the writers identified him with nature in a process of spiritual communion. Apart from civilization, the unspoiled wilderness became a serene sanctuary from that public world so zealously watched over by the clergy. In addition, violations of narrow doctrinal issues occasionally exposed literature to charges of anti-Catholicism. Yet the literary movement also admired the Church for its power to maintain social order, religious ritual, myths and traditions, and a definite hierarchy. Religion was important, not for its doctrine, but for its symbols and aesthetic forms. Catholicism thus came to seem at least a partial ally against the modernist threat to social morality and a sense of the divine. Science, progress, rationalism, industry, all these relied on the practical will and ignored religious feeling. Truths should instead be emotionally intuited, not intellectually derived, a matter for the soul and not the reasoning mind.

From this idealized view of the past and hostile view of the present, the literary movement could readily extract some clear conceptions about the nature of art. Industry was based on materialism; art should be spiritual. Technology was functional and rational; art should be heroic and passionate. Cosmopolitanism had diluted the roots and traditions; art should rely on memory and a sense of past and place. Progress had levelled the classes; art should stress hierarchy and excellence. The city had eliminated leisure; art should be serene, part of one's everyday habits, not confined to the museums. Science had become abstract and artificial; art should be concrete and natural. Civilization had made humanity complex and diversified; art should be

simple and ritualized. Commercialism had devalued art to the level of a utilitarian commodity financed by the philistines; art should be enjoyed by a learned elite. In their current tastes in reading, the Irish people seemed to prefer either a superficial romanticism of the past or an aggressive journalism advocating political and social change. The new national literature would create an authentic awareness of tradition and avoid the methods of propaganda, for within the social order, genuine art had the potential for great cultural achievement.

In deriving its view of history and art, the literary movement also had to confront some theoretical inconsistencies. There was a central confusion over what should come first, the restoration of a desired way of life, or the creation of a literature that would make such a culture possible but that also required the culture for its original, nourishing context. The writers envisioned an organic society and turned to artificial means for its realization. A unified social fabric was fundamentally unconscious, yet the movement sought consciously to change that fabric, in part by retreating from society. Despite their faith in uncontrolled nature, the writers desired control.

To resolve such doctrinal paradoxes, the literary movement could turn to its image of the hero, for he participated both in the idealized past and in the actual, imperfect present. The past could thus be accepted as a deliberate fiction allowing the artist a whole view of life. History or society might depart from the ideal, but literature would hold to the more unifying vision. Through Standish O'Grady's *History of Ireland*, for example, the writers could resurrect from Irish legend the heroic figure of Cuchulain. More "organic" and "natural" sources were at hand, such as nineteenth-century peasant culture. Yet the peasantry had largely ignored Cuchulain and dwelt instead on the legend of Finn MacCool, who seemed much less appropriate to the early Irish Renaissance and who thus had to await rebirth in Joyce's work.[4] Legends were fictions as deliberate as a literary concept of the past, demanding selection and subjectivity at those points where history or society had gone astray. As a more aristocratic hero than Finn MacCool, Cuchulain better corresponded to an idealized view of Ireland's past. Furthermore, he had suffered failure and loss and, in his tragedy, thus corresponded to the writers' more realistic appraisal of the present as well. History was progressing, Ireland was changing, and an artistic movement, however heroic, had little chance to stop it.

More optimistic visions of the future did, of course, emerge. With agrarian unrest largely resolved, it was hoped that Ireland would now settle for a consolidation of its material gains. As part of the

movement towards national independence, the agitation had proven necessary and useful but should now give way to the artistic renaissance. Yeats, beginning to turn aside himself from his visions of apocalypse, advocated just such a direction in a letter to D. P. Moran's paper, the *Leader*, in September 1900:

> I myself believe that unless a great foreign war comes to re-make everything, we must be prepared to turn from a purely political nationalism with the land question as its lever, to a partly intellectual and historical nationalism like that of Norway, with the language question as its lever.

"The partial settlement of the land question," Yeats went on, had defused that pressure for independence, and the "ten years of recrimination" following Parnell's death had so tarnished politics that "the people of Ireland will not in our time give a full trust to any man who has not made some great spectacular sacrifice for his convictions."[5] The problem of trust ran very deep, even within the cultural revival, for Yeats and Moran themselves had split sharply in the past over methods and goals. In a subsequent issue of the *Leader*, Moran issued a strong complaint against similar barriers to national progress: "The most deep-rooted faith in modern Ireland is the extraordinary Irish lack of faith in Irishmen. This perverted faith in Irish incompetence pervades the very atmosphere we breathe." On the same page and a different subject, Moran then unwittingly bore out his own complaint by describing the "curious modern Irish instinct for doing the wrong thing."[6] What, indeed, was the right thing? Given his nature and values, what was the hero now to do to regain the trust of Ireland, transform the country, and lead it into an ideal future? The question had occupied the Literary Revival from its outset and seemed inevitably connected with heroic sacrifice and loss. Further from an answer now than at the beginning of the decade, the writers could resolve even less their own deep distrust of Ireland and its ability or willingness to follow the paths they desired.

The ideals and goals of the Irish Renaissance thus resisted any lasting harmony with Ireland's political events or economic changes. The response of the poet to the decline of the Protestant Ascendancy differed from that of the politician, the shopkeeper, or the tenant, and even the desires for national independence elicited differing images of the hero. Yet the collective solutions of one social group originated in

problems perceived by the whole nation, and they closely related to and affected solutions of the others. Irish history over the latter half of the nineteenth century was not mere "background" to the literature, it was the shared social experience out of which the literature was born. The writers gave one kind of shape and unity to this experience, and their work cannot be dismissed with terms like escapist, decadent, or counter revolutionary. Yet the limitations of the writing can be clarified insofar as the artists and their work are seen to be alienated from much of the Irish society.

The situation of the Protestant Ascendancy, in particular, gave the writers a world view that forms many of the attitudes and values in the literature. Even more particularly, Parnell gave them a model of the aloof, aristocratic hero whose ideals, within the external realm of action, must inevitably fail. To sense the complexity with which these separate elements combine in the literature, we can consider the example of a theme as universal as that of love. Few of the major writers from this decade ever married, Yeats not until 1917 after years of transforming unrequited love for Maud Gonne into a major concern in his poetry. The decline of the gentry gave impetus to the literary motif of childlessness, as failure at action became analogous to failure at love. Parnell's calamitous relations with Katharine O'Shea seemed to demonstrate those connections even more conclusively. Among the intellectual groups, the tenets of Madame Blavatsky's theosophy further encouraged an idea of celibacy among writers and literary characters that, throughout the 1890s, relentlessly attacks any hope that love might bring success or happiness. In such a society, and doomed to failure, the hero finally could do nothing.

shadowy heroes

economics, religion, and society

To speak of the "Irish question" leads one to expect, somewhere, an Irish answer. British parliamentarians and administrators, rarely all that interested in Ireland, moved in the ponderous and unresponsive manner of any world empire's bureaucracy. Yet by the end of the nineteenth century they had proposed an ambitious array of answers: famine relief, coercion measures, local government reform, disestablishment of the Church of Ireland, improvements in education, increased voter registration, and a continuous series of land reform bills. Largely because of their piecemeal nature, however, none of the answers did what they were supposed — pacify Ireland. The social experiments England tried out on the Irish had been designed for single problems only, whereas the Irish question in the latter half of the century consisted of several interlocking parts: who was to govern Ireland, the English or the Irish; which religion would dominate in the society, Protestant or Catholic; and who was to own the land, the wealthy few or the large numbers of poor. Simplicity occasionally emerged from the tangle, as when the recurring periods of famine made land ownership a question of who was to survive. More typically, however, the Irish question just settled even deeper into the unmanageable bog of evidence collected by yet one more government commission.

What wonder, then, that many in England turned to on-the-scene commentators, such as William Carleton, whose popular literary accounts seemed to explain the Irish peasantry to his English audiences. Writers like Charles Lever and Samuel Lover further aided the British in categorizing their curious neighbors. There was Handy Andy, simple, innocent, and fun loving; or there was the savage, ape-featured terrorist. Conciliatory gestures towards the first, therefore, often went

1

hand in hand with coercive measures against the second, a combination sure to alienate almost everyone in Ireland in some way. During the Land War, increasingly violent and widespread forms of agrarian agitation also led the British to see the Irish question as a peasant problem. Measured against England's industry, progress, and shopkeeper prosperity, Ireland seemed headed backwards into dangerous and lawless primitivism.

This view contained some elements of truth. Outside of Ulster, Ireland was largely a poor, agrarian country relying on hopelessly outdated methods of farming and resisting any attempts at modernization throughout the century. The Great Famine that devastated the peasantry from 1845 to 1850 added tremendous weight, psychological as well as economic, to the demands for an equitable distribution of land. Yet even within the exploitative landlord-tenant system, Irish agriculture and the Famine turned many landowners into victims as well. Partly because of restrictions imposed by the land bills, owners often did little to improve their estates, content to let things run themselves in a manner that had some benevolent effects but that hardly followed the most efficient or profitable course.

Ireland's main problem by midcentury was the intense pressure of population on land. A competitive market had grown up that rewarded those who held land, so that increasingly smaller holdings proliferated and allowed several family members each to receive a fraction of an original holding, itself perhaps only marginally profitable. The cultivation of potatoes, one of the most labor-intensive of all agricultural practices, required little space, allowed for early marriages and large families, and led to a widespread subsistence-level existence on small plots to which the tenants clung with elemental tenacity. The potato crop made possible the large increase in population, yet the potato occupied exactly that point at which the culture of poverty was vulnerable. The rural economy lacked the ready capital available in Ireland's other economy, the maritime sector along the east coast, which was tied more directly to England and which enjoyed cheap labor imported from rural areas. Without enough flexibility to make more profitable risk investments, landlords and tenants could not respond adequately to shifts in the market structure. Although the trend from 1815 onward had been from tillage to pasture, this produced only marginal effects before the Famine. When the repeal of the Corn Laws in 1846 helped decrease wheat and increase cattle prices, the agricultural sector began a more rapid shift from an intensive to an extensive basis, one that could not absorb all the people from the countryside. With ruthless efficiency, however, the Famine years

would relieve the economy of much of the population it had previously tried to sustain.

In immediate and drastic ways, the Great Famine began the reshaping of Irish society. Between 1846 and 1851, the population dropped from 8.5 to 6.5 million, half of that loss resulting from disease or starvation, with another million people taking refuge in emigration and thus setting a pattern that continued to drain the country through-out the century.[1] The eviction of tenants reached unprecedented levels as landlords sought to resolve their own financial pressures by clearing the marginal, uneconomic plots and consolidating them into more efficient holdings. From 1849 to 1851 alone, 50,000 families were evicted,[2] and over the course of the decade, well over 300,000 holdings under five acres were wiped out.[3] The Irish landlords made local provisions for relief in many cases and still paid poor-law rates, al-though evictions reduced that liability. Yet they concerned themselves primarily with the question of how to salvage their estates. Exports of cattle actually rose at a steady rate throughout the Famine; the number of pigs, on the other hand, which depended on the potato crop and which were kept on the smaller holdings, fell sharply. In their search for increased revenues from abroad to supplement diminished rents, and in their apparent willingness to sacrifice the tenants, the landlords came even more to seem like alien oppressors in their own country.

The combination of falling rents, poor-law rates, and fixed expenses did ruin many landlords during the Famine. In its aftermath liquidation courts set up by the Encumbered Estates Act of 1849 sold about five million acres, one-fourth of the total area of the country.[4] As the new landlords and those who had survived the crises set about consolidating the estates, primarily into average farms of fifteen to thirty acres, subsistence-level agriculture began to disappear. The process of clearing and consolidation received added impetus from the nearly periodic failures of the potato crop throughout the century and from the tenants' own desire now to improve their status by using advantageous marriages as a way of combining farms. As children waited for their parents to turn over the land, they also married increasingly later, while those who failed to get an inheritance had few opportunities beyond emigration. Tenant-rights organizations began to lend assistance in the late 1840s but could do little for the now superfluous groups like the agricultural laborers. These men enjoyed higher wages when they worked, but employment was seasonal, and livestock did not require as much labor as crops. The gap between the established farmer and the landless man came to mirror the previous landlord-tenant divisions.

The visible effects of the Famine were staggering enough. A whole layer of people who could barely maintain a livelihood during good years underwent immense suffering and loss, and the whole character and practice of agriculture changed in a short period. Some less tangible effects also developed, however. The English had demonstrated their inability to help in any adequate way during times of need, thus alienating themselves still further from the Irish and carrying the landlords with them into the role of oppressors from the outside. In addition, emigration radically changed the nature of the Irish question by giving it a new international dimension.[5] Barbara Solow has demonstrated that post-Famine evictions and rack-renting were statistically not as common as popular accounts suggest, and that legal restrictions as well as self-interest discouraged the landlords from taking such steps. Between 1856 and 1876, by contrast with the Famine rate, evictions averaged fewer than 860 a year, and rent increases remained at a rate commensurate with price increases.[6] As F. S. L. Lyons notes in considering Solow's arguments on eviction, however, the landlords

> still did possess the power for non-payment of rent. There were enough examples of such eviction on the smaller, uneconomic estates for the mere threat of being turned out of their holdings to have an immense psychological effect on the tenant-farmers when times grew hard again.[7]

Within Ireland the idea persisted that land should belong to those who worked it, and this concept readily turned to the belief that eliminating the landlord-tenant system would significantly improve the whole country.

This last idea was extensively developed by James Fintan Lalor, who in 1847 began a scathing series of letters to the Irish press, primarily to the Young Ireland publication, the *Nation*. Lalor argued the importance of a "secure and independent agricultural peasantry," one that owned property and determined its use.[8] He placed the land issue squarely ahead of parliamentary concerns and, toward an improvement in agricultural conditions, advocated methods ranging from a general rent strike to violent clashes with those landlords who refused the necessary changes.

> It is a mere question between a people and a class, between a people of eight millions and a class of eight thousand. They or we must quit this

island. ... They form no class of the Irish people, or of any other people. Strangers they are in this land they call theirs, strangers here and strangers everywhere; owning no country and owned by none; rejecting Ireland and rejected by England; tyrants to this island and slaves to another; here they stand, hating and hated, their hand ever against us, as ours against them, an outcast and ruffianly horde, alone in the world and alone in its history, a class by themselves.[9]

The rhetoric creates a string of oppositions as relentless as the daily reports of Famine deaths, as determined to drum the landlords out of Ireland as they seemed to be in packing the emigrant ships. Lalor's proposals were highly radical, even for the Famine period, but his sentiments came more and more to threaten the landed class with the prospect that their position in Ireland might indeed be as alien as Lalor described.

The concept of peasant proprietorship had come up earlier in Thomas Davis' 1841 essay, "Udalism and Feudalism," one of his strongest and most important pleas for an agrarian economy based on a sturdy, landowning peasantry. Beyond this vision of a nation of yeoman farmers, Davis also advocated the guidance of an industrious middle class. While deploring English materialism, he saw the need for more extensive, and more benevolent, Irish industrialism, and much of the essay analyzed such economic issues as import duties and tariffs. The mystique of cultural nationalism, the concept for which Davis is most remembered, would supply the basis for such a nation. Even though he indirectly praised the dedication to violent resistance, Davis focused on methods substantially more gentle than those of his Young Ireland colleague Lalor.[10]

Despite Irish visions of a peasant proprietorship, even ones fitted out with concrete proposals for their realization, and despite losses during the Famine, the landed class held considerable power throughout the century. In the mid-1870s, twenty-five years after bankrupt landlords had begun to sell out under the terms of the Encumbered Estates Act, over 90 percent of the land still belonged to 6,500 proprietors, each with at least 500 acres, and with an average estate amounting to 2,700 acres; fewer than a thousand landlords owned half the country, their estates averaging 10,000 acres apiece.[11] At the other end of the economic spectrum, nearly 250,000 holdings in 1871 contained fewer than fifteen acres.[12] Such disproportions tended to blur the complex and overlapping class structure between the two poles, making England's task of finding any right answers that much

more difficult. A proprietor with 100 acres or more was considered a landlord, yet there was a fairly prosperous group of tenants on long-term leases and of middlemen who sublet land they rented. The largest rural group, tenants at will, held renewable leases of one year and, when they could, also sublet to a subtenant group. Cottiers took further minuscule sublet plots under living conditions far more primitive and uncertain than those of any group except the landless rural laborers.

The rural economic divisions inevitably blended into related cultural divisions, ones further conditioned by the effects of British colonization. The peasants in the West were hardly affected by the Anglicization that noticeably influenced tenants in other areas, while the urban middle class was both strongly Anglicized and resentful of the English influence. A small but significant group themselves in Ireland, the British stayed closely allied with the Unionist Protestants; yet this last group produced a sizeable number of defectors, Protestants alienated from their Ascendancy class, the Unionist cause, and the Anglicized manners of the native Irish. Each of these cultural groups identified with some common issues and disagreed over others. Meanwhile, back in Westminster, parliamentarians had to sort out the various needs and sympathies and decide which sector in Ireland was to be served by which particular piece of legislation.

For the poorer areas in the West, nothing seemed to help, and conditions there improved very little until the 1880s or even, in some cases, much later. On 11 April 1898, the *Freeman's Journal* wrote: "It is incredible that men like the Marquis of Sligo, drawing an income of £20,000 a year out of the district, should thus grind the faces of the poor, should rob the wretched widow of the last cow that gives milk to her starving children." The area from which Yeats was drawing spiritual sustenance led other eyewitness commentators, in letters to the *Freeman* and to *United Ireland*, to report famine conditions, eviction proceedings, and a seeming return to the old state of landlord-tenant affairs. The neighboring county of Mayo, poor in natural resources, likewise strained under a much higher population than the land could support in the latter half of the century. Much of the rest of Ireland, meanwhile, where population density and size of farms were moderate, had shifted into livestock. Displaced tenants and agricultural laborers from those areas, no longer able to find work within the new agricultural system, moved to counties like Mayo where the less advanced economy seemed to promise them employment and a holding of land. A continuation of pre-Famine patterns of early marriages also

kept the population increasing in the West, in marked contrast to the rest of the country. Where poverty helped restrict possibilities for emigration, the increase in numbers remained strong in the 1860s and did not begin a sharp decline until the 1880s.[13]

The Land Act of 1870 signalled a new direction in the course of the landlord-tenant relationship. Although significant as symbol, however, it achieved few concrete benefits. Tenants received the terms of "Ulster custom," the right to fair rents and credit for improvements, while landlords retained much of their old legal power, particularly the right to increase rents and to evict. The act further served to restrict landlord investment in agriculture at a time when ready capital from the owners could have significantly expanded and modernized agricultural practices. And it provided few incentives to sell or even buy land; under its terms only 877 holdings changed hands.[14] Even though the bill began the legal elimination of landlordism, many of the complaints heard during the Famine continued to be raised against landlords for years to come. The Richmond Commission, investigating agricultural conditions ten years after this legislative attempt to improve the plight of Irish tenants, still reported an excessive competition for land in the rural areas where there were almost no other means of earning a living. This competition occasioned such old and related evils as arbitrary rent increases and excessive subdivision of holdings.[15]

Landlords countered such reports by maintaining, with justification, that popular accounts exaggerated the power they actually possessed. Much of the clearing and consolidation of estates was carried out by simply buying up leases, a far easier process than the occasionally dangerous tactic of eviction. Although violence particularly characterized the Land War years of 1879–82, a threat of tenant retaliation was present throughout the century. Landless peasants especially felt they had little to lose by seeking revenge for landlord wrongs. The isolated position of the landlord and the amorphous nature of the hostility directed against him made rents difficult to collect when they were withheld, and evictions frequently required an armed squad of reluctant policemen. Landlord absenteeism did decline after the Famine, since many of the new buyers were native Irish; but as with other complaints against the system, absenteeism especially characterized the poorer areas in the West, where it acquired its greatest dramatic impact.

Irish landlords thus played a more passive economic role than their British counterparts. The tenants themselves resisted economic change, and the landlords tended to follow a live-and-let-live policy, benevolent at times, hopelessly inefficient over the long run, and disastrous during periods of famine. Farms stayed below optimal size, capital investments were restricted, and agricultural innovations were few. So that even though much of Ireland enjoyed more favorable prices and some definite measure of prosperity in the thirty years after the Famine, the tenants maintained only a fragile security, as the nearly total collapse of the agricultural economy in the late 1870s and early 1880s demonstrated. In those years, under a dismal stretch of weather, successive crop failures again forced many families down to the level of starvation, especially in the West. From 1876, the peak year for agriculture in the nineteenth century, the value of crops and livestock, and particularly the potato crop, fell drastically.[16] Greatly extended rail lines had made it possible to move products more quickly out to markets; now the same revolution in transport enabled Canadian and American producers to compete on the European markets and drive down prices. Similar circumstances in England reduced the need there for migrant workers. Private relief organizations mitigated a great deal of the suffering, but as in the Great Famine, government assistance again proved horribly inadequate. Opposition to the existing landlord-tenant system acquired new force, much of it violent.

The tenants did not want good landlords, they wanted none at all. Full control over the land they worked seemed the only acceptable offer, and the gentry and the British Parliament sought in vain to make do with less radical compromises. Since England was a more cohesive and unified country, landlords there had more influence on the attitudes of a rural society. But in Ireland the most widespread and cohesive social structure was Catholicism, and the Protestant gentry had no share in it. Nor did they have much faith in the increasing trend in England towards constitutional democracy, since religion, as the most important force in the lives of Irish tenants, only divided the landlords from the great mass of people. Religion was perhaps the least surmountable of all the barriers between the social groups, for economic, historical, and political reasons as well. Despite the relaxation of the Penal Laws in the latter years of the eighteenth century, and despite Catholic emancipation during O'Connell's political reign, the

Church of Ireland remained the official religion until its connection with the state was broken in 1869 by the Irish Church Act. The Anglican Church continued to enjoy much of its old wealth, social privileges, and power over education; but one provision of the act allowed tenants to obtain state aid for the purpose of purchasing church lands. Although it affected few people directly, it did suggest the idea that eventually would become the permanent solution to the land problem —pressure the gentry to accept hard cash and leave quietly.

Although the hierarchy of the Catholic Church was itself frequently aligned with England, the guardian of Ireland's temporal well-being, some key splits did develop within the Church leadership, primarily the division between the nationalists and the ultramontanists. Paul Cullen, Archbishop of Dublin from 1852 to 1878 and a conservative on Church matters, supported Vatican influence and the British connection in Ireland. Partly because of Archbishop Croke's support for the Land League, however, and partly because many of the parish clergy sympathized with the drive for independence at the parochial level, hierarchical power in the Church eventually passed to the nationalists. Their political alliances and compromises had the effect of lending Church support to those groups favoring constitutional methods rather than to the forces of agrarian agitation. Yet those separate political movements overlapped to a great extent, and even the advocates of agrarian reform relied on Church influence in the society. Despite proposals such as Michael Davitt's advocacy of land nationalization, agrarian agitation was directed towards an essentially peasant solution to the social problems. Many of the clergy came from the countryside and could easily identify with the problems of the tenants. They did actively discourage the more violent methods of agrarian agitation, and they tried to maintain their role as a force for order in a changing society. But the Church wanted to be involved in those changes. In 1884, therefore, an informal but effective clerical-nationalist alliance developed. The official Church opposition to radical groups like the Fenians led the parish clergy to offer even stronger support to the officially sanctioned nationalist activities such as Home Rule parliamentarianism. And no matter what the Church involvement in nationalist politics, it inevitably provoked the Protestant charge that Home Rule would mean Rome Rule.

Because of their greater education and experience, parish priests occupied major positions of secular as well as spiritual influence. After the Great Famine and disestablishment, a wave of increased religiosity in Ireland added even more to the Church's control

of its people's view of the world. In 1850 the approximately 5 million Irish Catholics were served by 5,000 priests, monks, and nuns; by 1900 their ranks had swelled to 14,000, while the number of Catholics had steadily fallen.[17] In what he terms a "devotional revolution," Emmet Larkin analyzes an increase in Church attendance from less than 40 percent to over 90 percent over this same half-century. The groundwork had been laid by Father Mathew's Total Abstinence Society and O'Connell's Catholic and Repeal Associations, which combined moral and political enthusiasm into strong, disciplined movements. After the Famine the Church began to acquire the machinery and material resources to direct this enthusiasm. Greater hierarchical control over the clergy, a greater ratio of priests to parishioners, and the economic power of the Church through its educational resources or goods and services to its membership all contributed to an increased moral and social influence. The Famine, Larkin feels, also crystallized a group identity crisis. In the context of a dwindling Gaelic heritage, therefore, the symbolic and unique language, rituals, and traditions, and the non-English nature of the Church became a powerful cultural substitute.[18]

With Gaelic Ireland and the culture of poverty broken by the Famine, the most influential social group that began to emerge, on the basis of its numbers as well as resources, was the Catholic tenant farmers with more than thirty acres. Larkin regards them as the "critical nation-forming class," the "dominant political and economic class after 1850 . . . the dominant social and cultural class as well." By providing the Church with its main financial support and by staffing it with their children, this group also came to make up the practicing nucleus of the devotional revolution.[19] A midcentury evangelical revival among Protestants led the already conservative seminary at Maynooth further to emphasize its own puritan sensibilities. More and more priests were being ordained from the poorer classes, and they, in turn, passed on the prejudices against early marriages that their economic experience with limited land resources had given them, now adding religious prejudices as well. The atmosphere of moral repression had its effect on the unmarried; a study of illegitimate births in fifteen European nations in the 1890s found the lowest rate in Ireland.[20]

The blend of nationalism and religion attained one extreme level in the religious fervor surrounding the Apostleship of Prayer, headed by Father James Cullen. The magazine voice of this movement, the *Messenger of the Sacred Heart*, began publishing in 1888; its circulation hit 47,000 by 1894, then 73,000 in 1904, and became the vehicle for

an ardent temperance crusade that elicited huge numbers of abstinence pledges. The Catholicism of the movement was militant and ascetic, the nationalism aggressive and emotional, and the rhetoric revolutionary, a combination of elements that made its way under such slogans as "Ireland sober, Ireland free."[21] The all-time hero of the temperance movement, Father Mathew, was honored with an 1890 centenary celebration that added a number of new statues of the crusader to inspire further pledges of Irish abstinence.

The Church maintained strict control over education as well, and governmental attempts to introduce nondenominational schools gained little ground. As late as 1900 the number of primary pupils in Church-affiliated schools was still at 65 percent. University education likewise split along sectarian lines, with Trinity College, Dublin, remaining a Protestant bastion. Even though teacher training remained rudimentary, the number of schools doubled in the last half of the century, and the number of people who could both read and write increased from 33 percent in 1851, to 84 percent in 1911. Yet even by 1911 only one child in seventeen attended school beyond primary grades. Like other social improvements in Ireland, education still had far to go.[22] Schools sought to make Irish pupils resemble as closely as possible their English counterparts, with Irish art, history, and culture receiving little attention. The Irish language also suffered in the standardized curriculum, since English was the tongue of social advancement. One exception to this British orientation in the National Schools was the Christian Brothers, whose primaries consequently produced many nationalist figures. But what varied little in education was the presence of the Church. Backwards in agriculture and industry, Ireland also maintained a traditional attachment to its religion, and the old social attitudes and views on morality remained largely intact. When the southern counties finally became an independent republic in the twentieth century, they still remained one of the most conservative states in Europe.

Like the religious influences, the differences in the society also ran deep. In the latter half of the nineteenth century, Catholics made up about 75 percent of the population, their numbers concentrated in the laboring industrial class and on the poorer farms. Anglicans dominated the ranks of the landed gentry and the professions; slightly fewer in number were the Presbyterians, who controlled the businesses and

the more prosperous farms.[23] Personal incomes highlighted the religious differences. Estimated per capita income rose form £7.9 in 1851, to £16.4 in 1891, yet of this latter figure, Protestants averaged £34.0, Catholics only £10.9.[24] Most government officials came from the Protestant Ascendancy; in 1886, for instance, one-half of all justices of the peace were landlords, while fewer than a quarter were Catholic.[25] These positions were supplemented by the resident magistrates, or R.M.s, who carried the increasingly centralized influence and legal control of Dublin Castle out into the countryside.

The social transformations during these years were more apparent in the cities than in the more populous countryside. The absence during the nineteenth century of any large urban middle class kept all social questions squarely within the agricultural sector. Only with the solution of the land question in the early years of the twentieth century did the conflict of proletariat and bourgeoisie move into the foreground, stimulated by increased urbanization. In 1841 approximately one-eighth of the population lived in cities; by 1911 urban migration had raised that fraction to one-third.[26] The new social problems became frequently as acute as poverty in the countryside. In the first years of the twentieth century, 87,000 people, 30 percent of Dublin, lived in slum dwellings, often the decayed shells of once elegant Georgian mansions that now lacked heat, light, and water.[27] Migration to the cities affected few urban centers besides Dublin and Belfast, with most of the smaller towns actually losing population. In Dublin the working class could expect only poor wages for occasional labor, women typically going into service and men working on construction projects or in the transportation and delivery of goods. The only effective degree of industrialization was achieved in the Lagan valley in the North. For the rest of Ireland, labor questions remained minor issues, since the proletariat consisted mostly of farm laborers and slum dwellers with few jobs and little political influence. The rural problems resolved themselves as the old feudal landlords gave way to a rural bourgeoisie of small farmers and shopkeepers; but in the cities, not until James Larkin and James Connolly was there any significant union organization or membership strength. The more extensive industrialization that might have provided the basis for a stronger working class never got started in the nineteenth century. Ireland had too many obstacles to it: a population decline, poverty, rural unrest, lack of raw materials, transportation costs, and competition from the outside, especially from England.[28]

Since the time of Daniel O'Connell, the strength behind nationalist politics had depended on the mass of peasantry. From the 1830s onward, however, the nationalist leaders, Catholic and Protestant alike, tended to come from the urban middle class steadily increasing in numbers and prosperity. Sean O'Faolain claims that nationalism, lacking the social content that a proletarian-industrial class would have added, developed instead as a social mystique. Politics as a technology, a blueprint for a better way of life, lay outside the range of such nationalist sentiments.[29] Yet this theory suggests that the rural classes had no clear notion of what they wanted and ignores the informed political consciousness begun by O'Connell's organizations. The emphasis on the mystique of nationalism, primarily separation from England, was cultivated by the political leaders themselves, socially at enough distance now from the mass of people in the countryside so that they could develop their own blend of agrarian reform and Irish independence. The social content was out there, in the economic issue of land; but the politicians found themselves more often intrigued by the nationalist issue of separation.

The political and economic order before the Famine had depended on a secure and powerful Protestant Ascendancy in control of a weak and impoverished tenantry. Over the latter half of the century, improved economic conditions, better education, improved purchasing power, and stronger political organization gradually changed this rural proletariat into a rural bourgeoisie. The land agitation in the late 1870s and early 1880s therefore grew in part out of an improved economic status that generated as much hostility as the poverty and exploitation had earlier. As personal incomes rose and as tenants acquired a greater economic interest in their holdings, they put increasing pressure on the landlords. Agrarian agitation resulted in political concessions and economic benefits and so was stepped up even more. Within the whole range of rural unrest, however, Paul Bew distinguishes measures such as boycotts, rent strikes, intimidation, and agrarian terror from the most important Land League policy, "different varieties of highly legalistic strategies."[30] The theory of a "frustrated revolution in rising expectations," according to Bew, thus only partly explains the actual violence, since many of the smaller tenants never enjoyed the increased prosperity of the post-Famine period. Economically as well as socially, the transition from tillage to pasture had failed.[31] Within the widespread feeling of antilandlord, religious, and nationalist unity, Protestantism became increasingly identified with Unionism. The economic competition thus took on much of the fervor

of a political and religious conflict, one fueled by the perceived injustices perpetrated by the landed class.

The rising middle class in the cities shared in the interests of the tenants for nationalist reasons, since many of them were only one or two generations removed from the land. But here, too, economics played a strong role. The advances of the middle class were tied much more closely to the tenantry than to the Protestant Ascendancy, and they thus had far more to lose if they identified themselves with the Ascendancy and became alienated from popular opinion. For the politicians, however, the related issues of land reform and political independence tended to separate. There were plenty of good reasons for this: it was feared that economic reform would defuse the desires for independence; or that there simply weren't enough party funds or political energy to coordinate and foster both issues; or that the British would play both issues off against each other without ever adequately resolving either; or that the crucial support from the Church would be lost in an agrarian campaign; or that a withdrawal from constitutional processes would fan anti-Irish sentiment in England; or that agrarian dissent might be used to justify British military intervention. The issue of Home Rule seemed more conducive to the highly prized state of "unity." If a less radical measure of land reform would end the agitation and bring the landlords into the nationalist ranks, Home Rule chances would improve. But there was also the fear, from the side of the peasantry, that the landed class would thereby be preserved in Ireland and that even the tenants' own political leaders held enough economic and social status themselves to lose sight occasionally of the conditions in the countryside or, worse, to desire that those conditions not change significantly further.

pOLITICS TRANSFORMED

Parnellism and the Landed Gentry

I rish politics in the latter part of the nineteenth century had a great deal of its structure, activities, and programs rooted in the period dominated by Daniel O'Connell. His Catholic Association was begun in the 1820s and succeeded by his Repeal Association, both huge but firmly controlled organizations that at times functioned almost as a self-government in Ireland and that eventually pressured England into the major concession of Catholic Emancipation. Using strategies such as consistent opposition to terrorism or dramatic parliamentary gestures to obstruct Westminster's activities, O'Connell managed to gain the support of the peasant masses, the Church, and the middle class. In much of Ireland, therefore, a relatively strong political consciousness developed fairly early in the century, one that included a commitment to unified power, democratic government, and political patronage.

By the mid-1840s, however, O'Connell's formula began to seem increasingly futile. The peasantry held firmly behind him, but younger nationalists turned more and more to the Young Ireland political writers, Thomas Davis, Charles Gavan Duffy, James Fintan Lalor, John Mitchel, and William Smith O'Brien. Faced with this initially mild insurrection and disturbed by Young Ireland's rhetoric of physical force, O'Connell counterattacked with the charge of anti-Catholicism. The Irish Renaissance would come to side with Young Ireland. O'Connell, it was felt, had compromised his position with the English by pushing Irish politics into expediency and personal ambition. Moreover, he had relied too greatly on the masses and the Church and, reacting to opposition from the writers, had turned to dogmatic quarrels and then political slander. His rivalry with Young Ireland created a pattern for many of the subsequent splits between writers and politicians at the end of the century: Protestants vs. Catholics,

intellectualism vs. vulgarity and philistinism, liberalism vs. religious morality, spiritualism vs. materialism, the select few vs. the indiscriminate masses.

Out of Young Ireland three distinct nationalist programs soon emerged. The armed insurrection wing, represented by John Mitchel, advocated a swift and violent break with England and the landlords. William Smith O'Brien favored a political revolution rather than a social one. But the most lasting influence emanated from Thomas Davis and his concept of cultural nationalism. Davis envisioned a people's republic that would unite all the different and usually squabbling Irish factions and inspire them to act at a higher and more noble level of spirit and identity. Unfortunately for Davis, it was O'Connell and his appeal to "Old Ireland" that commanded the mass following.

The Irish won major political concessions from England only insofar as they successfully welded widespread agrarian support behind a tightly disciplined party at Westminster. Although the combination also depended on strong political leadership and American funding, these two factors themselves failed to generate any parliamentary effectiveness after O'Connell's power had dwindled. Most Irish M.P.s closely resembled their British counterparts in actions and attitudes. While isolated members like George Henry Moore, the father of the novelist, did exercise some parliamentary independence in the early 1850s as part of the so-called Irish Brigade, they accomplished very little. They ignored the need for a popular movement behind them, a principle that O'Connell knew and that Davitt and Parnell rediscovered in building their own power base, and thus achieved nothing like a unified and independent party with any parliamentary clout. Even more than their colleagues who aped the English, factions like the Irish Brigade created a deep cynicism in Ireland about the efficacy of constitutional methods, a feeling that held on for several decades. The Fenian leader John O'Leary, dubious of Irish political efforts even at the best of times, described conditions after the 1865 election: "Parliamentary representation had reached that state in Ireland that no honest man ... could well see anything but the most disastrous outlook from it."[1] Under the leadership of Isaac Butt during these years, the party labored under Butt's moderate view of the role of a parliamentarian and directed almost no British attention towards Irish problems. The unity, discipline, and conviction that could have achieved any effectiveness had to await the arrival of Parnell.

The other end of the Irish political spectrum was occupied by the Irish Republican Brotherhood (IRB), an underground revo-

lutionary organization founded in 1858 and linked back to the republicanism of Wolfe Tone. Where the Irish M.P.s tended to become overly fascinated by Westminster, the IRB argued the necessity of armed insurrection. Never successful in any of their occasional uprisings, they nonetheless kept alive certain vital principles on the long movement towards independence. They resisted intrusion by the Catholic Church, established lines of support with the Irish in America, and enlisted a popular backing at home, including support from the lower classes at both the urban and rural levels. In cultivating the mystique of Fenianism, many writers depicted them as a lofty-minded but not very practical group in pursuit of a foredoomed goal, as in Yeats's portrayal of John O'Leary. Yet nothing in Fenian doctrine or practice was inspired by the lure of the lost cause, and even O'Leary scorned tactics or goals that could only end in failure. Never very many in number, poorly armed, opposed by the Church, and outlawed by the British, the Fenians still concentrated on what might be gained from violent resistance, not what would be lost.

By the year 1880 the face of political activities, not only in Westminster, but also in the Irish countryside, began to change under the pressure of three separate but related elements: the Land League, the Land War, and Parnell. The Irish electorate had begun to vote more along Home Rule lines than ever before, so that Davitt could write of the 1880 election that it "wrote the political doom of Irish landlordism."[2] Conor Cruise O'Brien's analysis of the restructuring of the Irish parliamentary party during this period indicates the extent of the changes. In comparison to the first election on the issue of Home Rule in 1874, the 1880 election returned markedly fewer landlords and members of the upper class. Their places had been taken primarily by Catholics from the lower-middle class, the farmers and shopkeepers, and this tendency grew far more pronounced by the election of 1885; the original two home rulers from the lower-middle class had grown to forty-four. The party became socially more conservative in its outlook, and in background and education it remained solidly within the English political tradition; but for the first time, it seemed capable of winning Home Rule for the Irish.[3]

The mass agrarian movement that finally lent some power to the efforts of the parliamentarians was the Irish National Land League. Founded in 1879 with Parnell as one of its first presidents, it was far

more effective than such previous organizations as the 1850 Tenant League or the local farmers' clubs. The Land League managed to unite behind it several diverse groups within Ireland; besides the tenants, who stood to gain the most from the League, many of the bishops and parish clergy, the politicians, the urban classes, and the newspapers also backed the policies of organized agrarian reform. At a less official level, hatred of English coercion and Protestant landlords frequently spilled over into agrarian violence called "outrages" in English legal terminology. In 1877 only 236 acts of violence accompanied the 463 evictions; by 1880, when evictions topped 2,000, the number of outrages reached 2,590 in the agrarian struggle that became known as the Land War.[4]

In its official, nonviolent function, the League helped support tenants faced with rack-renting or unjust evictions, including those who wished eventually to buy up their holdings. The policy of boycotting was also organized by the League. Parnell addressed this issue in 1880 when he advocated a "moral Coventry" against anyone who took over another holding from which someone had been evicted. The best response to such a person, Parnell suggested, was "isolating him from the rest of his country, as if he were the leper of old."[5] Within the year the policy was used so successfully against the Mayo land agent Captain Boycott that his name quickly became synonymous with the tactic. By mobilizing public opinion as well as massive demonstrations, the Land League contributed a great deal towards Parnell's early political successes and laid down the foundations on which many tenants became owners over the next thirty years.

By itself, without Parnell's political strategies and his ability to combine agrarianism with constitutionalism, the Land League would not have gained as much as it did. As it was, the League revolutionized the land issue, using social upheaval, especially during the Land War, to force political gains from the British. Hoping to placate the peasantry and thus eliminate popular support for the League and for nationalist goals, Gladstone's Parliament passed a Land Reform Bill in 1881 as one major part of the government aid measures for Ireland. The bill established the principle of copartnership between landlord and tenant along the lines of the "Three Fs": fair rent, fixity of tenure, and free sale of leases. A Land Commission created by the bill settled disputed rents and also provided credit for tenants to buy the land they worked. Initial reactions to the Reform Bill verged on the religious ecstatic. A. M. Sullivan, an Irish M.P., termed the bill "a charter of freedom for the long-oppressed tenantry of Ireland," and he recalled its parliamen-

tary reading into law: "As I sat there and listened to the words of the Premier, I felt as if I had, after the cruel toils and privations of the desert, been at length vouchsafed a glimpse of the Promised Land."[6] A similar exuberant optimism colored the memory of William O'Brien, another Irish M.P. and one of Parnell's chief lieutenants.[7]

Although Michael Davitt regarded the 1881 Land Act as "a legislative sentence of death by slow processes against Irish landlordism,"[8] he had doubts even before the passage of the bill that it could deal adequately with the conditions of extreme poverty he had witnessed in the West.[9] Davitt was the principal organizer of the Land League and the person who gave Parnell the issue of land reform to buttress the Home Rule movement. Davitt believed, however, that a system of land reform would be needed that went much further than Parnell's policies seemed to be heading, and he recalled an 1878 speech by Parnell that wavered between moderate and radical solutions "in a manner so cautious that it would leave him free to support consistently whichever scheme the country might make up its mind to prefer."[10] Within only a few years, Parnell had more definitely settled his course away from radical measures and from any further union of political forces with Michael Davitt.

Although it lowered rents about 10 percent across the whole of Ireland,[11] the Land Bill of 1881 failed to meet many of the economic needs of the tenants; only 731 holdings, with an average size of 42 acres, were sold under the terms of the bill.[12] One deterrent was the increasing risk of owning land. As in the Great Famine, falling revenues and fixed costs during the meager years of the 1880s made it more profitable to remain a tenant under a land bill that did little to help landlords. Evictions rose to levels higher than at any time since the Famine, with a corresponding increase in agrarian crime. Not only were private organizations and tenant committees required to aid many of the peasants, the landlords themselves needed their own relief groups during the Land War and its aftermath. The Irish Land Committee had been started in 1879 to oppose the Land League and to spread information defending the proprietors on agrarian questions. Two other protective agencies, the Orange Emergency Committee and the Property Defense Association, provided similar financial, legal, and moral support. Such groups were able to gain decisive benefits for the landlords in part because of disunity among the tenants. The Land League had failed to protect all the various and differing interests of its members, and class divisions further undercut measures like a mass "no rent" policy.

The landlords' main line of defense, however, remained the British government, and Parliament continued its opposition to agrarian agitation with harsh punitive legislation to quell the outrages. Debate on one such coercion bill erupted into a major parliamentary uproar in 1880, with Parnell at its center. The traditional Irish policy of parliamentary restraint had produced few results in the past, but several of the Irish M.P.s, including Parnell, had since discovered the effectiveness of O'Connell's old policy of obstruction. The filibustering, endless points of order, and roll calls all were brought to bear against this newest coercion bill. Yet the strategy was also aimed at minimizing Parnell's responsibility for the forthcoming Land Act of 1881. Balanced between the opposing extremes on the land legislation, he avoided expressing either full support or full opposition. He had finally to face the possibility of seceding from Parliament in 1880, seeking a general rent strike, and thus provoking a full-scale conflict with England and the landlords, a conflict Davitt felt would then have succeeded in crushing landlordism.[13] Instead, Parnell opted for the constitutional rather than the revolutionary path, counting on substantial land reform as an acceptable accompaniment to the coercion bill.

Parnell's course remained obscured by the events of the next year. He continued his policy of parliamentary obstruction, and finally, in October 1881, the British arrested him and several followers. F. S. L. Lyons believes that the arrest was "exceedingly convenient":

> If he had remained at liberty he would either have had to continue at the head of an agitation which was becoming steadily more violent and thus risk a head-on clash with the authorities, or else break with the land movement and at one stroke lose much of the prestige he had gained in the past two years. His imprisonment . . . won him the halo of martyrdom for the cause and kept him out of the way while the League was in its death-throes.[14]

Although his separation from Katharine O'Shea led him to seek a release from prison, a letter to her immediately after his arrest mentions exactly the strategy that Lyons analyzes.[15] In Kilmainham Jail he could avoid responsibility for the land legislation until its concessions had eroded much of the determination behind the land agitation.

Six months after Parnell's arrest, in the so-called Kilmainham

Treaty that created the Liberal-Nationalist alliance, he finally offered his support for the bill as a solution to the land question. In exchange, the government announced an end to the coercion, an expansion of the Land Act benefits, and the release from prison of the leader of the Irish parliamentary party. Although Parnell's gestures and rhetoric in Ireland remained revolutionary, he began systematically to curb the agrarian movement even as he detached himself from it in characteristically aloof fashion. The shift in emphasis from agrarian agitation to Home Rule was partly influenced by limited party funds, since the agrarian policies necessitated major expenditures to support the tenants. Parnell had also made some major decisions about his own political philosophy, however, and in Davitt's opinion, the shift in position broke the back of a potentially successful revolution:

> It was the vital turning-point in Mr. Parnell's career, and he unfortunately turned in the wrong direction. He had hitherto been in everything but name a revolutionary reformer, and had won many triumphs at the head of the most powerful organization any Irish leader had at his back for a century. He now resolved to surrender the Land League, and to enter the new stage of his political fortunes as an opportunist statesman.[16]

The final phrase is bitter, for Davitt felt a betrayal behind the strategy shift; yet Lyons' assessment of the turning point in his biography of Parnell substantiates each of Davitt's points.[17] The more revolutionary wing of the agrarian movement, dismayed at the compromises, nonetheless kept silent as Parnell set out to stop the violence still going on despite the virtually defunct status of the Land League. The Ladies' Land League, established by Anna Parnell while her brother was in prison, was another organization Davitt felt had performed effective and necessary work in the absence of the imprisoned male leaders. On his release, Parnell quickly shut down the group as a public embarrassment and nuisance.

His creation of a well-disciplined political party, during this period and throughout the 1880s, did win for his country the grudging British recognition that the Irish might indeed be capable of self-government. One of his main achievements, this had to be balanced against his suppression of the revolutionary direction of Irish nationalism. His sympathy for both tenants and landlords complicated his view of the Irish question. A landlord himself, he accepted before many of his peers that the old system of land tenure had to change and

Avondale, Parnell's family home in County Wicklow.

that the tenants had to receive justice. Robert Foster, in his study of Parnell's early years, concludes that he had "a 'modern' outlook where industry was concerned, and a readiness to accept the ending of the old land system (which had never proved profitable in his own case)."[18] His social conservatism inclined him to temper proposed land reform with the desire that landlords should not face unnecessary or excessive losses or threats of violence. If the tenants could be placated with lesser substitutes for land ownership, such as greater financial security, then compulsory land purchase, which Parnell never endorsed very strongly, might well be avoided. Under the best of conditions, the agrarian movement would have had little success in a direct conflict with landlords backed by armed British support.

In Parnell's view, land reform by this time had become a decidely secondary issue. He spoke in August 1882, of the "great object of reform which has always possessed the heart of the Irish people at home and abroad—I mean the restoration of the legislative independ-

ence of Ireland."[19] He saw the possibility that a land settlement would erode tenant support for Home Rule and hence chose not to seek a solution to the land issue until after such independence had been won. The decision did not lack for good arguments. O'Leary likewise saw few chances for a land settlement as long as the English connection remained intact, and he admitted having little "agrarian ardour" himself in the drive for Irish freedom.[20]

The strategy did succeed in transforming Home Rule from a vague ideal into a serious parliamentary issue, and in the process Parnell also gained the support of Gladstone and a major English political party. Throughout this decade Parnell's popularity in Ireland was unshakeable. A statement of support in *United Ireland*, a Parnellite newspaper, sounded a common note on 23 December 1882, when it claimed: "If it be hero-worship to follow such a man as trustfully as a Pillar of Fire, the Irish people are not likely to shrink from the imputation. . . . High above the tumult and doubts of the moment rises that serene figure." The paper did not need the Christmas season from which to draw its imagery; to his own people Parnell was the Messiah who would lead them over into the Promised Land.

The departure from an agrarian to a constitutional stance manifested itself in the organization known as the National League, established in 1882 to replace the Land League and to emphasize parliamentary Home Rule over land reform and agrarian agitation. The Franchise Bill of 1884 more than tripled the Irish electorate and boosted Parnell's power even more, so that the 1885 general election returned him with a political party tailor-made to his purposes in Westminster. A rival political group, however, the Plan of Campaign, did pose a potentially dangerous threat to Parnell's constitutional alliance with Gladstone's Liberals. Formed by John Dillon, William O'Brien, and Timothy Harrington, the Plan developed as a tenant assistance group in response to worsening agrarian conditions in 1886 and 1887. Parnell immediately branded it as extremist, and the English, fearing a resurgence of the Land War, passed a new Crimes Act and even enlisted the aid of the Vatican as a way of suppressing this new organization. A further landlord syndicate came together in early 1889, combining the resources of about a dozen wealthy Irish and English landowners. Their financial support to those in difficulties because of the Plan stiffened landlord opposition to the agrarian wing. The Irish clergy, while resisting Rome's intrusion, could not unite on any position on the Plan; but Parnell, seeing it as a nonparliamentary diversion, never ceased his opposition.

The Liberal alliance nonetheless failed to gain much more as an alternative. After the defeat of Gladstone's Home Rule measure, the 1886 elections returned a parliament even less inclined to vote for any degree of Irish independence. The weakness behind the Home Rule legislation was not wholly caused by the voters in England, however. Lyons analyzes Parnell's position after 1882 and concludes that "by turning his back on the land agitation he isolated himself from the mass support in Ireland without which a parliamentary leader at Westminster was, if not impotent, at any rate extremely vulnerable."[21] The popularity and support were there if Parnell had chosen to use them fully, as he did in building an original power base. But agrarian agitation also implied social changes and economic readjustments more substantial than he wanted to allow.

The divorce ended Parnell's leadership of the Irish party in December 1890. His relationship with Katharine O'Shea had removed him increasingly further from the day-to-day party business, a vacuum his lieutenants had to fill from about 1886 onward. In the months just before the scandal became public, his leadership had deteriorated "almost to the vanishing point,"[22] Lyons writes, and adds the further charge, more serious than that of no management, that "he had subordinated his judgement to that of his mistress and in so doing had recklessly jeopardized the important national interests committed to his charge."[23] Yet no one aware of these sins could have anticipated the coming storm of retribution.

The day after the O'Shea verdict, the British press opened the attack, piling stock anti-Irish copy upon lurid anti-Parnell divorce transcripts. Fearing a loss of voter support because of the outraged religious sensibilities of the Nonconformist British middle class, Gladstone followed with a demand for Parnell's resignation, and shortly afterward, Davitt's *Labour World* became the first Irish voice raised against the offender. Parnell hit back with a manifesto "To the People of Ireland," an unexpected assault on the British Liberals that completed the break with them and seriously damaged any hopes for Home Rule in the near future. The manifesto quickly increased the anti-Parnell ranks within his own party. In addition, a few days before the showdown in Committee Room Fifteen, the issues of personal morality and public politics became hopelessly entangled by the Irish bishops. Seeing a chance for greater Church control within the party, they joined the solid political lines already formed, abandoned their deliberate policy of silence on the issue, and presented a united front against the proven adulterer. As the most organized of Parnell's oppo-

nents, the clergy also proved the most effective. One Church voice, the *Irish Catholic*, set early standards for a religious rhetoric that gloated over foul demons caught in their own vices.

Parnell's allies were equally prompt and enthusiastic. The *Freeman's Journal*, on 18 November 1890, challenged: "Let him who is without stain among you cast the first stone." Religious imagery was not the sole property of the bishops, and the *Freeman* pursued its line: "He has brought [Ireland] out of bondage. He has led her within sight of the Promised Land." Over the next several months, under the refrain that "Our business with Mr. Parnell is political," the *Freeman* continued to argue that Ireland dare not betray its leader at this crucial period in the struggle for Home Rule and that his private business was immaterial to his public achievements and abilities. Parnell was too noble and aloof, the *Freeman* claimed, to allow such matters as Katharine O'Shea or the divorce scandal to influence his judgment, and so "You are requested not to speak to the man at the wheel." For those readers who demanded an answer from the captain regarding his private life, the *Freeman* had extraordinary theories to offer: "It is living in England which has contaminated Mr. Parnell, and were he living at home in Ireland he would never have fallen into the O'Sheas" (21 November 1890). In any case, the British were the true villains. "A Catholic Priest Abroad" wrote home to praise Parnell as a man "of the household of Pharaoh," one who should not be exiled because of a few "Pharisees and Scribes" in Ireland and England.[24] And the image of the Messiah had not yet even approached its zenith.

The anti-British line of defense was taken up more soberly by John O'Leary, his credentials solidified by occasional criticism of Parnell in the past. Just before the vote on the party chairmanship, O'Leary claimed that Parnell was the only fit leader in Ireland and that he shouldn't be thrown over simply because "the whole howling voice of prurient British hypocrisy has been heard."[25] Supporters within his own party argued that accepting Gladstone's ultimatum of Parnell or Home Rule would make the party wholly dependent on the Liberals for any future gains and would be a humiliating condition with which to live. The party should instead stand behind Parnell and continue his effective policy of shifting alliances from one English party to the next, depending on where the concessions could be obtained. Writers like Yeats and Joyce would later take up O'Leary's point, while transferring the hypocrisy from the British to the Irish. For Parnell and his party, however, things were no longer that simple, and shifts in political alliances no longer feasible. Ever the pragmatist, willing to com-

promise long-term goals for short-term gains, Parnell abandoned this tactic in helping bring about his own personal disaster. He clung tenaciously to the leadership and refused to negotiate any bargains such as temporary resignation. Faced with the damaging effects of Parnell's manifesto, the Irish members who voted him out of the leadership were practicing what Parnell himself had taught them, that the interests of any individual member were secondary to those of the party.

The controversy split the country as well as the Irish party into rigidly opposed factions whose acrimonious debate during the next year frequently spilled over into shouting and shoving matches. The anti-Parnellite seceders, it was charged, had turned on and dumped Parnell only "because a section of the English people called upon them to throw him overboard."[26] During a by-election in North Kilkenny, in which Parnell, Davitt, and Tim Healy were each physically roughed up, Justin McCarthy defended the rebellion with the startling claim that Parnell "was a dictator of the worst type, a tyrant in council, and a man who commanded the fetish worship of his followers."[27] The vicious political campaign raged across the whole country. One casualty was the previous union of Catholic and nationalist forces, now completely sundered as the Church hierarchy held fast in their opposition to Parnell, even though some rank-and-file clergy continued their support. In an exhausting campaign during the months following the leadership vote, Parnell attempted to rally a following and regain his lost power. Against his formidable enemies in the Church and professional classes, he appealed, albeit ambiguously, to the Fenians and to "the dumb multitudes with whose concerns, if the truth be told, he had not greatly occupied himself for many years past."[28] Lyons adds to this assessment that the Fenian appeal "powerfully reinforced the later tendency to mythologize him as the forerunner of a more extreme nationalism. ... his whole career belied the wishful thinking of the militants who claimed him for their own."[29] His erratic and irrational behavior in the final year of his life created the fear in many ordinary people, as well as in the clergy and politicians, that he was irrevocably destroying any chance for Home Rule.

In September 1891, the *Freeman's Journal* drastically reversed its backing of Parnell and decided that he now concerned himself solely with his own political problems, that he was destructive of "unity," that he had lost the support of the people, and that, except for the pro-Parnellite *United Ireland*, all the Irish press was now against him. *United Ireland* responded with the taunt, "Fallen Journal." In the gen-

eral election of 1892, the Parnellites won only nine seats, the anti-Parnellites seventy-one. Lyons writes: "The verdict of the electors was a verdict in favour of the liberal alliance, and against the policy of independent opposition so consistently advocated by the Parnellites."[30] But by the time this verdict was in, Parnell was dead.

In reporting Parnell's death in October 1891, the Irish press, with few exceptions, tried to call off the fighting right there. The *Irish Times* voiced the common hope that "The controversy as far as it had a personal character is absolutely at an end" (8 October 1891). In the same issue Justin McCarthy told an interviewer of the "universal feeling of regret among Irishmen" and assured him: "All feeling of passing hostility will be swallowed up in that regret." But the *Daily Express* wrote of Parnell's "superiority" over his opponents in the Irish party and went on to accuse them of "national ingratitude," domination by the clergy, and responsibility for Parnell's death.[31] A more important exception to the attempts at harmony was *United Ireland*, and this paper made it immediately clear that the hostilities, of a highly personal character, would continue for a long while yet. In black-bordered columns, the paper took up its campaign:

> Slain, sacrificed by Irishmen on the altar of English Liberalism he, the greatest Chief that this land has known in the struggle of centuries against English domination, has been murdered by the men whom he dragged from obscurity and who hated him, even whilst they fawned upon him, because they could never repay all that he had done for them personally. Murdered he has been as certainly as if the gang of conspirators had surrounded him and hacked him to pieces. . . . Shall Ireland exact no punishment for what has been done? (10 October 1891)

Later issues, ignoring the protests and the pleas for unity, reprinted this outraged cry for vengeance. The Irish, *United Ireland* argued, had "wandered in the wilderness" long enough in their painful search for independence and now, as a "predestined nation," demanded a fierceness of purpose in achieving freedom; the time for compromises was over.

United Ireland ran its black-bordered issues on the anniversary of Parnell's death for the next several years. Extensive interviews, personal recollections, and an endless stream of poetry periodically resurrected Parnell's memory in those issues, always accompanied by renewed attacks on the Catholic priests and bishops, the "seceders"

who had voted against Parnell, and especially Tim Healy as prime villain. The myth of the martyred Messiah grew more well defined with each year. Some major groundwork for this had come from no less a source than Parnell's own mother, who, following his death, told an interviewer: "My son is descended from the line of a tribe of Judah.... Charles died a martyr; he died as Christ died, hounded to death by those who should have stood by him."[32] *United Ireland's* memorial issues trotted out all the stock versions of this myth. Parnell had lifted the Irish "from the slough of despond to the heights where hope was shining, and he brought them within sight of the Promised Land" (8 October 1892). That same year, however, brought out a newer variation of the messianic theme: Parnell was not dead, he "cannot die while the land he toiled for is unfreed" (15 October 1892). The popular legend of the coffin filled only with rocks was not far behind.

W. B. Yeats's "Mourn—And Then Onward!" (10 October 1891) is only the best known of the many poems to fill out the *United Ireland* columns on the theme of Parnell. Yeats envisioned a guidance emanating from the grave in the form of a pillar of flame. To William Boyle, this spirit looked rather more like "the still unconquered dust of the martyr's tomb."[33] Katharine Tynan's poems "A Wandering Star" and "The Dead Chief" evoked even more of the messianic trappings, including martyrdom and faith in Parnell as a Christ figure who was not yet dead after all (17 October 1891). Later writers would have an aesthetically easier time refining and developing Parnell's myth, for after only a few years, the main elements were already well known.[34]

In 1897 *United Ireland* ceased its memorial issues and began instead to argue its policy of "National Unity." The theme had become almost an obsession in Ireland during this decade, when no one could seemingly agree on anything. The Irish Race Convention met for several days in Dublin in September 1896, for the purpose of creating unity among the Irish factions. The proceedings, the *Freeman's Journal* announced hopefully, "lift the Irish question into the pure air of patriotism high above the squalor and tumult of petty personal factions" (2 September 1896). That same year the Childers Commission offered an even stronger rallying point for the fragmented Irish nation: the British had been mistakenly overtaxing Ireland for years to the tune of over two million pounds annually. Committees were formed to organize meetings, protests, and policies, and the newspapers fanned the common outrage through much of 1897 under headlines such as

"British Plunder of Ireland." The opposition to England lent itself readily to the "National Unity" policy advocated by such political leaders as John Redmond and Timothy Harrington and supported by *United Ireland*. In 1898 the Wolfe Tone Centenary provided the occasion for yet another try at piecing together the splinters of Irish public life.

The divisions that formed within the Irish parliamentary party after Parnell's death and that lasted throughout the 1890s were only the most disenchanting aspect of the country's inability in that decade to control its own future. John Redmond, author of a manifesto then adopted by the Parnellites, appropriated the tone of the divorce debate in his accusations of "treason." The seceders, "in obedience to foreign dictation," had disrupted the party and subsequently "loaded with calumny and hounded to death the foremost man of our race." With such as these, there could be no possible future fellowship.[35] The charges of adultery and countercharges of betrayal gave way to an unseemly struggle for new leadership positions, control of policies and constituencies, and even direction of party funds and newspapers. Three main factions developed, headed by John Redmond, Tim Healy, and Justin McCarthy, with even the anti-Parnellites splitting over the issue of Church influence within the party. The British Liberals won a small majority in the 1892 election, and Gladstone dutifully shepherded another Home Rule bill through the House of Commons, only to have the Lords soundly knock it down. In the 1895 election the Tory-Unionists achieved an overwhelming majority, leaving the Irish with no bargaining power at all. The constitutional road to Home Rule had been rendered impassable.

John Sweetman, an Irish M.P. writing on the stagnation of politics in the 1890s, conceded the existence of a parliamentary vacuum: "In Ireland there is a general apathy, the people have practically lost confidence in all members of Parliament, and I cannot say I am surprised, as we are doing nothing for Ireland."[36] The "constructive unionists" at Westminster took the opportunity to develop the hope that relations between their country and Ireland might somehow be improved by offering substantial concessions and perhaps getting Home Rule "killed by kindness." Irish nationalists feared the effects of better government for the same reason that British officials placed their hopes in it: shorn of economic immediacy, the demands for independence might dwindle to nothing. Disillusioned with political processes, nationalists now turned instead to new expressions of independence, emphasizing Irish cultural identity and consciousness in ways more articulate and far reaching than before.

The constructive unionists forged ahead, however, and concessions on land ownership began rapidly to shift power and influence away from the Protestant Ascendancy and toward the discontented tenants, who increasingly aspired to and gained middle-class status. Successive land bills in the past had failed to alter land ownership on any wide scale. Under the Land Acts of 1870 and 1881, for instance, only sixteen hundred tenants in fifteen years had bought their holdings. The Ashbourne Act of 1885 and its sequels accounted for 25,000 more sales, and the 1891 and 1896 acts added 47,000 more. But in 1903 the Wyndham Land Act assured tenants that purchase payments would stay below rents; over the next fifteen years, nearly 280,000 holdings were sold, nearly half the total area of the country, with whole estates often going to the previous tenants. In 1870 only 3 percent of Irish landholders owned their holdings; by 1906 that figure had reached nearly 30 percent. [37]

As the prosperity and influence of the Ascendancy declined over the final decades of the century, that of the middle class steadily rose. A similar pattern had been operating in England since the 1860s, as economic and social changes there gradually transformed the aristocracy into an anachronism. Newer social groups won representation in Parliament, and it was these middle-class forces with which Gladstone aligned himself in England and which benefitted from land legislation in Ireland. Yet the figures for land sales do not show a Protestant gentry in full-scale retreat. Despite land transfer and the accompanying shift of local government out of the hands of old county families, the Ascendancy went on dictating many of the concerns of Irish society, especially at its upper levels, until well into the twentieth century. Dublin Castle continued to sustain a social elite that drew much of the professional class into its aura of prestige and gentility.

Some spokesmen for the Ascendancy found such a function horrifyingly trivial and shortsighted. Standish James O'Grady launched his rhetorical campaign to awaken the landed class to its fate with an 1882 pamphlet appropriately entitled *The Crisis in Ireland*. He damned the landlords for squandering their wealth, power, prestige, traditional heritage, and so on. In their cowardly dependence on England, they had turned weak, selfish, and downright rotten. This hardly meant, however, that such a class should be cast aside. If Ireland eliminated its aristocracy, a much greater danger threatened the coun-

try. Independence would follow and then, in due course, lead to "an Ireland gross and materialised."[38] And democratic, he could have added, for O'Grady knew about democracies:

> [T]his waste, dark, howling mass of colliding interests, mad about the main chance — the pence-counting shopkeeper; the publican; the isolated, crafty farmer; the labourer tied to his toil, or tramping perhaps to the polling booth . . . at his *disposal*, the whole property of the island.[39]

O'Grady accepted the inevitability of dissolving the large estates, but he pleaded that the aristocrat himself be preserved as a "wise statesman looking only to the welfare of the country."[40]

Within but a few years, O'Grady felt compelled to restate his unheeded warning. *Toryism and the Tory Democracy* (1886) repeated the attacks on spineless defeatism among landlords and on mob rule by greedy barbarians. But with time running out and with further land acts plus a possible resurgence of agrarian violence at hand, O'Grady's "wise statesman" began to seem far too inadequate for the crisis; a messianic hero was called for now: "[E]ven amongst Irish landlords, amidst this ignoble herd of men . . . brave men and true are there, though transformed. . . . Dear friend, you must deliver them; you, or no man."[41] Just who this savior might be that could rally the exhausted troops, O'Grady could not yet say, although the closest candidate seemed to be the Tory demagogue, Lord Randolph Churchill. O'Grady may also have envisioned a nobler model along the lines of the legendary Irish hero Cuchulain. O'Grady had given Cuchulain a prominent place in his earlier *Histories*, works that would eventually gain him a solid reputation as one of the fathers of the Irish Renaissance. As an aristocratic ideal, Cuchulain might also serve politically to inspire the Ascendancy to abandon their vulgar, materialistic new habits and to cease parlaying with peasants and shopkeepers. Such barbarisms as the Land War need never have happened had the landlords disregarded both the economic demands of the mob and their own greedy impulses.

Lord Randolph was clearly not Cuchulain, nor did any other Messiah step forth from the aristocratic ranks. The tradition of idealistic social services among the landed classes had languished throughout the nineteenth century, ever since the Act of Union in 1800. Besides an abdication of responsibility and a related diminishment of national function involved in turning over the government to the British, the

Act of Union reflected what Oliver MacDonagh calls a "failure of
nerve" among the Ascendancy.[42] Sir Samuel Ferguson had discerned
their weakened plight as early as the 1830s, finding the Protestants
"Deserted ... insulted ... threatened ... envied ... plundered ... robbed
... driven abroad by violence."[43] By the end of the century, a doom-
sayer like O'Grady could do little more than rail against the impotence
of his class.

Two years after the Childers Report on overtaxation, the various committees headed by the Ascendancy to decide on a course of
action had not yet done anything at all. O'Grady's "The Great Enchantment" tried sadly to explain why such things could be:

> They [i.e., the aristocracy] might have been so much to this afflicted
> nation; half-ruined as they are, they might be so much to-morrow, but
> the curse that has fallen on the whole land, seems to have fallen on
> them with double power — the understanding paralysed, the will
> gone all to water, and for consequence a sure destruction.[44]

O'Grady could not understand such paralysis; perhaps it was occasioned by guilt. Past exploitation of the peasantry should not deter
the aristocracy from acting now, however, for in O'Grady's view, as
later in Yeats's, the Irish masses needed strict control, longed for it, in
fact. The peasant had virtues beneath his occasional violent moods:
"Poverty, simplicity, religion, including respect for priests and
bishops."[45] His only chance of behaving in a moral way lay in the
willingness of the aristocracy to force him in that direction.

Despite such pleas and aristocratic ideals, the gentry were
using their remaining political power, and it was still considerable, to
settle on a course quite unlike the one envisioned for them by
O'Grady: the exchange of their land and influence for solid cash. The
Irish Landowners' Convention provides one index. In 1888 the Convention petitioned England for a readjustment of their fixed costs. By
1895 they affirmed that the final solution to the land problem was the
sale of estates to tenants. A series of articles appeared in the *Daily
Express* in early 1899 entitled "The Case of the Irish Landlords." The
author, "One of Them," argued that the costs of land reform should be
borne by the whole country and not just by the landlords. Compulsory
purchase was too slow and costly. The economics of creating a peasant

proprietary clearly dictated a policy that "shall mean to the Irish land-lord not a loss but a gain" (17 June 1899). On O'Grady's ideals of public spirit and generosity, such proposals remained silent. Even a bill as revolutionary as the Wyndham Land Act provided very favorable terms that solved the financial problems of many landlords. Their estates, for instance, would now be purchased with cash and not, as had been the case before, with stock that could easily fluctuate.

The 1890s saw numerous government aid measures designed to improve relations with Ireland. Westminster established public health plans, a Board of Works to supervise public projects, and provisions for reform of national education and local government. The Local Government Act of 1898, reversing previous patterns by which government reform had meant increased centralization, created councils that were heavily represented by Catholics and nationalists and that transferred significant political power at the local level away from the gentry. The Congested Districts Board promoted local industries and assisted those who moved to economically more advantageous parts of the country. The Board helped improve agricultural conditions by amalgamating holdings, demonstrating improved farming techniques, and developing the concept of the cooperatives.

The old problem remained, however: the Irish question demanded an answer that addressed the issues of economics, religion, and independence simultaneously. The failure of the constructive unionists to offer such an answer in programs like the above can be seen in the example of the Irish Agricultural Organisation Society, the IAOS. Sir Horace Plunkett, founder of the Congested Districts Board, wealthy landowner, and staunch Unionist, created the IAOS in 1894. He built the organization around his concept of the cooperative, one that dealt with economics rather than politics, with questions of production and distribution rather than land tenure. The Department of Agriculture and Technical Instruction worked with Plunkett for a time, and the results slowly caught on and proved successful within limited spheres, as in the reorganization of the dairy industry. The cooperative programs were propagandized in the *Irish Homestead*, now known primarily for its editor, George Russell, who also worked as an organizer for Plunkett. Yet the IAOS had no extensive effect on economic or social conditions, and Plunkett never ceased thinking of politics and nationalism as irrelevant to economics.

Plunkett was wrong. In 1898, fearing that the land issue was becoming one of technique rather than tenure, William O'Brien founded the United Irish League. Tapping a strong vein of agitation

and unrest, the League resumed many of the tactics of the old Land League, including advocacy of compulsory land purchase. By 1901 O'Brien had 100,000 members and a major swell of popular support.[46] The success of the League indicated not only that full peasant proprietorship remained a live issue, but also that the social improvements of the 1890s still had very far to go. Poverty remained widespread in the West, and for the rest of Ireland, prosperity had become possible in part because the bottom layers of society had simply been eliminated through starvation or emigration. From its 1845 high of 8.5 million, the population was nearly halved, to 4.7 million, by 1891. In England and Wales for the same period, the population had more than doubled. Despite urban migration, more than 60 percent of the Irish still belonged to the rural classes, compared to approximately 20 percent in England. Was there an Irish answer? For those in the countryside, concessions by the constructive unionists had proven inadequate economically and had been used to subvert the desires for independence. The nationalists had little more to offer, however, for in their concern with Home Rule, they tended to isolate themselves from the economic problems and political support of the masses.

         Throughout the latter half of the century, therefore, two distinct strands, of land reform and of Home Rule, had run through Irish politics, each rendered increasingly less effective the greater its separation from the other. In the early stages of his career, Parnell used the land question to establish his political base, then began a circumspect withdrawal from the desires for a radical change in the old system of landlord and tenant. To certain of the nationalists, Parnell seemed to hold open the possibility that once the British connection was severed, Ireland would look much as before, except that different people would govern it. The landlords and Ascendancy might still hold a solid position in the society and perhaps a strong representation in the new government as well. Even Standish O'Grady came to discover that Parnell, now dead, had possessed admirable political qualities:

> Parnell was no out-and-out revolutionist. Born and bred an aristocrat he knew that his class were the possessors of certain moral and intellectual qualities without which Ireland as a nation would be the poorer. I think he had planned out ways and means for preserving the Irish gentry.[47]

The Fenians, of course, preferred to talk about Parnell as out-and-out revolutionist, and one can readily speculate on both views. O'Grady was clearly right, however, in assessing history's judgment of the divorce scandal: "Posterity will easily forgive Parnell and like him probably all the better for his weakness."[48] As a literary theme, Parnell would enjoy a long and illustrious career to come.

The writers of the 1890s identified much more closely with the Home Rule strand of nationalism than with land reform. As a political issue, it had more romantic appeal as a heroic struggle for freedom against oppressive England. Especially when linked to the charismatic personality of Parnell, nationalism took on a mythic aura that seemed ready-made for artistic expression. And the charisma had existed long before the final, desperate year of struggle. William O'Brien, one of Parnell's lieutenants, described an 1886 meeting that took place in a heavy fog. O'Brien felt entranced by the "overpowering fascination" of Parnell's features in such a mysterious atmosphere: "It was the apparition of a poet plunged in some divine anguish."[49] Several months before the divorce scandal hit the press, the *Freeman's Journal* described Parnell as "one of the men with that strange atmosphere, that indefinable fascination, the nimbus by which these beings are surrounded that have the mighty force of will to control the minds and acts of multitudes of their fellow men" (21 July 1890). T. P. O'Connor's brief *Charles Stewart Parnell: A Memory* (1891) appeared shortly after Parnell's death and already intoned the list of qualities that would pass into literature: resolute strength, reserve, passion, nervous energy, tenacity, an impassive exterior, iron self-control. In 1898 R. Barry O'Brien published a more complete biography, *The Life of Charles Stewart Parnell, 1846–1891*, but one that helped foster the same mythic qualities. When based on the final year of his life and on Parnell's furious but doomed campaign to regain power, the aura of superiority received tremendous impetus from the resulting "legend of the prophet sacrificed by his own people."[50]

The mythic substance, however, obscures the more specific and mundane aspects that attracted the literary movement to Parnell, aspects such as his economic conservatism, his politics of compromise, and his suppression of agrarian agitation. Many of the writers from this period were directly affected by the violence of the Land War, as well as by the long-term implications of land reform. The decline of the Protestant Ascendancy seemed to demonstrate a general decay of the whole country, into a condition of dull, middle-class materialism on the one hand, and unchecked lawlessness on the other. Parnell offered solu-

tions to these fears. He had opposed violence, offered a measure of support to the gentry, and sought the national independence that might have kept land reform from making too drastic a change in the face of Irish society. He was, as Lyons writes, "neither a creative thinker nor a radical innovator."[51] Yet his politics sufficiently resembled those of the writers, so that by the end of the decade they had enveloped the "King" in a mantle of heroism, martyrdom, and messianic devotion to Ireland's national consciousness, often selectively omitting questions of the politics or economics.

The legend depicted Parnell as a great leader betrayed by the followers he had created, a genius sacrificed to mediocrity, a hero rejected by the mob. It was English treachery that destroyed him, or religious bigotry, or Irish paralysis. For the writers of the 1890s, although Parnell did represent the hope of a better Ireland than the one they saw emerging, he also represented their recognition of the futility of their position. Their ambitious literary projects, even those inspired by the possibility of influencing economic values or political directions, never wholly escaped the same deadening feeling of paralysis that the artists attributed to their society. They sought an active role in Ireland's affairs while simultaneously cultivating the posture of the Irish hero who failed at action. Or who simply failed to act. In an interview on Parnell, Lyons noted that "his charismatic quality . . . is now, in my view, considerably reduced by his lack of judgment and his strange, almost wilful lethargy."[52] His reluctance to make clearly defined commitments or to follow decisive courses of action helped Parnell as much as his personal magnetism in welding together the disparate Irish social and political factions. To the writers, Parnell's avoidance of public action held out, however faintly, the promise of a halt to the changes in Irish society; but they also came to believe that the only response to such inevitable change was to avoid it, to withdraw from the processes of history, to create instead an aloof, ideal world of heroic personality and spirit. The writers could understand Parnell's lethargy as well as his charisma, and in much of their work in this decade, they seek to retreat from, or even to annihilate, their experience of modern Ireland.

--◦❖{3}❖◦--

celticism anò the vision of unity

h istorians and poets alike had sought to link the concepts of Irish nationalism and culture years before the Literary Revival began developing this combination into doctrine. James Macpherson's Ossian poems in the 1760s launched a European interest in Celticism, some of it solid scholarship, some of it laboring under the same spurious romanticism propagated by Macpherson's literary hoax. By the 1890s the Irish writers had come to look much more directly to Matthew Arnold for their phrases and categories. In his essay *On the Study of Celtic Literature* (1867) Arnold refined Macpherson into a text the Irish could use as a working outline, one including even key poetic terms. The Yeatsian word "gay" was Celtic, Arnold had already explained,[1] and "Gael" originated in a word meaning "wind" and signifying "the violent stormy people" (p. 82). Arnold described "The Celtic genius, sentiment as its main basis, with love of beauty, charm, and spirituality for its excellence, ineffectualness and self-will for its defect" (p. 115). Arnold's positive qualities seemed "the first valuable compliment [the Celtic world] had received from an English source in several hundred years."[2] As for the negative ones, they could be turned into virtues as well, for ineffectualness seemed to demonstrate an idealistic, willful refusal to compromise with modern materialism. For all his dislike of philistinism, surely Arnold sympathized with what he saw as a Celtic reaction against the "despotism of fact" (p. 102).

Arnold's politics required more dexterity from the Irish, however. Writing in the year of the unsuccessful Fenian rising, he had taken as an epigraph for his essay a line from Ossian: "They went forth to war, but they always fell." The literary movement, itself disturbed by Ireland's potential militance, remained in substantial agreement with this dim view of Celtic violence. Yet Arnold also saw the need to join the separate temperaments of Celt and Teuton into a union that

37

meant solidifying the English connection. One obviously had to read Arnold selectively. His distinction between the masculine, energetic Teuton and the feminine, artistic Celt, although disturbing in its plea for unity of the wrong sort, did forecast the frequent presence of women as central characters in work from the 1890s. To refer now to the hero as "he" may be a useful stylistic convenience for the critic, but as often as not, it is a misleading one.

In an 1897 essay, "The Celtic Element in Literature,"[3] Yeats refers both to Arnold's work and to that of Ernest Renan, who also based the concept of national identity on that of culture in an 1856 study, *The Poetry of the Celtic Races*. Renan looked for the essence or soul of a culture within its spiritual principles and heritage, and where these held strong, the country seemed weak politically. Ireland, for instance. In the Irish past Renan felt a key element had been Rome's failure to conquer the island and thus to corrupt the native culture. On the other hand, he discovered far more laments of defeat from the Gaelic bards than songs of gaiety and victory. As with Arnold's work, this interpretation was more accessible and attractive to the literary movement than the authentic Gaelic poetry itself. In one of his final studies, from the late 1880s, Renan turned to the people of Israel, an interest shared by those Irish who saw their plight as similar to that of the Jews. Another favorite cultural parallel was with ancient Greece, and for this idea one could turn for scholarly support to 1880s studies by John Rhys and Henri D'Arbois de Jubainville.

Among Irish scholars, Sir Samuel Ferguson developed an influential concept of cultural nationalism in his 1830s essays on James Hardiman. Ferguson sought to reconcile Protestantism with Celticism into a union that would produce a national literature based on an authentic Irish tradition. His work directed the Ascendancy's attention toward the native culture and also laid the foundations for a distinctively Irish style of writing in English. Ferguson was a dedicated Unionist, however, and it took Thomas Davis in the 1840s to enlist the notion of cultural nationalism in the cause of national independence. Davis appropriated Ferguson's distinction between English reason and Irish emotion and developed it into a sharp critique of the commercialism and industrialism emanating from England and corrupting Irish spirituality and imagination. His call to action brought religious and class issues into the dispute as well:

> Modern Anglicanism, i.e., Utilitarianism, the creed of Russell and Peel ... this thing, call it Yankeeism or Englishism, which measures

prosperity by exchangeable value, measures duty by gain, and limits desire to clothes, food, and respectability; this damned thing has come into Ireland. . . . it is the very apostles' creed of the professions, and threatens to corrupt the lower classes, who are still faithful and romantic.[4]

This argument worked its way from Young Ireland up to the 1890s via such figures as Sir Charles Gavan Duffy. John O'Leary, too, records that his reading of Davis in 1846 led to a kind of "conversion,"[5] and he would, in turn, convert writers like Yeats, Douglas Hyde, and Katharine Tynan in the next generation.

The young movement gained further direction from earlier translations of Irish poetry by Hyde, George Sigerson, and James Clarence Mangan, and especially from Hyde's scholarship. But if anyone can be named the actual father to the Irish Renaissance, Standish James O'Grady has perhaps the strongest claim. Ernest Boyd calls O'Grady's two-volume *History of Ireland*, published in 1878 and 1880, the "starting-point of the Literary Revival."[6] O'Grady introduced to his audience the legendary Cuchulain, a heroic ideal from the past who seemed to promise an exalted heritage for the future. O'Grady's Cuchulain lived in a pastoral aristocracy devoted to beauty and craftsmanship, poetry and courtly bearing. Although he kept his passionate nature under tight reserve and depended solely on himself, Cuchulain was governed by absolute ideals and loyalty to his society. With marital infidelities also to his credit, he came more and more in his readers' minds to resemble their own modern hero, Parnell.

O'Grady established the principle of Irish history as imaginative recreation, a precedent that Yeats and others would readily adopt. The writers had more than literary reasons for recasting history, however, and Stopford Brooke's essay on "The Celt" places Arnold's and O'Grady's ancient Gael squarely within the more immediate context of modern social issues. Lecturing to the Irish Literary Society of London in October 1899, Brooke first recounted the usual characteristics. The Celtic race had never suffered inglorious failure or commonplace success. Its people had been undaunted by defeat, tenacious and unchanging, fiercely individualistic, passionate, sensuous, yet always yearning for something beyond the senses. Then Brooke went on: "The Celt was essentially aristocratic. . . . There is no trace of any democratic feeling such as grew up in the English towns. . . . This too was the element which lasted on, in another form, as landlordism, and gave it power for so long a time."[7] The mass of Irish peasantry seemed

much more manageable, within political as well as literary bounds, when invested with a Gaelic tradition of simple values and a strict social order. The gradual rise of the middle class after the Great Famine had created not only a literary movement, but also a whole economic segment that, like the landed gentry, had its own fears of being trapped between two cultures. Material advances and cultural interests separated it from the peasantry, nationalism from England. Even Davis' *Nation* had not been written in Gaelic. It therefore seemed necessary to construct a Gaelic tradition and imaginatively impose it on a tenantry that, in the process of driving out landlords, was clearly and dangerously in violation of its spiritual heritage.

The Gaelic past also offered a respite from the religious differences that unsettled Irish visions of unity. Vivian Mercier, in considering the influence of the Protestant religious revival on the Irish Renaissance, finds a strong evangelical impulse behind the interest in Gaelic. Figures like O'Grady, Hyde, Yeats, and Synge all had direct family connections to the ministry. After Disestablishment in 1869 and a fading, in the late 1860s, of the evangelical revival, Protestant religious energies took a more broadly cultural turn. Knowledge of Gaelic had previously been used in translating the Bible and in proselytizing among Catholic tenants. Now other ways of uniting Protestant and Catholic could be found, as in those elements, such as emphasis on Scripture, shared between the Church of Ireland and the early Celtic Church. To those still imbued with fundamentalism, the Gaelic religion seemed pure and uncorrupted, free from all religious or ethnic differences. Mercier further sees evangelicalism, in the latter part of the century, merging into theosophy or the religion of art. Action, or works, became replaced by faith, rationalism by anti-intellectualism, history by myth.[8]

The founders of the 1890s literary organizations conceived of their movement as a unifying alternative to the divisive controversies that followed Parnell's death in 1891. W. P. Ryan, Literary Society member and author of an 1894 history of the movement, described "our quiet little haven of literature" within the "seething agitation" of the Parnell controversy.[9] More ambitiously, it was hoped that the national sentiments inspired by Parnell's charismatic personality could now be channeled into nonpolitical efforts. Yeats later preferred to remember Parnell's death as the fulfillment of a prophecy and as the occasion for a

"supernatural insight" on his part, "the sudden certainty that Ireland was to be like soft wax for years to come."[10] Many people, politically disoriented in this acrimonious period, did welcome a movement that seemed capable of putting the country back together again. Writers, politicians, professional and rural classes, all were to find a common ground somewhere "above" the disillusionments of politics.

In late 1891, therefore, Yeats and T. W. Rolleston met with the Southwark Irish Literary Club and organized a merger, formally created in 1892, called the Irish Literary Society of London. That same year, aided by John O'Leary, Yeats brought together a similar organization, the National Literary Society, in Dublin. The new societies determined to reach a much wider audience than any previous group, with the general hope of shaping Ireland's direction over the next several years. Weekly public gatherings would stimulate a broad cultural discussion of their issues. In libraries all across the country, nationalist reading rooms would add depth and scholarship to the discussions. To make sure the people understood which Irish values were most important, the Dublin society hoped to publish a new series of Irish books. Perhaps an Irish theatre group could even be organized to tour the rural areas.

Yeats's insight, however, fails to account for very much of the beginning stages of the movement. The Southwark group had been formed as early as 1883, and it developed many of the ideas that later became the official policies of more notable organizations. Besides turning out the usual lectures, essays, and concerts, Southwark members staged dramatic performances, wrote contributions for the press, and planned the publication of low-priced Irish literature, which could then be sold or else distributed through lending libraries. Another prototype organization, the Pan-Celtic Society, came together in 1888; in the same year under O'Leary's guidance, the first official anthology of the new movement appeared, *Poems and Ballads of Young Ireland*. The London Rhymers, who were attracted to Celticism as an imaginative, poetic culture opposed to that of Victorian England, began meeting in 1890, and theosophical organizations had existed in Dublin since 1885. Parnell's death may have catalyzed several factors, but they had already begun developing toward similar coalitions before.

John O'Leary also served as a major catalyst in the late 1880s. Among the various connections between Irish literature and nationalism during this period, O'Leary's meeting with Yeats in 1885 stands out as a nearly perfect example of how productive those connections could become. Released from British prison, O'Leary returned to

Ireland in 1884 and immediately began devoting his energies to educat-
ing and organizing the Irish youth, especially the writers. With his
links to famous nationalists of the past and with his own incontroverti-
ble reputation as a romantic patriot and martyr, he soon attracted an
impressive following. Yeats, Hyde, Tynan, and Maud Gonne all borrowed books from him, learned from him, and soon began translating
his influence into their own writings. He seemed to promise a whole
new range of uniquely Irish subject matter to young poets struggling to
launch their careers. In some cases, as when O'Leary helped raise the
money to publish Yeats's *The Wanderings of Oisin* in 1888, service in his
ranks became directly profitable.

Another part of O'Leary's appeal to the writers lay in his
discouraging of any political involvement that violated their devotion
to literature. One could follow O'Leary without actually having to
enter the distasteful world of politics or engage in any potentially
dangerous activities. O'Leary generally opposed violence, particularly
the individual acts of terrorism that had marked the Land War, for
agrarian agitation seemed to him as strategically ineffective as the
efforts of Irish parliamentarians. The pursuit of his romantic ideal
required no tangible political results as a measurement of success.
There was a slight internal contradiction: truly apolitical writers would
tend not to align themselves with any organization. One did not have
to declare one's political allegiances in O'Leary's group, however; that
kind of choice, in a country sharply divided and potentially revolutionary, could mean nothing but trouble.

Writers like Yeats, Rolleston, and John Todhunter also balanced their nationalism against the aesthetic inclinations of the Rhymers' Club. The Young Ireland tradition had a compelling energy but was
constraining in its simplistic rhetorical impulses. The Rhymers, despite
their tendency toward aesthetic decadence, did reinforce Yeats's interest in technique and an elaborate style. On a more local level, the
Dublin theosophical organizations provided a crucial meeting ground
for the artists and intellectuals who came to form the Literary Revival.
Yeats's friend Charles Johnston helped found the Dublin Hermetic
Society in 1885, and a year later the Dublin Lodge of the Theosophical
Society received its own charter. A blend of psychic research, mystic
and Eastern philosophy, and arcane ritual, the theosophical movement
centered around its Russian founder Helena Petrovna Blavatsky.
Madame Blavatsky had organized her idiosynchratic studies into an 1876
treatise, *Isis Unveiled*, a religious handbook that her followers used to
replace the Christian ritual they had rejected. The all-encompassing

intellectual system attracted figures like Yeats, O'Leary, Sigerson, George Russell, and John Eglinton, and theosophical journals such as the *Irish Theosophist* influenced the Revival throughout much of the 1890s.

When the literary societies began forming in 1891, therefore, the mechanism for such groups was already well established, from the Young Ireland strategies transmitted by O'Leary to the elite coteries of the Rhymers. The main difference with the new societies lay in their hope of reaching a much broader public and of promoting Irish "unity." As late as December 1896, Alice Milligan, a Belfast writer, could still apply this hope even to the troubled North. Class war had declined there, Milligan claimed, and so had religious differences. All the Irish in Ulster could soon unite around the recognition of "alien rule at the root of their poverty," and the literary movement could foster and direct this outburst of unity.[11] Northern Presbyterians and Unionists, had they taken notice, must have believed Milligan mad; Lord Randolph Churchill and the "Orange card" had long since brought economic, sectarian, and political rivalries to the brink of a holy war in Ulster. The literary societies had proposed to stay out of politics, not to remain ignorant of them. And in Ireland in the 1890s, one could not utter the word unity without calling up a host of political reverberations, not even if one qualified it as "Unity of Being."

The hope of keeping the movement separate from politics, and from the disunity a political commitment would engender, held strong throughout the decade. Writing at the end of the 1890s on organizations like the Irish Literary Society, the National Literary Society, the Irish Literary Theatre, the Féis Céoil Committee, and the Gaelic League, Yeats asserted: "All these organisations have been founded since the fall of Parnell; and all are busy in preserving, or in moulding anew and without any thought of the politics of the hour, some utterance of the national life, and in opposing the vulgar books and vulgarer songs that come to us from England."[12] The statement sandwiches literature between political forces while claiming its aloofness from them. Yet the politics of the hour, Parnell and the English alike, were part and parcel of the national life. A writer who truly took no thought of those politics had a long way to go in convincing an Irish audience that he spoke for the country.

The writers, of course, could not remain nearly as distant from

political conflict as Yeats's or Milligan's statements suggest. They sought to distinguish between literary and political nationalism in part because of recurrent demands from nationalists that literature subordinate itself to Ireland's political causes. Even beyond their refusal of the methods of propaganda, the writers envisioned a completely new Ireland, one that would rise out of the ashes of politics and history. It would reject the materialism of England, the commercial aspirations of a decadent empire, and cling instead to its spiritual past, its small,integrated, agrarian communities, even its own language. Ireland, said Yeats, "will always be a country where men plow and sow and reap." Its people would keep alive "the ideals of a great time when men sang the heroic life with drawn swords in their hands."[13] The writers hoped to direct their country back toward such ideals by avoiding "politics," the mundane, day-to-day maneuvering, compromising, and calculating that ended so badly for Parnell. In the Ireland of Parnell's time, however, the drawing of swords meant not heroic song, but the bitterness and conflict of Committee Room Fifteen. The goals and values of literary nationalism inevitably blurred into those of political nationalism in a confusion of policies that dogged the Irish Renaissance from its start.

Yeats, writing of the period several years later, still had not resolved some of the internal tensions of the movement. He had feared that the leadership of the country might pass into the wrong hands after Parnell's death: "I dreaded some wild Fenian movement, and with literature perhaps more in my mind than politics, dreamed of that Unity of Culture which might begin with some few men controlling some form of administration."[14] Unity of Culture was indeed in Yeats's mind and would remain an important concept for him long afterward. In statements like these, however, it remains inexorably connected to the very experience, the disturbing power struggles of the 1890s, that it professes to transcend. His qualifying use of "perhaps" suggests an awareness of just such a connection. Language here transforms political activities into literary ones, thus justifying the choice of the cultural leaders from an enlightened "few men" rather than from dangerous revolutionaries. By further transforming this select administration into "Unity of Culture," the sentence completes the process by which dread gives way to dream. The politics of the 1890s literary movement lay in just such a willingness to sweep aside the barrier of the visible world and set in its place a myth of the poets' making.

Observers from outside the literary societies recognized the political implications of the movement almost immediately. *United*

Ireland hailed the founding of the National Literary Society as a "re-markable meeting" in that it brought such differing political elements together "on the same platform in serving the Irish National cause." Then the newspaper had some cautionary advice for the gathering: "Mr. Yeats," in his speech on the creation of informed Irish public opinion, "declared that the means . . . were nobler and better than the end; but . . . let us not put too much faith in books. . . . We are most certainly for the end" (18 June 1892). Already a bit too suspicious of Yeats, the paper erred in its report; the editorial citations come from George Sigerson's speech delivered at the same meeting. But the message was clear enough: literary movements had political potential, and the writers should use that potential for the right, i.e., nationalist, cause.

United *Ireland's* initial enthusiasm for the societies continued for several years. Nationalist verse like Katharine Tynan's appeared frequently in the columns, along with serialized novels, articles and letters from Yeats and others, literary-political commentary by Sir Charles Gavan Duffy, and extensive coverage of all the frequent sessions of the literary societies. And all the while the suspicions grew. *United Ireland* supported Duffy over Yeats in the dispute about the "New Irish Library." John McGrath's review of Yeats's *The Celtic Twilight* hinted that Yeats sometimes tended to stray too far from Celtic paths (23 December 1893). In an article of 17 August 1895, "Mr. Yeats on Irish Literature," the paper decided a few things needed clarifying once and for all. In his tastes in Irish poetry, as in *A Book of Irish Verse*, Yeats was guilty of "logrolling," a charge Yeats himself was sensitive about. He wrote too much like the decadents and aesthetes of England, the paper charged, and his attempts to separate literature from nationalism only alienated him from the Irish nation:

> [W]e are of opinion that if ever Irish Literature is loved for its own sake it must be at a time when the people will have no concern with politics. . . . While the struggle for our National rights goes on politics is indispensable. It might be best for the cause of Literature if its votaries so fostered it that it would tend to make the National struggle short. Davis made it serve that purpose.

A year later *United Ireland's* interests in the literary movement began quickly to fade. The paper's impatience with Yeats reflected a growing and widespread hostility towards the writers. Over the course of the

decade, the early feeling of harmony between poetry and nationalism gave way to a paralyzing antipathy that occasionally exploded, as in the arena of the national theatre, into deadly verbal warfare.

Celticism became an appealing movement in part because it seemed capable of defusing such conflicts; as with Arnold's original lectures, discussions of the "Celtic note" usually dealt very soon with an accompanying look at "unity." The Gaelic tradition offered to the imagination a period in which cultural differences and antagonisms faded away. Ancient chieftains and heroes were clear enough, their place in society made plain by the lengthy Irish sagas; it became somewhat harder to envision how such harmony would look in modern Ireland, whether in an actual society or even a particular poem. Katharine Tynan, still in the first flush of her recent discovery of Irishness, gave some early guidelines: "By the Irish note I mean that distinctive quality in Celtic poetry the charm of which is so much easier to feel than to explain." She mentioned naive "simplicity" as a feature, "a light touching of the cords as with fairy-finger tips." One might recognize "a shade of underlying melancholy" in this poetry of the twilight, or an "undertone," or perhaps a "shadow." The Celtic note produced "a rainbow of all colours where none conflict; a gamut of all notes which join to make perfect harmony."[15] Although it tempted them into a quaint, precious, and imprecise fairyland, Celticism did offer, to Tynan and to other young poets in O'Leary's coterie, a rich and unique subject matter for their work. Could this same heritage inspire a whole nation into a feeling of harmony?

Perhaps, offered D. P. Moran, but certainly not on the terms of Tynan and Yeats. Instead of being a "grand symbol of an Irish national intellectual awakening," Celticism was "one of the most glaring frauds that the credulous Irish people ever swallowed." No promotion of harmony here. Moran instead found a hope for Irish unity in the link between the Gaelic revival and the actual Gaelic language, a not unreasonable idea except to those who found Gaelic linguistically difficult and economically impractical. Despite their nationalist claims, English-speaking members of the Literary Revival, in Moran's view, talked *about* the Celtic note instead of *in* the Gaelic language and thus gained for Ireland little more than a "bit of English patronising praise."[16] Edward Martyn, a fellow activist in the Gaelic League as well as one of Ireland's two leading playwrights at the time, filled out the argument with a letter to Moran's paper, the *Leader*:

[The Irish] are always ready to inveigh against England, and then to fall down and worship her, and imitate her customs, and swallow her abominably vulgar literature, and neglect every artistic movement whose object is to strive to save the country from the level of cosmopolitanism and vulgarity in which it is settling.[17]

Moran's own journalistic columns in the *New Ireland Review* and the *Leader* consistently ridiculed anything tainted by Anglicization, and he based his militant proposals for economic improvements, independence, and Irish art firmly upon the language issue. The Gaelic League, with its broad-based support in the new classes emerging in Ireland, seemed to him to contribute much more to an Irish consciousness than the intellectual elites started by Young Ireland and reborn in the present Literary Revival. In a style that echoed Moran, the Gaelic League concurred: "[W]e shall have occasion to expose the artificiality and insincerity of the so-called Celtic note and Celtic spirit of the so-called Celtic renaissance in the English language."[18] Once more the swords were drawn. *United Ireland* made its own contribution to disunity when it began a regular column in 1896, "Irish Language Notes." The lead-in quotation, from Tacitus, could not but have rankled the non-Gaelic members of the Revival: "The language of the conqueror in the mouths of the conquered is the language of slaves."

By this time, however, the language of the conqueror had nearly eradicated that of the native. At midcentury perhaps a million and a half people still used Gaelic, but over the next several decades famine, poverty, and emigration decimated the Irish-speaking tenantry. Education was modelled on the English system, and English offered the language of profitable employment. At a hearing on education in 1899, Dr. Robert Atkinson, a professor at Trinity College, testified against Gaelic as a subject for schoolchildren. Besides being too difficult and often morally unfit, the Irish sagas had nothing worthwhile to offer the nonspecialist; and "spoken Irish would not be of the remotest commercial value."[19] Atkinson had his overall cost-benefit ratios correct; the dominance of English over Gaelic could no longer be reversed. Yet he failed to recognize the perceived need for Irish instruction and the enormous contribution of the Gaelic League to a national consciousness. People who did not use their native language could still identify with it and did so now in large numbers. Founded in 1893, the Gaelic League grew to 107 branches in 1899, and to nearly 400 by 1902. Even the clergy offered major support, for they associated English with Protestant England and its potential for spiritual destructiveness.

A precursor organization, the Gaelic Athletic Association, had been founded in 1884 by Joyce's Cyclopic "Citizen," Michael Cusack. The GAA, with its Fenian connections and hostility to "Foreign Games," aroused intense nationalist interest at the local, rural level. Cusack's followers were largely lower-class, and they tended to exclude Protestants and the middle class from GAA functions. O'Leary found himself a place among them, but to most of the leading Celticists, the GAA seemed nothing more than a crowd of unruly, albeit patriotic, sports fans. An organization like the Gaelic League would give Irish nationalism more intellectual respectability. Its founders dedicated themselves to preserving and extending Ireland's national language and to cultivating a modern literature in Irish. And, in the interests of harmony, the League pronounced itself decidedly non-political.

As the first president of the Gaelic League, Douglas Hyde represented an early hope for strong, unifying connections between the language and literary wings of the Irish Renaissance, for in 1892, a year before the League's founding, he had also been named first president of the National Literary Society in Dublin. That he became a major influence on the entire cultural movement is indisputable; Dominic Daly claims: "Whatever is rooted, traditional, distinctively Gaelic in Irish life today owes its survival in whole or in part to him."[20] The son of a Protestant minister, Hyde spent the first twenty years of his life in County Roscommon in the West, absorbing from his family the classical learning and manners of the Ascendancy, and from his neighbors the language, folklore, and customs of the native Irish. His Gaelic sympathies at first almost completely dominated his links to the Ascendancy. By his late teens he had developed a fiercely anti-English, pro-Fenian posture, writing poems in Irish that proclaimed the need for violent revolution to secure independence. Even in his first years at Trinity College in Dublin, Hyde's early thoughts about entering the ministry were undermined by his suspicions that Protestantism served the cause of the Anglo-Irish establishment.

Hyde came into John O'Leary's circle in the mid-1880s, an influence that completed the replacement of his earlier Fenian views with those of a more cultural nationalism. His interests by this time had become almost solely identified with the Gaelic language and its survival. He had been active as early as the 1870s in the Society for the

Preservation of the Irish Language; then, in 1893, the Gaelic League seemed to offer much richer possibilities. Although he recognized the necessity of maintaining English because of its economic importance and saw the impossibility of transforming Ireland into a thoroughly bilingual nation, even among the peasantry, Hyde felt that Gaelic needed the chance to survive as a minority language and in certain areas of the West. He published *Beside the Fire* in 1890, a collection of stories translated from the Gaelic. His most significant work from this period, *Love Songs of Connacht*, appeared in 1893.

That year was significant for Hyde in other ways than the *Love Songs*: "The greatest thing I did in the past year—indeed, the greatest thing I ever did in my life—was that I got married."[21] His bride was Lucy Kurtz, daughter of a German scientist, graduate of Trinity College, so much in his thoughts at this time that a journal entry recounted one of their outings and concluded: "I came back and we established 'THE GAELIC LEAGUE' to keep the language alive among the people."[22] The importance of the personal event could allow the public one to be summed up, in his journal, between a shopping trip and "Dinner with Lucy." In a literary movement remarkable for its avoidance of marriage and suspicion of the success of love, Hyde's sentiments were as radical as his signature, in Irish, in the marriage register in England.

In other social respects, Hyde had also moderated considerably from his earlier Fenian sentiments. Building on his family background, Trinity degrees, and membership in the Royal Irish Academy, he began cultivating the role of the country gentleman in the Protestant Ascendancy circles. On the contrast between these social contacts and Hyde's activities in the broad-based Gaelic League, Daly notes that "in private life his preference was for the aristocratic and urbane."[23] The Ascendancy was welcome in the Gaelic League as well. Feeling that the parliamentarians and nationalists had allowed the language to decay still further and that Irish unity was now crucial, Hyde successfully worked to keep the League apart from the controversies of conventional politics. Its membership included Unionists and Orangemen as well as the more nationalistic Irish, a cultural meeting point that held until 1915, when the militarist and revolutionary elements began assuming control of the League. In the face of severe factionalism, Hyde finally resigned the presidency he had held since the League's founding. A further opportunity to serve the cause of national unity came in 1938, when Hyde received his highest honor, becoming the first President of Ireland.

The crucial force behind the revival of Gaelic, Hyde also exercised a strong influence on the Literary Revival through such works as the *Love Songs of Connacht*. Padraic Colum, Lady Gregory, George Fitzmaurice, and most spectacularly, Synge relied on his work as their model for peasant speech. Hyde's themes, too, became a rich source for the writers, his Gaelic mode and peasant realism a valuable corrective to the misty romanticism of the Celtic note. Yet he had never tried to shape the Anglo-Irish strand of the movement, seeing English primarily as a useful medium by which to disseminate Gaelic. Although he sought a distinctively Irish way of translating the Gaelic poetry, he did not feel committed to creating a distinctive idiom. As the preface to *Love Songs of Connacht* noted, Hyde's main concern was with accuracy and authenticity, the reproduction of the "vowel-rhymes," "exact metres," "interlineal rhyming," and "Irish idioms" of his originals.[24] Besides John O'Daly, Edward Walsh, and particularly James Hardiman, Hyde's preface acknowledged the early nineteenth-century translator J. J. Callanan, one of the first to strive for the metric and rhyme effects of Gaelic. The most immediate influence on Hyde's translating style, however, and the man to whom the *Love Songs* were dedicated, was George Sigerson, whose contribution to the field, as in *Poets and Poetry of Munster. Second Series* (1860), Hyde regarded as enormous. In *Bards of the Gael and the Gall* (1897), itself dedicated to Hyde and Sir Charles Gavan Duffy, Sigerson refined his style in an anthology of verse translations that superbly captured the Gaelic rhythms. Even more than Hyde's, these two works established a major link with James Clarence Mangan, Sir Samuel Ferguson, and the beginnings of the literary movement.

Much of the appeal of the *Love Songs* lay in their confirmation of many already current attitudes within the Literary Revival about what Hyde termed, in his opening remarks, "the Gaelic nature." Central to this was "a melancholy spirit" ever engaged in "making a croon over departed hopes, lost life, the vanity of this world, and the coming of death." The *Love Songs* were the fourth chapter of Hyde's songs of Connacht, the previous three, including drinking and sporting songs, having appeared in the *Nation*. The wild and careless spirit of the earlier poems, however, did not catch the Revival's fancy as well as Hyde's love songs. When he wrote that "The life of the Gaels is so pitiable, so dark and sad and sorrowful," he added one more scholarly imprimatur to the poetic conception of Ireland's ancient past.[25]

Another responsive Celtic chord was struck by Hyde's identification of many of the songs' composers as women. The first song,

for instance, "If I Were To Go West" (p. 5), is a woman's lament about the failure of her love: "I denounce love; woe is she who gave it/To the son of yon woman,who never understood it." Her heart is "bruised, broken," like "a young maiden after her marrying." Men are completely absent from the poem, and even her beloved can no longer be found. One of the better-known songs, "My Grief on the Sea" (p. 29), which Stephen uses as a model for his *Ulysses* poem, was given to Hyde by "an old woman named Biddy Cussrooee (or Crummey in English), who was living in a hut in the midst of a bog in the County Roscommon." Like many of the songs in the collection, it expresses the despair and sorrow of love that remains unrequited. Lovers are typically false and inconstant, like "The Tailoreen of the Cloth" (p. 37), who shapes lies as skillfully as he does fabric. Or the two may be separated by harsh circumstances, the sensuality of the descriptions of a beloved confined to hopeless longing in the imagination.

Yeats's reaction to the volume was enthusiastic. Not only had Ireland found a poet of power, but Hyde had found a world rich with poetic promise. In the world of the peasants, Yeats noted in his review, "Everything was so old that it was steeped in the heart, and every powerful emotion found at once noble types and symbols for its expression." The people of the modern "world of whirling change" could only regret their existence, locked as it was in the "stubborn uncomeliness of life." Divorced from nature, they had little chance to mend the splits within their symbols. Yeats's remarks, his offhand characterization of the peasant world as "beautiful if somewhat inhospitable," seemed to have far more to do with the difficulty of being a poet than with the difficulty of being Biddy Crummey in the midst of a bog.[26]

If Yeats had missed an essential point in Hyde's depiction of the peasantry, however, he had misjudged Hyde's commitment as well, only two years later coming to the sad conclusion that the poet in Hyde was now overwhelmed by the dry, unimaginative scholar.[27] Worse, Hyde seemed absorbed in propagandistic journalism. Yet English, to Hyde, was merely a means of spreading his gospel of the Gaelic revival. He continued to lend some support to Yeats's cause, as with his play *Casadh an tSugan (The Twisting of the Rope)*, produced in 1901 as the first Gaelic work of the national theatre. But his primary interest was the language itself. Later, looking back on his work, he wrote: "My aim was to save the Irish language from death—it was dying then as fast as ever it could die — and that ambition did not lend itself to English writing except for propagandist purposes."[28] In that aim he was more successful than he had any right to hope. Yeats could have faulted

Hyde for his adherence to an essentially poetic solution to Irish problems. Hyde's faith in Ireland's willingness to reject English "materialism" was a tacit endorsement of the economic system from which
the mass of the Irish sought to escape. But Yeats, guilty of the same
faults in his own vision of Ireland's future, was not likely to make such
a charge.

Although it drew heavily from the Irish consciousness inspired by Hyde's Gaelic League, the Literary Revival thus stressed a
different note, Celtic rather than Gaelic, the creation of an Irish literature in English. It was this heresy that occasioned D. P. Moran's
spirited prose, and it was a consequent difference in tactics that separated writers like Yeats and Hyde. In the inaugural lecture to the Irish
Literary Society of London in March 1893, Stopford Brooke delivered
one of the first major claims for English in "The Need and Use of
Getting Irish Literature into the English Tongue." Brooke advocated
Anglo-Irish literature as the logical successor to ancient Irish, and his
speech, according to Ernest Boyd, constituted "a complete manifesto
of the principles and aims of the Literary Revival."[29] Yeats argued the
same point as Brooke and with the same problems of definition that
Tynan had earlier: "Can we not keep the continuity of the nation's life
. . . by translating or retelling in English, which shall have an indefinable Irish quality of rhythm and style, all that is best of the ancient
literature?"[30] People like Professor Atkinson, in Yeats's view, were
hopelessly out of touch with the times, victims of the Trinity College
syndrome of alien imitativeness. Yet even though he hailed the strong
sales of Irish-language books in attacking the academics, Yeats also
wanted to secure a place for Irish works in English.

Ideally, Irish readers would buy such books along with those in
English. The Celtic note was better attuned to English reading tastes,
however, with the Catholic Irish more interested in an anti-English
nationalism and militance characteristic of novels like Canon A. P.
Sheehan's *Luke Delmege* (1901). Yeats published in Catholic journals like
the *Irish Monthly* and *Irish Fireside* in the mid-1880s, yet the gap between him and his audience seemed at times unbridgeable. The barriers created by his problems with the language were at least partially
clear to him: "I might have found more of Ireland if I had written in
Irish, but I have found a little, and I have found all myself."[31] That
little, for someone like D. P. Moran, was hardly enough, and Colin

Meir even finds discrepancies in Yeats's claimed admiration for Irish poetry in translation. His later poetry does gain a clarity of language from Hyde or James Callanan; but "Yeats's early work shows very little evidence of being influenced by the translations from the Gaelic which by 1895 he was praising as the main line of his native tradition in verse written in English."[32] English tastes, now with a renewed interest in the Irish question, tended to draw the Celtic movement towards London and the Continent. In Yeats's own case his nationalist style gradually gave way to a European and Romantic mode in the 1890s. Reacting against "the several historical cultures which were competing for his identity," he began piecing together the "perennial elements of a new and in large part imaginary civilization," one concerned with what Allen Grossman analyzes as the Wisdom tradition. With the constraints of Irish history and the process of "archetypal self-finding" behind him, Yeats then entered a new phase of his career after 1900.[33] Celticism did produce a number of major works, by Yeats himself, George Russell, George Sigerson, Nora Hopper, and William Sharp; but after the 1899 publication of Yeats's *The Wind Among the Reeds*, the movement was kept alive, over the next fifteen years, only among the lesser writers.[34]

The lack of an Irish audience plagued the Literary Revival from the beginning. It seemed impossible to gain a sympathetic hearing for new ideas or modes of expression that failed to conform strictly to traditional Catholic values or to the nationalist aversion to anything Anglo-Irish. Yeats publicly complained in 1892 that the Irish "buy no books," their respect for poetry being mere lip-service: "They are proud of being a more imaginative people than the English, and yet compel their own imaginative writers to seek an audience across the sea."[35] T. W. Rolleston not only complained that the literary societies lacked the support of Irish critics and readers, he also emphasized English as the more proper language of the movement.[36] Rolleston's lecture drew a sharp response from the Gaelic League; yet the criticism against the writers was not entirely political and did expose some genuine contradictions within Literary Revival doctrine. Despite the influence of the Gaelic translations, and despite the ideal of a national literature as the voice of a whole country, many of the writers sought literary models from outside Ireland. Rather than cultivating simplicity and directness, their work was often consciously aesthetic and esoteric.

The poet Lionel Johnson, an English convert to Celticism, defended the movement from such charges in a lecture on "Poetry and

Patriotism." He rejected the political view that Irish literature should take Young Ireland as its model, and in demanding freedom from nationalist coercion, he claimed that an aesthetic interest in form and style was neither "British" nor "decadent."[37] The people in Ireland most likely to accept Johnson's premises, however, belonged to the Protestant Ascendancy. Yeats later sketched out the problem and a potential solution in "Reveries over Childhood and Youth." The Catholics seemed to lack good taste and decency, while the Protestants seemed mostly to think of getting on in the world. He would have liked to join the two halves and unite nationalism with a freedom from provincialism.[38] He had earlier noted a Protestant interest in "Irish things" in describing the superiority of "Unionist" reading choices over those of the Catholics: "These people are much better educated than our own people, and have a better instinct for excellence."[39] Mindful of the declining numbers of the Ascendancy, Yeats nonetheless saw their interest as a hopeful sign. Unity of all the political factions might yet come and with it a greatly expanded audience for Irish writing.

The hope was ill founded, both for politics and literature. The tastes of the Catholic readers continued in the mold of Thomas Davis, a materialist and positivist mold, as the writers saw it, one designed to produce specific gains and not universal truths. And the Irish writers themselves, "unless they are satisfied with a purely local reputation, are obliged to publish in England."[40] By this time, however, Yeats had grown weary with "this endless war with Irish stupidity"[41] and was turning to a more exclusive audience among the intellectual elite. In Yeats's view Hyde had sacrificed his artistic nature for linguistics and scholarship, and the Gaelic League seemed hostile and far from nonpolitical. Perhaps the man of genius in Ireland might still hope to reach the masses, not through such ventures as the New Irish Library, but through a select few whose ideas gradually shaped the rest of the society.

Literary projects like the New Irish Library, although publicly discussed in terms of literary goals and aesthetic criteria, never rose very far above the economic issue of readership. The Library grew out of the Irish Literary Society during 1892, with Yeats taking the initial lead in plans and negotiations for a series of popular, low-priced books on Irish subjects. O'Leary also supported the idea, and it was thought that Gavan Duffy's name would lend even more weight, so he was invited to direct the Library. Sir Charles had ideas of his own, however, ones that had not progressed much beyond his Young Ireland days.

In an 1892 address to the Literary Society he evoked the tradition of Thomas Davis and the value of "good books," those that "make us wiser, manlier, more honest, and what is less than any of these, more prosperous."[42] The progression itself was startling enough, but not nearly as unsettling as Duffy's continued insistence that literature must lead to specific, realizable gains. The foundation for a major dispute was laid.

Yeats had been right on one point in the decision to call on Duffy: his venerable name did gain respect and support for the whole movement. Perhaps even too much support, and not exactly of the right kind. The *Freeman's Journal* hailed the Literary Revival as a return to "the enduring lessons which can only come from those who are apart from the passing political strife of the moment" (30 August 1892). No quarrel from Yeats here, except in the *Freeman's* choice of the "most admirable leader of such an enterprise," the man who already threatened to bury the New Irish Library in political oratory, Sir Charles Gavan Duffy himself. Yeats tried a different angle and proposed a committee to advise Duffy on prospective titles. The *Freeman's* position became unequivocal: "[T]here is one danger to be guarded against, and Sir Charles Gavan Duffy is a safeguard; the danger is lest the new company should be used as a propagandist machine for sectional ideas and principles in conflict with the sentiment of the people. Such a danger lurks in Mr. Yeats's proposal" (7 September 1892). Duffy had strong support from the eloquent lawyer J. F. Taylor, from Sigerson and Rolleston, and from the clergy and the press. A year after the dispute opened, *United Ireland* still called him "the most prominent figure" in a literary movement that could well "transform and remould our whole National existence" (24 June 1893). There was no mention of Yeats, by now completely outmaneuvered in the publishing venture he had started.

Although he lost this particular battle, Yeats did irreparable damage to the brand of Young Ireland literary taste that Duffy tried to propagate. Duffy himself never gave up the belief that literature should have practical benefits, arguing in 1893 that readers' "lives might become fruitful" through a proper selection of books. His example for this proposition was an agricultural pamphlet on improved farming practices, and Duffy hoped someone would write such a work for his Library.[43] In the *Irish Homestead*, George Russell would later alternate poetry, imaginative essays, and farming tips with some success. Duffy never found any effective combination, however, and his polemical choices for the Library proved deadly boring. The first offer-

ing, as Yeats predicted, did spectacularly well, for the distribution mechanism was well established. When buyers realized how tedious and rhetorical the works were, however, they had little to do with any subsequent volumes. Yeats enjoyed the luxury of writing several reviews critical of Library titles, but it was hardly a solace:

> I recognize with deep regret ... that the "New Irish Library" is so far the most serious difficulty in the way of our movement, and that it drives from us those very educated classes we desire to enlist, and supplies our opponents with what looks like evidence of our lack of any fine education, of any admirable precession [sic] and balance of mind, of the very qualities which make literature possible.[44]

Not only had Yeats's pride suffered, but an audience for the kind of Irish writing he envisioned had failed to materialize. If his ideals conflicted with the "sentiment of the people," and Duffy's tastes with their level of endurance, it was difficult to see where such an audience might be found.[45]

With the problem of readership so deeply involved with the problem of how to create a national literature, the Irish writers sought to clarify the theoretical relationship of art to society throughout the 1890s. Two overriding questions emerged: that of language, whether Gaelic or English, and that of the writer's primary duty, whether to nationalism or art. Within these broad outlines the movement dedicated to unifying the Irish nation found ample room for internal quarrels, few of which ever reached any adequate resolution. Three slim volumes of essays from the period contain nearly every major theoretical question raised during the decade: *The Revival of Irish Literature* (1894), *Ideals in Ireland* (1901), and *Literary Ideals in Ireland* (1899). The chronological progression illuminates very little. Sir Charles Gavan Duffy's two essays in the earliest collection advanced the literary values that drove Yeats out of the New Irish Library, and by 1900 literature was still defending itself against the same demand that it serve specific nationalistic ends. Perhaps the only offering that resists relocation is George Moore's unique miscues occasioned by his late arrival on the scene.

In addition to Duffy's two contributions, *The Revival of Irish Literature* included Hyde's "The Necessity for De-Anglicising Ireland,"

a highly influential keynote address to the National Literary Society in November 1892. Hyde described the Irish paradox, felt particularly keenly by the nationalist middle class and the writers themselves, of alternately imitating England and then resenting that imitation. To prevent further decay of Irish language, traditions, and national identity, the nation must re-establish a continuity with its own cultural heritage, "must strive to cultivate everything that is most racial, most smacking of the soil, most Gaelic, most Irish."[46] The soul of Ireland, Hyde asserted, lay in the common people themselves, the hewers of wood and drawers of water, and he was confident they would reject English materialism before it overwhelmed Ireland. Hyde's strong appeal grew out of the inclusiveness of his vision. Not speaking to the common people on this occasion, he nonetheless offered his audience spiritual links to the whole country and an understanding of their Irish-English ambivalence. They did not have to throw off England, did not even have to be most Gaelic, for he had added a further category, most Irish, which embraced even the non-Gaelic strand of the Literary Revival. As an emphasis of poetics in a political climate, George Sigerson's essay, "Irish Literature: Its Origin, Development, and Influence," also attracted considerable attention. The press hailed his address as a major step in establishing a scholarly basis for ancient Irish literature, and the young movement would come to profit both from the scholarship and from the ambitious claims for the power of literature.

The collection of essays Lady Gregory edited in 1901, *Ideals in Ireland*, covered a broader range, but with the common theme of Irish nationalism contrasted with English cultural incursion. D. P. Moran set the appropriate tone with "The Battle of Two Civilizations," an analysis, like Hyde's, of the Irish-English ambivalence in Ireland. Moran envisioned an apocalyptic resolution of this conflict, a new Ireland rising up from the foundation of the old Gaelic civilization. In his essay Yeats followed Hyde's early lead in denouncing materialism as a national temptation, then spelled out more clearly than Hyde the ideal of Ireland as a land of the poor but content: "Ireland has no great wealth, no preoccupation with successful persons to turn her writers' eyes to any lesser destiny." One could have asked about the Irish writers who had sought a "lesser destiny" in the English marketplace, but Yeats's eyes were not to be turned this time. Irish poetry, he

claimed, dwells "on ideas living in the perfection of hope, on visions of unfulfilled desire, and not on the sordid compromise of success. The popular poetry of England celebrates her victories, but the popular poetry of Ireland remembers only defeats and defeated persons."[47] Within this state of affairs there were no doubt a great many malcontents, writers, merchants, and politicians alike, who would have preferred the compromise of success and the chance for a few victories. With the exception of Moran, however, the contributors to *Ideals in Ireland* had little time for speculations about economic or political progress.

The lost cause, with Parnell as its patron saint, received more radical expression from George Russell. In "Nationality and Imperialism" he took up Hyde's concept of a racial and national consciousness, distinct from English materialism and linked to the Irish language. Other goals seemed to Russell even loftier than that of Irish identity:

> Some... protest against our movements as forlorn hopes. Yet what does it matter whether every Celt perished in the land, so that our wills, inviolate to the last, make obeisance only to the light which God has set for guidance in our souls? Would not that be spiritual victory and the greatest success? (p. 20)

It was difficult to tell just where Russell's guiding light might lead, or who would still be around to enjoy the victory. But there were other surprises in the collection. Hyde asked: "What is the chief cause that has put Ireland so much back now compared with other countries on this side of Europe?" (p. 55). And then, to those who worried overly much about poverty, landlords, and English repression, he offered an answer: "bad teaching." The writers seemed to have only poetic solutions to Ireland's problems, solutions directed toward an elite that cherished the values of the past, and all in the interests of literature.

George Moore, newly arrived from London and not yet fully conversant with all the issues, knew enough to protest against commercialism, plead for a revival of the Irish language, and evoke the ideal of "small peasant states." Regrettably ignorant of the language himself, he closed with the offer to pay for Gaelic lessons for his nephews. Moore was not finished yet, however, and before *Ideals in Ireland* went on sale had an addendum slip put in confessing that at the time of his address, "he did not know of the extraordinary revival of the

Irish language in Dublin." Hostile critics like Susan Mitchell had their fun with Moore, seeing him as wholly misplaced within the movement while appreciating the punch lines he handed them ready made. More serious critics of the Literary Revival, however, could wonder what other extraordinary things the writers did not know about the country for which they were so busily creating a national literature.

The third collection in this group, *Literary Ideals in Ireland*, was indebted to T. P. Gill, editor of the *Daily Express*, who devoted extensive coverage in his paper to the activities and opinions of the Literary Revival. Early in the decade the *Express* had followed the customary policy of Irish newspapers in printing only a small weekly column on literature, art, and music, almost all of it from England and the Continent, and none of it given any nationalist tinge. The main exception, *United Ireland*, closely followed the literary scene through much of the decade. When its interest faded, Gill took up the slack and, in September 1898, radically expanded his paper's coverage and space for contributions. Almost immediately, the *Express* became the forum for a literary controversy, one less spectacular than the Yeats-Duffy split, but one that dealt more fully with the basic issue of the place of art in society. Having discovered his talent for open literary warfare, Yeats was in the middle of this debate, too, along with John Eglinton, George Russell, and William Larminie. *Literary Ideals in Ireland* reprinted a series of letters exchanged by these four.

Eglinton's essay, "What Should Be the Subjects of a National Drama?" opened the discussion. He demanded from national literature "a strong capacity for life among the people,"[48] and toward that union of art and society, rejected the attempts to transplant ancient legends "into the world of modern sympathies" (p. 11). His later offering, "National Drama and Contemporary Life," stated the case against misdirected artistic values more sharply: "The poet looks too much away from himself and from his age, does not feel the facts of life enough, but seeks in art an escape from them" (p. 27). By implication, such poetry as *The Wind Among the Reeds* was on the wrong track. In responding to Eglinton's theories, Yeats injected a more overtly personal note with his essay, "John Eglinton and Spiritual Art." He split with Eglinton on the issue of "aesthetic" over "popular" poetry, categories he had originally derived from his review of Arthur Hallam's essay on Tennyson.[49] Popular poetry, Yeats claimed, "is the poetry of the utilitarian and the rhetorician and the sentimentalist " (p. 35). Yeats

wanted to "liberate the arts from 'their age' and from life, and leave them more and more free to lose themselves in ... the accumulated beauty of the age" (p. 36). In relying on ancient myths and legends, the poet would function as a visionary seer, like Villiers de l'Isle Adam, for instance, "the principal founder of the symbolist movement" (p. 32). Yeats's subsequent essay, "The Autumn of the Flesh," further discussed his ideal of an art that would fill "our thoughts with the essences of things, and not with things" (p. 74). In realizing his proper role, the poet should now assume the task in society previously administered by the priests. In Yeats's view the Church concerned itself more with the social than the spiritual order and so had fallen into the same materialistic values held by the people themselves.

Eglinton rejected the charge that he advocated a utilitarian poetry of the marketplace, but he took up Yeats's personal note in his reply, "Mr. Yeats and Popular Poetry." Subsequent directions in art and critical theory would undercut Eglinton's devaluation of ancient myth as subject matter and his insistence on a persuasive moral tone in poetry. In claiming that poets like Yeats could not afford to regard modern life as gross and materialistic, however, he struck close to home: "Art which only interests itself in life and humanity for the sake of art may achieve the occult triumphs of the symbolist school, but humanity will return its indifference in kind" (p. 46). In Ireland by the end of the century, humanity had shown not only indifference but, on occasion, outright hostility to the school of Mr. Yeats.

The depth of Eglinton's philosophical concerns, ones that Yeats admired, found little room in this overly reductive dichotomy of aesthetic vs. popular, or idealist vs. materialist. Eglinton's earlier work, *Two Essays on the Remnant* (1894), had adopted a strongly idealistic tone in its attacks on commercialism and the artificiality of modern life. The "Remnant," Eglinton felt, must retire to the wilderness to renew its poetic inspiration. The same belief in the artist as solitary visionary re-emerged in his *Pebbles from a Brook* (1901). As Chosen People, the poets should listen to the oracles within themselves and then seek to restore humanity to its once lofty aims. The Heroic Age was lost, humankind had fallen, but the possibilities for moral regeneration still remained. What this meant for Irish literature was clarified in Eglinton's 1902 essay, "The De-Davisisation of Irish Literature." Davis had reacted against English materialism with his alternative vision of Celtic Ireland; now, Eglinton maintained, a new, more cosmopolitan direction was needed, one that did not concern itself primarily with nationalism, but with the individual person.[50]

Yeats found a bit here that he liked, and a great deal more that he did not. Eglinton's reliance on the cultural achievements of cosmopolitan literature seemed dangerous, an artistic sanction of Anglicization and Unionist politics. De-Davisisation, however, was long overdue, and the poet as priest also struck him as a worthwhile proposition. Yeats admitted in 1901 an original annoyance with the 1894 "Remnant" essays but now saw some value in the Remnant as leaders of the "great instinctive movements that come out of the multitude."[51] Eglinton's was a less messianic view of art than Yeats preferred; but then, in Yeats's opinion, Eglinton had written a number of things merely out of irritation, things Eglinton himself did not actually believe.

In his own contribution to the *Daily Express* row, George Russell tried, vainly as it turned out, to smooth over the differences between Yeats and Eglinton. In "Literary Ideals in Ireland" he claimed that both men actually sought the same spiritual essence in literature and that both would, properly, use literature as revelation rather than literal depiction. Later in the controversy, when he submitted "Nationality and Cosmopolitanism in Literature," Russell fell back on the dichotomies already established by the two main combatants. He opposed Eglinton, and by this time Larminie, for their adherence to an "actual Ireland" rather than to an "Ireland in the mind" (p. 83). Eglinton was for cosmopolitanism, but Yeats was for nationalism, and Russell agreed that what Ireland needed now was its own sacred, national ideals. With the opportunity to foster these ideals at hand, poetry should seize it. As Eglinton had compared the Irish to the Jews, Russell now drew a parallel with the ancient Greeks. As for the Irish themselves, they could well ask by this time what had happened to Ireland in all of the lofty evocations of ideal Greece and divinely chosen Israel. The debate on the artist's place in society had occupied the writers throughout the decade. *Literary Ideals in Ireland*, besides drawing together the main outlines of this issue, also suggested an increasing distance between the Irish Renaissance and the actual concerns of the Irish people. Eglinton linked an interest in "life among the people" to cosmopolitanism and finely wrought philosophic prose. Yeats tried to bring nationalism under the same roof with arts that "lose themselves in beauty." The theories about a truly national literature seemed more than a little confused and misdirected.

Opposing voices did arise from within the movement, ones more sympathetic to the desires for economic betterment or political action. In a contribution to the *Daily Express* a few months after the above exchange, Maud Joynt sought to reconcile industrialism with idealism. She opened with the familiar definition of humankind as visionary beings always longing for higher values, then expanded this view with the unusual claim that "Material progress does not necessarily mean materialism." Quite the contrary, the industrial progress in Ireland should be "one of the brightest signs to those who cherish great hopes for her future, for it is the material counterpart and embodiment of the changes taking place in higher planes."[52] On the exclusion of political commitment from the literary movement, "Iris Olkyrn" (Alice Milligan) asked in 1893:

> Should men of culture and taste, for the sake of developing Irish literature, leave the noisy field of political warfare, and attempt to develop their art in some quiet paradise apart, or should they bring into the conflict the keen intellectual weapons which can do good service there, though the edge will be blunted and the lustre dimmed by hacking of coarser opposing blades?[53]

Lest her readers might mistake the rhetorical drift, Olkyrn specifically identified Yeats as one of those writers who had succumbed to the temptation of faeryland. The issue, for Yeats, was clear; art should not sacrifice itself for politics. Nor does faeryland begin to explain the region he took for his work in the 1890s. But neither do the pejorative associations behind "materialism" begin to explain what material progress meant to Ireland in the late nineteenth century. Joynt's essay suggests another kind of aesthetic blunting and dimming, an oversimplification of historical processes, a rejection of the idea that higher spiritual values could manifest themselves in a material Ireland the writers found so difficult to accept.

Two separate issues lay at the bottom of these various literary discussions, that of language and that of artistic responsibility, and the tendency of the debates to confuse the two made satisfactory resolutions even more difficult. A great deal of Irish writing in the early phases of the movement had to be in English, and on this point men like Hyde and Yeats could agree. Was this authentic Irish literature, however, and was it eventually to be supplanted by a literature wholly in Gaelic? The two sides by this point were far apart and both drifting into the second issue: could an Irish artist write what he liked?

Nationalists outside the intellectual circles maintained that art must administer to patriotism and deal with those themes deemed politically most pressing. Literature would function as propaganda, not only in the choice of theme but in the manner of expression. No complicated symbols or foreign models allowed.

The artists rightly condemned this as too restrictive and parochial, and they proved their point by creating a brilliant outpouring of literature. But how national was their movement? Already made uneasy by their inability to use Gaelic or to avoid foreign literary influences, they needlessly oversimplified the second issue by claiming that art's responsibility was solely to art, the artist's responsibility solely to his vision. In so doing, they distanced themselves, not only from narrowly nationalist priorities, but also from broad sections of the whole nation. The politicians wanted to rely on literature for contributions to economic progress or political power, and the artists could justifiably brand such expectations as philistine. Yet politics did not equal Ireland, and the gradual feeling of antipathy to the writers that developed over the 1890s extended through much of the whole society. For this the writers could blame the politicians, but they could blame themselves, too. They did not, however, tending eventually to shift the burden of responsibility over to the "Irish." This position conveniently overlooked the fact that they and their work were, as they had claimed, and as nearly every poem, novel, and play had demonstrated, also Irish. The historical specifics of time and place made up an essential element in the literature, and the writers could ill afford not to understand those specifics completely. Insofar as they alienated themselves from Ireland as artists, their work suffered as art.

somerville and ross

T he most complete fictional account of the decline of the landed
gentry in nineteenth-century Ireland comes from the novels of
Somerville and Ross, writers who had almost no contact with the
"official" members of the Irish Renaissance, who, in fact, regarded
such organizations as the Gaelic League as "secretly highly disloyal."[1]
Yet their combined experiences brought to their collaborations an epic
breadth that depicts the Protestant Ascendancy in relation to every
other major social force in Ireland and that produced, in *The Real
Charlotte* (1894), perhaps the greatest Irish novel of the nineteenth
century. The Somervilles of Drishane and the Martins of Ross, the
house whose name Violet Martin attached to her share of the authorship, both suffered the economic and political losses that systematically eliminated the Irish landed gentry. The two cousins recognized
the place their own families occupied in the decisive social transition—
within the span of only three generations, Ross House slipped from
financial stability into abandonment and near ruin. In writing of such
processes, Somerville and Ross maintain a realistic, detached, often
ironic tone. But the fiction cannot overcome a deeply felt regret for the
lost way of life; their sympathies and point of view remain bound to
those of the Big House.

The latter part of the nineteenth century is portrayed most
completely in the novel Edith Somerville rightly called the "best of our
books,"[2] *The Real Charlotte*. The novel preserves the atmosphere of an
aristocracy in the brilliant and idle autumn of its power. The Dysarts of
Bruff, wealthy Protestant landholders and the center of social activity
in the town of Lismoyle, host and attend a season's worth of teas,
picnics, tennis parties, and outings on the lake with the British officers.
The Dysarts form only the top layer of a society that includes wealthy
farmers and land agents, extends down through shopkeepers and

tradesmen, and reaches to the servants and finally to the beggars. The authors range widely. But always they control the separate elements with familiarity and realism; with a precisely directed prose style; with contrasts that balance one class against another; and also with the complex strength of one central character, Charlotte Mullen.

Charlotte unites the novel's cross section of classes and interests. Closely involved in all the shifting balances of power, she uses her shrewd plots to influence the fortunes of many other characters, for good as well as for ill. She converses as easily with the inner circle of Bruff's aristocracy as she does with the Catholic tenants and beggars. Early in the novel she inherits a sizable amount of money that provides much of the capital behind her swift rise in the society, from the level of tenant to that of an actual landed proprietor. Even more than on the useful financial backing, however, Charlotte relies for her successes on a powerful will, intelligence, and social audacity. When she ultimately fails, therefore, the loss cuts deeply into every level of the society whose fate she has linked with her own. She may resort to underhanded tactics or bully her opposition into acquiescence, but her most ambitious scheme has the sensible and sympathetic goal of marrying her cousin Francie into the Dysart family and thus continuing the aristocratic line. Her inability to carry through her plan both results from and helps perpetuate the decay weakening the whole society — the declining fortunes of the Protestant Ascendancy.

Somerville and Ross follow most of the Irish writers of this period in attaching more weight to the internal decay of the Ascendancy than to the newly emerging economic and political structures beyond its control. Although Charlotte does not belong to that class, she represents a rejuvenating strength that might succeed in restoring the power of the Big House. The gains of the Irish middle class came in large part out of the pockets and privileges of the upper class. In their opposition to these gains, the authors depreciate the value of Charlotte's materialistic goals and cause her ultimately to fail at what she wants most. Yet the hope that Charlotte's vital practicality may unite with and inspire the Ascendancy balances the authors' suspicion of the rising middle class and brings to Charlotte's character a unity of attractive and repulsive traits that is psychologically and aesthetically effective. Charlotte's plan for her cousin's marriage holds out the distinct promise of success and renewal. Human action, however, has little effect on restoring the dwindling power of the Big Houses; the old feudal order cannot be joined to new sources of energy. With the old values extinct, no one wins any meaningful control over Ireland's

future, not the gentry, and not the middle classes who acquire a material power that has lost its moral worth. The authors can finally only stand back and observe this failure, much as they did within their own families, with an attitude of sometimes amused, sometimes horrified, dismay.

Somerville and Ross frequently placed their own experiences against a broad background of major social processes. In "The Martins of Ross," an essay on her family written only a few years before her death in 1915, Violet Martin described her father's funeral in 1872 as the final tableau in a tragic drama: "With the death of my father the curtain fell for ever on the old life at Ross, the stage darkened, and the keening of the tenants as they followed his coffin was the last music of the piece."[3] James Martin's death became for her the nation's loss as well as her own, yet the rhetoric, coming as it did nearly forty years later, appears strikingly misplaced, more melodrama than sadness. Edith Somerville likewise regarded the death of her grandfather in 1882 as a representative event: "With him ... passed the last of the old order, the unquestioned lords of the land."[4] The old landlords of Ireland were indeed dying out; still, the authors looked to their past as to an ideal dream world that language might preserve. In words that weave the spell of the Celtic Twilight, Martin wrote of Ross estate:

> The quietness of untroubled centuries lay like a spell on Connemara ... the old ways of life were unquestioned at Ross, and my father went and came among his people in an intimacy as native as the soft air they breathed. ... All were known to the Master, and he was known and understood by them. ... as a system it was probably quite uneconomic, but the hand of affection held it together, and the tradition of centuries was at its back.[5]

The "happy marriage," as she further characterized it, between tenant and landlord ended in the crucial year of 1872 when the Ross tenants, no longer willing to suffer the uneconomic system in affectionate and unquestioned intimacy, broke custom and voted for a Home Ruler over the landlords' candidate. She blamed her father's death on this act of supposed treachery: "It was not the political defeat, severe as that was, it was the personal wound, and it was incurable."[6] The tenants, in Violet's view, were the first to break faith.

Ross House, on the shore of Ross Lake, County Galway. This was the family estate of Violet Martin ("Ross" of Somerville and Ross).

Up to this time the estate had relaxed under the benevolent hand of James Martin, and "the subdivisions of the land were permitted, and the arrears of rent were given time."[7] Even though "eviction was unheard of," however, the laissez faire policies had some effects the essay fails to mention. Subdivision added more voters to the landlords' side at election time; it also created large numbers of subsistence-level holdings that, during the periodic crop failures, could not support a family. Violet Martin singled out as the real villains the spokesmen for the tenants, the false prophets who led the Master's sheep astray. A priest mandated against the landlords in the pivotal 1872 election, and later it was Parnell who furthered the collapse of the dream world. She wrote about the years 1881–82: "Ireland was falling into chaos. Arrears of rent, Relief Committees, No Rent manifestoes, Plan of Campaign evictions, Funds for Distressed Irish Ladies, out-

rages, boycotting, and Parnell stirring the 'Seething Pot' with a steady hand."[8] Even before this difficult period, with her father dead and her brother Robert unwilling to manage the estate, Violet and her mother had been forced to abandon Ross in 1872 and move to Dublin. The estate had passed through the difficult period of the Famine and remained solvent; James Martin, however, lacked the financial abilities of his father and quickly ran up debts of several thousand pounds. When Robert chose to pursue his London career as a journalist and politician, leaving his inheritance in the hands of a poorly qualified land agent, businesslike competence such as that which Charlotte Mullen was to possess must have appeared to Violet very desirable indeed.

Despite Violet Martin's distaste for the vulgar modernity of city life, the problems of the estate and the seemingly demonic agrarian agitation had changed her world into something threatening. She saw the demands for Home Rule as the beginning of barbarism in Ireland and as a potential surrender of the country to Parnell and his supporters. In "The Martins of Ross" she noted: "From 1877 it was Parnell who carried the horn, a grim, disdainful Master, whose pack never dared to get closer to him than the length of his thong; but he laid them on the line, and they ran it like wolves."[9] With her love of hunting and her respect for the leader who could command the hounds, Martin grudgingly acknowledged Parnell's strength; but he and his followers represented a much greater threat to her family than did the Charlotte Mullens. In 1882 Robert Martin became an officer in the Property Defense Association to assist boycotted landlords. At the request of the Irish Unionist Alliance, Violet Martin and Edith Somerville campaigned during the 1895 General Election. In 1912 Martin suggested that "under Home Rule there would first be Vatican Law, and after that, the sure revolt against it—a bad business too."[10] The decline of the old order seemed a collapse of all social structure; the onetime masters of the hunt had become the quarry.

The Somerville family likewise suffered as landlords. Edith, sharing Martin's political metaphor, wrote of her parents that

> somehow they ... pulled through those bad years of the early 'eighties, when rents were unpaid, and crops failed, and Parnell and his wolf-pack were out for blood, and the English Government flung them, bit by bit, the property of the only men in Ireland who, faithful to the pitch of folly, had supported it since the days of the Union.[11]

The essay containing this passage nostalgically idealizes the Somerville parents, who sacrificed both for their tenants and their children during the hard times. The tenants received seed potatoes, which they had to eat because they were starving; Edith received art lessons in Düsseldorf and Paris. She was profoundly aware of the suffering, writing in her diary in January 1891: "Rode round the Lickowen country. Sickened and stunned by the misery. Hordes of women and children in the filthiest rags. . . . felt helpless and despairing in the face of such hopeless poverty."[12] But this was the heart of the British Empire in 1891, and once more, just as they had so frequently in the past, people were starving under an economic system that had long since played itself out. Somerville noted the sacrifices, the price of her art lessons among them, that the landed families made for Ireland; there were other observers who found such sacrifices too selective.

The us-against-them dichotomy, Ireland of the Big House versus Ireland of the Cabins, is present in Somerville and Ross's work, but without the intensity of a cause. The "personal element" that reigns supreme in stories such as "Poisson D'Avril" also moderated their views of the public element, replacing the hasty passions and overly rigid categories of political rhetoric with a more generous sympathy for real people and actual experiences. When the Somerville estate at Drishane was forced to adopt "unusual defensive precautions" against Fenian activities in the mid-1860s, Edith, then a girl of ten, preferred to idealize the rebels and act the part of an Irish nationalist herself. Her dissenting role was expanded when the English dragoons offered her brother a ride on their horses; Edith, only a girl, was ignored: "I think that from that hour I became a Suffragist."[13] Yet the various causes, whether women's rights, anti-Parnellism, nationalism, or unionism, never invade and restrict the literature. There the mildly rebellious and critical attitudes attach more significance to the internal weaknesses of the gentry than to the shifting economic and political forces outside its control.

Even as she continued to support the old economic system, therefore, Somerville also recognized the part that the gentry had played in its own ruin. Her 1925 novel, *The Big House of Inver*, uses the Prendeville estate to chronicle the entire history of the Protestant Ascendancy of the nineteenth century. From its earliest beginnings in nobility and splendor, the family line soon became corrupted by marriages into the lower class and, even more so, by its own brilliant but debilitating extravagance. She does not withhold admiration for the aristocratic gallantry of their lives, for all the epic waste; yet she feels

the tragedy of it as well. The landed class had dealt too recklessly with its resources and by the end of the century had none left to fall back on. Never feeling as committed as Violet Martin to the old way of life, Somerville wrote in 1917:

> Things are better now. . . . Inspectors, instructors, remission of rents, land purchase, State loans, English money in various forms, have improved the conditions in a way that would hardly have been credible thirty years ago, when, in these congested districts, semi-famine was chronic.[14]

Yet the deep-rooted sympathies and instinctive assumptions that had shaped *The Real Charlotte* in 1894 remained firm throughout both their lives. Prosperity for the large mass of people and bureaucratic thoroughness do not necessarily create moral ideals or provide acceptable substitutes for the cast-off traditional values. Somerville and Ross could understand the passage of the old order into history and appreciate the new social institutions; but their first and strongest loyalties remained always with the Big House.

They recognized, years before most members of their landed class, that the old system of land ownership and social privileges was nearing its end, paralyzed by its own feudal sensibilities and extravagances. Yet historical perception formed only one part of the authors' sense of their class. Literature also gave them a way of evoking the past and using it to measure and judge the new, rising interests. Their recreation of the old social order continues to mourn the loss of that way of life, even as it admits the loss. With all its strengths and limitations, the vantage point of the Protestant Ascendancy serves as the dominating center of their work. They accurately describe the fate of many once great estates, yet their work passes, perhaps too lightly, over the fate of the large mass of the peasantry. While estates might go bankrupt, the tenants faced eviction and starvation. People who remembered these harsher sacrifices more vividly than the relief payments, emergency supplies, and financial losses of the gentry increasingly saw the Big Houses of Ireland as a symbol of exploitation rather than protection.

The two cousins met for the first time in 1886; Martin was then twenty-three, Somerville twenty-seven. By the end of that summer

they had become close friends, and by 1889 their literary career was firmly under way. Somerville held to her original intention of becoming a painter, producing illustrations that accompany many of their works. But writing now came first. On the mechanics of their collaborations, she wrote that

> our work was done conversationally. One or the other — not infrequently both, simultaneously — would state a proposition. This would be argued, combated perhaps, approved, or modified; it would then be written down by the (wholly fortuitous) holder of the pen, would be scratched out, scribbled in again.[15]

Their collaborative talents did not extend into service for the Literary Revival, however. Martin first met Yeats in 1901, on Lady Gregory's estate. Not a bit impressed, she wrote an amusing vignette of Yeats's awkward attempts to shield her from the wind while she lit a cigarette. And she resisted Lady Gregory's suggestion that she assist them in the creation of a new play for the Literary Theatre.[16]

Until Martin's death in 1915, the two writers frequently lived and traveled together, sometimes gathering material for a book or article on their excursions. Even when separated, as during Martin's efforts with her mother to reopen and restore the poorly managed Ross mansion in 1888, the two regularly corresponded on various writing projects. Their first novels, *An Irish Cousin* (1889) and *Naboth's Vineyard* (1891), rely heavily on sinister family intrigues that threaten sentimental love affairs. Critics took little notice of the works, although the *Lady's Pictorial* printed the second novel as well as two of the travel books that brought the authors the most attention in the early 1890s.[17] Their greatest success came with the publication in 1899 of *Some Experiences of an Irish R.M.*, reprinted five times the year it appeared. Two other collections of R.M. stories followed: *Further Experiences of an Irish R.M.* (1908), still riding the wave of the earlier work's popularity, had a first edition of 10,000 copies; *In Mr. Knox's Country* (1915) completed the series of marvelously comic stories. Although the approval of the British readers gave the two authors their first established degree of financial security through their writing, the commercial successes could not head off the rising economic burdens of the old family estates. With Somerville's parents both dead by 1898, she had assumed control of Drishane and discovered the depth of the problems facing the estate. But the money did release them from the demands of the

journalistic ventures that had previously consumed so much of their writing time.

Major Yeates, the Resident Magistrate (or R.M.), is a decent and innocent Englishman assigned to judicial duty in an Ireland that persistently defies his reason and comprehension. The first account of his adventures, *Some Experiences of an Irish R.M.*, opens with his acquisition of one of the marginally less dilapidated country houses in the West. Unknown to him, the squatters who previously enjoyed the house move to the attic and, fortified now with the Major's whiskey as well as the game from his estate, go on with their poaching practice. Their activities inevitably and hilariously come to light, but the pattern continues to plague Yeates throughout the book: even in the comparative safety of his own home, he is not immune from the shrewd but questionable schemes of the native Irish. The well-meaning representative of legal authority, he fails to keep even himself from becoming an accomplice, unwilling or unwitting, in later plots of dubious legal or moral nature.

Because of his professional status, Major Yeates is also compelled to participate in frequent social events not of his choosing or liking. His wife Philippa organizes many of these, in blithe disregard for her husband's longing for a little peace and quiet. In his marriage as well as in his dealings with the neighbors, Yeates most commonly finds himself manipulated by life's circumstances. He does enjoy fox hunting, however, and in their attention to complicated, madcap action in this work, Somerville and Ross achieve their most poetic effects in the many descriptions of the hunt. The Irish Literary Revival could easily dismiss them as witty observers of gentry sporting-life. For their many readers, on the other hand, the hunting scenes became the most characteristic and best-loved feature of the R.M. stories.

Part of the work's appeal, outside Ireland, lay in its reinforcement of the stage-Irish characters previously found in Charles Lever or William Carleton. The peasantry can be very helpful on hunts, battering down rough walls for the horses or hysterically shrieking directions for the riders. In other affairs, however, they resemble old Handy Andy — unreliable but good natured, untrustworthy but colorful in their voluble explanations. One story, "The Holy Island," recounts the predictable fate of a shipwrecked cargo of rum. Despite the best efforts of the police, the peasants manage to loot the casks and either get totally drunk or sneak the plunder off for a profitable resale to the pubs. Ireland is a holy island, the authors ironically suggest, only in the minds of the most naive of its inhabitants.

The character of Flurry Knox unites these stories as much as that of the Major. His main occupation is horse dealing, for Flurry can scheme and maneuver with the best. Unlike Yeates, but similar to Charlotte Mullen, Flurry makes things happen, moving easily up and down the various levels in his society as circumstances require. He changes over the course of the stories, however. Just as Yeates becomes more the knowledgeable local, Flurry becomes more domesticated and serious. His marriage is the final event in the work, another intricate scheme that accompanies his inheritance of his grandmother's large estate. On the wedding day the shockingly cultivated dress and behavior of Slipper, the omnipresent idler and notorious poacher, suggest huge changes in the state of the world. Normality quickly returns to the landscape, however. Slipper is discovered the next day, drunk as usual, his trappings of respectability scattered in the ditch.

The world of the Irish R.M. resists change, and therein lay a good part of its appeal, both to the English readers and to Somerville and Ross themselves. Their Irish people exist in an innocent and good-humored past, in an imagined period before such characters as resident magistrates had become the intensely hated alien representatives of English law. In *Wheel-Tracks*, a 1923 collection of earlier pieces and autobiographical sketches, Somerville described the Irishman who had supplanted those like Slipper.

> America and National Schools have created a new variety of Irishman, with his sense of humour drugged by self-conceit, with not enough education to reveal to him his ignorance, and with the bad manners inspired, apparently, by Democracy, which seems to act as an auto-intoxicant, with a result that is an indifferent substitute for the generous power of hero-worship.[18]

The Irish of the R.M. stories, for all their exasperating foibles, at least kept their sense of humor. And, more importantly, they kept their place. With an epic scope more complete than that of any other writer of the Irish Renaissance, Somerville and Ross captured the dilemma of the Protestant Ascendancy, its apprehensive and indefinite position between the native Irish and alien English. Their own sense of humor, however, came under increasing strain. In late 1898 Martin took a fall from a horse and suffered the severe back injury from which she never wholly recovered. Her health made the sustained and taxing effort of another serious work like *The Real Charlotte* seem out of reach for the

remaining years of their collaboration. The depleted resources of Ross and Drishane further demanded more of the R.M. stories that had proven so successful commercially. The fate of the old social order, turning increasingly to the tragedy that had marked *The Real Charlotte*, instead helped lead the two writers deeper into the comic world of the R.M.

The Real Charlotte began as a skeleton scenario in 1889. A year later Somerville and Ross were hard at work on the novel and finished it in the summer of 1892; revising and editing took another year. Publishers proved reluctant to take the manuscript, but Ward and Downey finally bought the rights for £250 and published it in three volumes in May 1894. Uneasy about their first three-decker and their most serious and ambitious work so far, the authors felt disappointed by some of the first reviews and the reactions among members of the two families, who disliked the "unpleasantness" of the novel. Within a year, however, the initial opposition gave way before the critics who acclaimed the work as perhaps the finest Irish novel of the century.

The Real Charlotte is about failure and loss (or, "unpleasantness"). It studies a broad section of Irish society of the late nineteenth century and finds that society characterized by decline, victim to a relentless string of defeats and dispossessions. No one gains anything substantial through his or her efforts, and only a few characters just manage to break even. The staggering record of failure needs emphasis early in a discussion of the novel because of the ease with which we as readers overlook it. In one measure of its success, the novel lures us into the same kind of ill-fated dreams that entangle the characters. The frequently light, witty tone conceals the underlying darkness, as do the dreams themselves, many of them attractive and sensible, seemingly within reach. But always a plan that has such promise ends in shambles, or a sympathetic character fails at some crucial point. Until the very end we believe that something will turn out right. And as events sweep aside even the final hope, we, like the servant who brings the last piece of tragic news, like the authors themselves, can only turn aside helplessly from the ruin.

In leading up to each failure or loss, the novel frequently creates situations of contrast: someone's external appearance versus his inner motivations, or his present status versus his past, or his own behavior versus that of another character who, although in similar

circumstances, belongs to a different social group. The contrasts partially define by negation and elimination, by determining what a character is not. "Washerwomen do not, as a rule, assimilate the principles of their trade."[19] This statement contains much that is characteristically Somerville and Ross. The artificially elevated diction and point of view establish an ironic contrast between language and experience. The qualifier "as a rule" adds to the irony and also gently tempers the directness of an already indirect statement. The authors distance themselves through such techniques from the world of the novel just enough to prevent too complete an identification with any character. As detached, critical, slightly amused observers, they finally refuse an entanglement in the potentially disappointing outcome. No character, therefore, earns unqualified admiration and sympathy. For us, the irony, the qualifiers, and the statements of negation, the whole manner of definition, reveal enough through indirection to make the characters engagingly attractive, bad habits and all. Only gradually do we learn of the futility of their efforts, something the authors have foreseen all along.

The novel emphasizes the differences common to many characters between their inner and outer selves. With the definitions of character originating from such a distanced point of view, Charlotte requires the most attention. Because of her more complex motives and more intelligent schemes, the "real" Charlotte emerges only after a wide range of observations, and then only dimly. She resembles

> some amphibious thing, whose strong, darting course under the water is only marked by a bubble or two, and it required almost an animal instinct to note them. . . . but people never thought of looking out for these indications in Charlotte, or even suspected that she had anything to conceal. (III, 89)

She thus functions as a limiting force on the other characters in the novel; if one could succeed in comprehending Charlotte, in charting the subsurface movements of her nature, then one could exercise some control over the various influences pressing in on the society. Action could become effective. Instead, only rare and easily overlooked signs hint to the others that the real Charlotte differs from what she seems.

One of the most vividly realistic of the early pictures of her reveals Charlotte keeping a lonely watch over the sick-bed of her dying aunt:

> Probably at no moment of her forty years of life had Miss Charlotte Mullen looked more startlingly plain than now, as she stood, her squat figure draped in a magenta flannel dressing-gown, and the candle light shining upon her face. . . . The lines about her prominent mouth and chin were deeper than usual; her broad cheeks had a flabby pallor; only her eyes were bright and untired, and the thick yellow-white hand that manipulated the hair-pin was as deft as it was wont to be. (I, 15–16)

The description follows the sequence of other characters' perceptions of Charlotte. Her unattractive shapelessness at first appears pathetic and vulnerable, the candle light and deep-red dressing gown only emphasizing a loveless existence that will never lure a man to her bedroom. Yet Charlotte's eyes betray her intensity and strength. In a novel whose characters so often lack energy and the ability to act decisively, her deft competence arouses our interest and makes her increasingly sympathetic and attractive as the central figure.

Charlotte directs her usually successful schemes with a quick intelligence, but even more with her powerful will. In the most straightforward of her major plans, she wants ownership of Gurthnamuckla, a particularly valuable holding on the Dysarts' large estate. Julia Duffy occupies the farm but has let it slide progressively deeper into ruin, thus completing the decay of her family's position, a loss of respectability even more humiliating in comparison to Charlotte's rise in society. Although Charlotte claims that at one time her ancestors ranked with the Dysart family, Julia and the Lismoyle society rather think of her as the daughter of a national schoolmistress and the granddaughter of a "barefooted country girl."

Beneath its veneer of poverty, Gurthnamuckla remains an attractive piece of property. With it, Charlotte could become even more important in Lismoyle as a landed proprietor and the "lady of the manor." The farm's pastures offer rich grazing land and an opportunity to work more closely with Roderick Lambert, to "stable our horses together," as Lambert suggests. Formerly a pupil in her father's house, he managed to acquire the position of land agent for the Bruff estate. Her long, deeply felt love for him has proven "more costly to Charlotte than any other thing that had ever befallen her" (I, 163). The passion she has had to repress when Lambert once rejected her brings to Charlotte's plots even more emotional intensity. For a woman of her position, intelligence, and abilities, Ireland in the 1880s would have offered few opportunities outside the financial consolidations of a

shrewd marriage. As an example of what women had to face in other professional endeavors, Charlotte could have taken a lesson from Parnell's perfunctory suppression of the Ladies' Land League in 1882, an organization headed by his own sisters.

Lambert thus becomes the highly desired object in a further major scheme, and marriage seems a real possibility when his wife dies. Charlotte simultaneously hopes to arrange a marriage of her first cousin, Francie Fitzpatrick, to Christopher Dysart and that family fortune. The highflown, at times outrageous, ambition of these schemes actually detracts little from our agreement with Charlotte that they make a lot of sense. Lambert is a cheap, flashy opportunist, and a petty embezzler besides; but he's more pathetic than evil or despicable. Despite his conviction that he has "raised himself just high enough from the sloughs of Irish middle-class society to see its vulgarity" (I, 180) and to feel slightly repulsed by Charlotte, he has already wed once for money. Marriage could break the spiral of disappointment in Charlotte's personal life. And through the second plotted match, Francie could inspire Christopher to shake off his personal lethargy, his lack of "confidence in anything about himself except his critical ability" (I, 186), in a marriage that would both renew and carry on the Dysart family line.

But too many forces work against success, and nothing turns out right. Francie rejects Christopher and thus occasions one of those spasms of fury when "the weight of the real Charlotte's will, and the terror of her personality" (III, 13) burst through to the surface. Charlotte's strength of will later faces a much harsher test with the news of Lambert's betrayal: he has somehow won Francie's hand. The first loss leaves society the poorer; the second cuts Charlotte personally and goads her truly to revenge. Her last and most inspired plot, fueled by her despair and rage, finishes by destroying Lambert, Francie, even Charlotte herself. She not only gains crushing financial power over Lambert, she offers to Francie the possibility of leaving him and running off with the superficially romantic British officer Hawkins. Lambert finally realizes the horror of what Charlotte has done to him, but their confrontation, and the novel, end abruptly with news that appalls them both: Francie has been killed in a fall from a horse. Charged in her aunt's dying wish to care for Francie with the inheritance that Charlotte instead used primarily to foster her own social advancement, Charlotte must now confront her most awesome personal failure.

Francie offered the cheeriest possibility for a happy ending of some sort. She possesses boundless energy and charm and an irre-

pressible optimism that more than compensate for her lack of serious-
ness and cultivated taste. An orphan, raised in Dublin, she brings the
city's intensity to Lismoyle when she comes under Charlotte's care.
Vulgarity, one of the novel's recurrent concepts, clashes with the more
traditional standards of the agrarian community, but Francie injects
some badly needed imagination and freshness into a fading society.
Somerville wrote of her: "We knew her best; we were fondest of her."[20]
Her fatal spill, the last of five deaths, seems the most tragic, especially
when we recall the energy and success that characterized her initial
escapades.

The frequent social events provide contrasts between many
characters. Their breeding and cultivated poise, or lack of those crucial
qualities, emerge from such affairs as the tea party given by the
Beatties. We first see how Lady Dysart manages her lawn tennis party
and thus can more accurately gauge the Beatties' upper-middle-class
affair, the awkward uncertainty beneath their show of gentility. Charlotte's tea party falls to a lower level still, and even the servants have
their social rituals. The comparisons, the details peculiar to each level,
define a good part of the class differences and also suggest the relative
worth of each. Francie, riding on her background in such democratic
institutions as the Dublin Sunday School, which "permeates all
ranks," proves capable of shifting freely from one class to the next. The
unaffected luxury and quiet, meditative elegance of Bruff not only
awes her, it offers her a way of life the authors see as qualitatively
better.
    The ease with which Christopher Dysart becomes fascinated
with Francie and then idealizes her abilities and talents suggests the
possibility that she might well move among the aristocracy as his wife
some day. In teaching her about poetry, "he had found out subtle
depths of sweetness and sympathy that were, in their responsiveness,
equivalent to intellect" (II, 194). The irony does not entirely mask the
sexuality of the language. Even though Christopher continues to appear "infinitely remote" in Francie's mind, "her pliant soul rose
through its inherited vulgarities, and gained some vision of higher
things" (II, 255). She can shed the limitations of her class more easily
than she can her fascination with Hawkins, however. Although the
suave, irresponsible officer once seemed to her a star "of unimagined
magnitude," Francie finds him more comprehensible than Chris-

topher. Feeling comfortable within the conventional language he uses in their love scenes, she allows herself to be overpowered by his sheer animal charm. Christopher, by comparison, speaks often of kindness in wooing Francie. He respects her more than does Lambert and his smothering, selfish concern. When she puts up a front of independence, therefore, one that Hawkins would have brushed straight through and Lambert stubbornly waited out, Christopher acknowledges it.

Lambert, least likely of the three, finally marries Francie. Her flirtation with Hawkins resulted in her expulsion from Bruff, followed by Charlotte's anger that Francie refused Christopher's proposal. Packed off in disgrace, Francie suffers the final blow when she learns that Hawkins, more in need of money than love, has returned to an original betrothed who will pay off all his debts. Lambert, dull but persistent, represents to her the only link to the happy summer in Lismoyle and an escape from the drudgery and poverty of her aunt and uncle's house in Bray. In his role as savior, however, Lambert has very limited range. After he had earlier capsized his yacht and was floundering helplessly in the lake, Christopher was the one to save Francie from drowning. The lake is much more his element than Lambert's; or Cursiter's, who chugs meaninglessly back and forth across it in a steam launch; or Hawkins', who runs the launch aground. Why, then, does Christopher, with his hidden strength, with his unselfish concern for Francie, rate "small claim to respect or admiration" (I, 190) from the authors?

The judgment belies much of the respect and affection Somerville and Ross have for Christopher but does point to what they see as crucial inadequacies. He is a failed artist, a creature "so conscious of its own weakness as to be almost incapable of confident effort" (II, 255). In his hobby of photography he seeks a mechanical proficiency otherwise immobilized by his own self-doubts.

> His fastidious dislike of doing a thing indifferently was probably a form of conceit... it brought about in him a kind of deadlock.... Half the people in the world were clever nowadays, he said to himself with indolent irritability, but genius was another affair. (I, 186–87)

Frustrated by the conviction that he lacks superior qualities, Christopher refuses halfway measures and insulates himself from any risks, social or emotional. Yet both the social and the emotional situations call for strong, decisive action. Francie represents one way, seemingly the

only way, for Christopher to break free of his paralyzed isolation. As with other characters, notably Lambert, scenes of natural beauty signal a fairly conventional mood of lyrical reverie for Christopher. But while Lambert accepts these emotions and momentarily escapes from convention, Christopher always questions his feelings as "mere self-conscious platitudes." Francie changes that, arousing in him renewed faith in "the mysteries of life into which he had thought himself too cheap and shallow to enter" (II, 256). She complements his failings, transforms him into a stronger, more decisive and active person, allows him success. And equally important to the novel, marriage would assure his family line.

Several factors contribute to Christopher's failure. One is simply his personal weakness, his inability to win Francie even from someone as shallow as Hawkins. And the tremendous pressure of circumstances proves too complex, too firmly locked into a downward-turning spiral. The collapse of his relationship with Francie cuts even deeper into the power of an already failing landed class. Attractive as Christopher may be, he shares in the debilitating weakness and ineffectuality paralyzing the Protestant Ascendancy and dooming it to ever greater decay. Nor does the future of the newer, rising classes appear substantially brighter. In her victories over both Julia Duffy and Lambert, Charlotte resorts to the hated methods of the Irish "gombeen men," usury and financial coercion, to drive her victims into ruin. Yet her gains cost her a great deal and fail to bring her what she wants most.

The choice of a spinster as a main character raises biographical issues closely related to the social character of *The Real Charlotte*. The novel relies on many obvious biographical details, such as the resemblance of Lough Moyle to Lough Corrib, the Galway lake marking one edge of Ross estate. Gurthnamuckla housed a Ross tenant, a widow in arrears on rent. And Somerville explained that her mother provided the model for Lady Dysart: "She, as we said of Lady Dysart, said the things that other people were afraid to think."[21] Charlotte only seems to practice such honesty. More speculative, and more crucial to the novel, is the resemblance of Robert Martin, Violet's brother, to Christopher Dysart. Robert wrote plays requiring the participation of the whole family, as does Christopher's younger brother Garry. He frequently sailed Ross Lake. He had the romanticism and sensitivity that mark Christopher as eccentric. And his reluctance to carry on the Ross estate after James Martin's death in 1872 necessitated its abandonment. In their ambivalence about Christopher, Somerville and

Ross temper their affection with the judgment that, like all the other men in the novel who have abdicated responsibility or proven ineffectual, he is not the strong, masculine hero needed to carry on the Dysart family line.

His sister Pamela, too, we sense, will never marry. Spinsterhood proves an accurate metaphor in defining the dilemma of the landed gentry. And marriage fails to offer any successful alternative. As an institution, it takes a relentless beating in *The Real Charlotte*, with one character after another demonstrating, whether by word or in practice, that wives and husbands have a miserable time of it together. The unmarried states of Pamela and Christopher coincide with the internal weakness of the gentry, its failure to propagate its aristocratic tradition and values. With Charlotte, spinsterhood points up an even broader deficiency in the society, the inability of vital, decisive action to reverse the decline of the old way of life.

There remains a vast gulf separating Christopher from those who possess, as do Francie or Charlotte, the energy of renewal and who offer him an escape from his paralysis. The personal weakness preventing him from winning Francie also makes him no match for Charlotte's brisk practicality and business schemes. At their meeting to discuss the affairs of the Bruff estate, he and Charlotte appear together as "two incongruous figures on the turf-quay, one short, black, and powerful, the other tall, white, and passive" (III, 205). Christopher can master the surface of the lake, can even save Francie from its depths. But he can never hope to comprehend the murky, mysterious forces suggested by the turf-quay hidden along the shore and whose dark recesses Charlotte, as distinctively Irish as the Dysarts are British, knows so well.

The universality of failure in the novel serves a warning to those in Ireland who value too much the kinds of materialistic gains Charlotte wants. Such a rise in society can bring nothing but disappointment; the middle classes should therefore seek more idealistic and spiritual goals than those that serve only self-interest and that so often come at the expense of the gentry. Even more importantly, Somerville and Ross see failure as the distinguishing feature of their own dilemma, and of the whole state of crisis within the landed class. Feeling that they themselves could never marry, they could at least create a literary character who attempts marriages for other people. In the interests of their class, they hold out the hope that such matchmaking will restore the fading power of the landed families. In the interest of their art, and demanding from themselves a clearer vision of their

experience, they had no alternative but to depict such hopes as futile.

Edith Somerville recorded an incident from her years with Violet Martin that struck them both, at the beginning of their literary career, with the force of a supernatural vision. They were leaving from a visit to the family of an old estate when they glimpsed, in a secluded window of the mansion, a white face:

> An old stock, isolated from the world at large, wearing itself out in those excesses that are a protest of human nature against unnatural conditions, dies at last with its victims round its death-bed. Half-acknowledged, half-witted, wholly horrifying; living ghosts, haunting the house that gave them but half their share of life, yet withheld from them, with half-hearted guardianship, the boon of death.[22]

The shock seemed to them an inspiration, a signpost towards the kinds of realism and authenticity they should strive for in their work. The theme of the lonely figure on the margins of his society became more pronounced in Yeats's writing from the 1890s, and over and over in the literature of this decade there recurs the image of the person trapped between life and death, the real and the ideal, the waking nightmare and the visionary dream. The landed gentry in late nineteenth-century Ireland found themselves isolated in just such a fashion. An alien class in their own society, heirs to a noble past and a desolate future, they felt unable to repair their failing fortunes, yet felt equally unable to accept the lot that history offered them.

GEORGE MOORE

In his biography of George Moore, Hone records that in 1893 Moore wrote to his brother Maurice to request information about their family history. This renewed interest in the Moore ancestry, George felt, was somehow associated with the "preposterous" love for England then inspiring his writing of the novel *Esther Waters*.[1] Since 1873 he had lived only intermittently in Ireland and later wrote that, when there, he "always experienced a sense of being a stranger in my own country."[2] With Moore Hall and the family estate falling increasingly into decay, Paris or London seemed more attractive, more conducive to art, more sympathetic to Moore himself. If the Irish landed gentry similarly felt like strangers within their own country, he had taken pains to protect himself against such a position. Attachment to England, criticism of Ireland, devotion to art—all served to distance him from a culture he found alien and restrictive.

In cultivating his role as artist in exile, however, Moore could never wholly escape Ireland. When Yeats and Martyn first proposed to him the idea of a new Irish theatre, he found their hopes absurd, for "to give a Literary Theatre to Dublin seemed to me like giving a mule a holiday."[3] The initial skepticism did not last, however. A later telegram from Martyn read, "The sceptre of intelligence has passed from London to Dublin,"[4] and Moore hurriedly packed his belongings and followed along. He had, in his view, already rescued the theatre rehearsals from the bumbling amateurism of Martyn and Yeats. Ireland contained his own experience within its past, might yet be a fresh subject for his work, might even offer him "A new language to enwomb my thoughts."[5] Perhaps even Moore himself was to bear the sceptre of intelligence that would save his country.

This idea, too, struck him as a bit preposterous. Yet the whole range of his long relationship with Ireland was dominated by unresolved ambivalence. Outraged by Republican forces who burned

Moore Hall in 1923, he would write: "No country is so foreign to me as Ireland."[6] A similarly clean separation of sensibilities from his country of origin had earlier allowed him to pronounce *Esther Waters* "the most English of all novels."[7] Yet the same affection for Moore Hall that turned to bitter grief at its destruction also binds *Esther Waters* to his family estate in Mayo. Although set in England and concerned with the life of an English servant woman, the novel takes its directing consciousness from experience that is uniquely Irish. It not only dramatizes, several years before Moore heard of such things as national theatres or language revivals, the state of mind that eventually drew him back to Ireland and its flourishing literary movement; the work also helps to identify some of the central feelings underlying that artistic renaissance and to locate those feelings within particular transformations of the Irish political, economic, and social structures.

Esther Waters describes what happens to a person who attempts to succeed, in the way that would make her happiest, within a society that precludes success and streaks of luck. Not visibly in a state of decline itself, the society of the novel nevertheless inexorably forces each of its characters into failure and hardship. They have no way of reversing their fates and can at best only recognize the futility and irrelevance of action in the face of such complex and powerful environmental forces. Those desires for happiness that depend on outside means inevitably end in ruins. People find contentment, Moore suggests, not by seeking external success, but by turning inwards, beyond the range of action. As she comes to rely less and less on a society that takes more than it gives, Esther finally rests upon the simple and life-sustaining core of her personality, one too solid for the world to break. Yet even when defined on her own terms, her character emerges primarily from the experiences of deprivation, calamity, and loss. The answers she gains for herself demand a withdrawal from and rejection of the world in which she has found little more than suffering.

In exploring the theme of defeat in the world of action and society, Moore took up problems that grew out of his own roles as both a novelist of insecure financial and aesthetic means and the landlord of a large estate in late nineteenth-century Ireland. The novel's depictions of the emotions and consequences of failure draw much of their immediacy of feeling from his anxieties about his status within the circles of artistic talent and landed power. Moore Hall faced the same economic pressures threatening thousands of large Irish estates at that time: how to control its own fortunes during the major social transition increasingly eroding the wealth, power, and privileges of the landed

gentry. Although he never approached Esther's extreme poverty, Moore well understood the fear of one day ending up with nothing and the desperate hope of somehow breaking into the streak of fortune that would reverse the decline.

Moore Hall had never enjoyed a very secure economic foundation, especially in the wake of the Famine. When Moore was nine, however, one of his father's race horses began a streak of luck for the estate by winning a major race and initial purse of nearly £20,000. Much of the new wealth helped expand the racing facilities, and for George and his brother Maurice, "there was no life except the life of the stable-yard."[8] Money also became available now for George's education at British schools like Oscott, a less happy experience, both academically and emotionally. Dismal progress seemed to bear out his parents' joking but ill-considered ridicule of him as stupid, ugly, and doomed to failure. He dreamed of winning acclaim as a gentleman jockey and found himself directed towards a military career instead. Then, in 1870, his father died unexpectedly; as with the horses, chance had again intervened, whether for good or bad, George could not decide, for "I suddenly found myself heir to considerable property . . . and then I knew that I was free to enjoy life as I pleased; no further trammels, no further need of being a soldier."[9] The circumstances resemble those preceding the death of Violet Martin's father. George Henry Moore had won a parliamentary seat in 1868 with his support for land reform and certain principles of tenant rights. When his own tenants conspired to withhold rents, however, he returned from Westminster determined to insist on the rights of a landlord. His threats of mass eviction were cut short by a fatal stroke.

Like Violet Martin, Moore's son George also felt quite sure who bore responsibility for the loss to the family. He wrote in a preface to Maurice's biography of their father: "He died killed by his tenants, that is certain; he died of a broken heart."[10] The estate at that time comprised more than 12,000 acres, with yearly rentals worth £4,000. The eldest son returned home, freed from military school into the role of young Irishman about town. In 1873, when Moore turned twenty-one, he moved to Paris, liberated into a new life of aesthetic circles and affairs with models and actresses. He had an annual income of £500 to invest in his burgeoning interest in art, and Ireland had come to seem threatening and artistically stifling. The year 1870 for Moore seemed to

mark a turning point in the status of his landed class. An uneasy complex of views began to emerge for him, a combination of enlightened land politics and tenant treachery, an enforced and unwanted career replaced by the freedom of art, new social responsibility coupled with new financial benefits, all somehow united within the experience, awesomely subject to chance and fate, of an unpredictable and incomprehensible Irish tenantry and his father's sudden death.

Supported in fairly lavish style by rents from the estate, Moore soon gained introductions into the artistic circles of Parisian café society. As a regular at the Café de la Nouvelle Athènes, he eventually met all the major French artists of the period, impressionist painters as well as naturalist novelists. His extravagant life style failed to produce much evidence of any talent for painting, so in 1876, and feeling occasional financial pinches, he turned to writing. *Flowers of Passion* appeared in 1878, *Pagan Poems* in 1881, poems nearly smothered in the imagery of the Pre-Raphaelites and the shock appeal of Baudelaire. But despite his verbal flamboyance and outrageous poses, Moore's personal life retained a fairly respectable base. A Parisian friend, Théodore Duret, explained: "He tried to shock and astonish people; but he was always the gentleman, and would never associate with those whom he thought to be below his rank as an Irish landlord."[11] The two sides of his character, the decadent aesthete and the cautious, sensible landlord, meshed with a disquieting tension that generated brilliant verbal energy in such works as the *Confessions of a Young Man* (1888). Only rarely in his early writing, however, could he direct that energy with any artistic sureness and excellence.

The crash came in 1880. His uncle and financial manager Joe Blake wrote that the estate was on the brink of another rent boycott and possibly bankruptcy. Malcolm Brown, in his book on Moore, claims: "The traumatic shock of Blake's letter was the most memorable experience of Moore's life."[12] It crystallized all his worst fears about the collapse of everything he valued. The ruin of his whole landlord class by such means would begin the final stage in the decline of what little remained of civilization, that island of art and high culture, refined thought, good taste, elegant manners, everything precious to him that the barbarian masses threatened and now seemed certain to destroy. He saw himself thrown back upon a talent as yet untried, condemned to pander to the philistines for his very survival. The self-irony of the *Confessions* only partially defuses his hysterical protests about such a fate: "That some wretched farmers and miners should refuse to starve, that I may not be deprived of my *demi-tasse* at *Tortoni's*; that I may not

be forced to leave this beautiful retreat, my cat and my python — monstrous."[13] But leave he did, and a year later had settled into a lower standard of living as a frugal and laborious professional writer in London. The estate continued to produce a modest income, and to get even that much, he lived in constant horror that the tenants might at any time capriciously refuse to pay and so plunge him into poverty.

Moore started out with several literary odd jobs, writing reviews and articles while working on more ambitious novelistic enterprises. Love affairs with society women such as Mrs. Pearl Craigie and Maud Burke gradually won him entrance into London's upper circles. Like many of his own literary characters, however, he consistently managed to avoid any relationship that became too entangling or demanding. Helmut Gerber sums up this period: "His relations with women always seemed to be carried on at a distance, often by correspondence, or he chose as his objects of affection women who were for various reasons unattainable."[14] The men and women Moore created in his novels similarly fail to achieve any enduring happiness or ideal union through love. He patterned *A Mere Accident* (1887) on his friend and cousin Edward Martyn. The hero, against his celibate inclinations, finds himself pressured into a marriage engagement; he is spared, however, when his fiancée conveniently kills herself after being raped by a tramp. Written as an exercise in Walter Pater's prose rhythms and sentiments, the novel elicited no more than a mild protest from Pater against the careless use of such lurid material. Whether in love or high society, the ambivalence eventually won out. Society women got him the necessary introductions; in the mid-1890s he even became a member of Boodles, a club for London aristocrats. But even then his eccentricities alienated most of the club set. Art offered more secure emotional ground.

During the 1880s and early 1890s, however, art had as yet no financial security to offer, no tangible proof of his talent and worth as a writer, no comforting release from anxieties about surly tenants and timid, ineffectual landlords. Moore cultivated Pater's influence for a time, an interest that he dated from his 1885 reading of *Marius the Epicurean* and that lasted until about 1893. *A Mere Accident* was only one of several "aesthetic" novels written during his discipleship to Pater,[15] but several works outside this period also took artists as their main figures and depicted failed attempts to translate imagination and sensitivity into artistic expression. Much like Christopher in *The Real Charlotte*, these characters feel paralyzed by their own worldly cynicism and by the suspicion that they lack the necessary spark of genius

to justify their efforts. Lewis Seymour of *A Modern Lover* (1883), Frank Escott of *Spring Days* (1888), the *fin de siècle* hero of *Mike Fletcher* (1889), and later Mildred Lawson of *Celibates* (1895)—each is an artist *manqué* who falls short of greatness because of frustrating doubts and dilletantish indecision. John Reid, the Swinburne-like poet turned labor organizer in the play *The Strike at Arlingford* (1893), comes to recognize that his sympathies with the common mine workers are all wasted pretense. Hubert Price of *Vain Fortune* (1891) endures a long period of poverty, abuse, and the misery of artistic creation, then does manage to produce a work he considers great. But his elation soon fades before the realization that these efforts too have been futile, and he sinks back into his original, stagnant insecurity: "See him reading and re-reading the few lines he has written, knowing them to be worthless, tortured by a prescience of the perfection required, and maddened by the sight of the futility that is . . . the pained, pinched look of impotent desire."[16] Such frustration points toward the personal need Moore felt for a character like Esther Waters, one who allowed him both to depict accurately the hopelessness of her situation and still to keep her immune from the horror of failure or mediocrity.

With unflinching self-recognition, he wrote to his mother regarding his novels from this period: "The bitterest thing is what I think of myself:—it is not the work of genius, not that of great talent. It is the work of a man affected by that most terrible of all maladies, a dash of genius."[17] Several years later, in 1890, he confessed to his brother Maurice: "I do not think I shall do anything of real value. . . . I have the sentiment of great work but I cannot produce it."[18] Artistic inadequacies further became analogous to an inability to form a satisfactory love relationship. Locked within their own frozen emotions, his characters cannot commit themselves either to artistic expression or union with another person. Their dread of failure finds its chief expression in an attitude of aesthetic ennui. In his own role as an Irish landlord, Moore likewise faced the debilitating pall of defeat. If the landed gentry was indeed doomed, if decisive action and committed heroism could make no difference, then the man of sensibility had best recognize and learn to face the collapse, even if only from behind a mask of indifference and melancholic lethargy.

In the *Confessions of a Young Man*, the first of several autobiographical works, Moore turned even more directly to the theme of himself as the artist in the process of trying to consolidate his talent. Within a constantly shifting maze of insecurity and doubt obscured by outrageous verbal bluffs, of giddy success plunging to dispossession

and pessimism, he charts his early stages as an artist, particularly the French influences. For only in Paris, Moore suggests, can the artist find the combination of atmosphere and companionship necessary to stimulate greatness. Elsewhere, uniformity and democracy soon condemn genius to exhaust itself within the limits of a too common humanity.

> Humanity is a pigsty, where liars, hypocrites, and the obscene in spirit congregate. . . . Far better the blithe modern pagan in his white tie and evening clothes, and his facile philosophy. He says, "I don't care how the poor live; my only regret is that they live at all;" and he gives the beggar a shilling.[19]

Despite his ironic distance, Moore enjoys playing the pagan and the snob. Throughout the work, however, shrill declarations of superiority echo off his own doubts about his ability to succeed as an artist.

In his attempts to resolve such uncertainty once and for all, Moore begins in the *Confessions* the mental process that, by the early years of the twentieth century, had firmly enshrined art as his supreme value. If society condemns its members to follow predetermined patterns, the artist can create and command his own, patterns more beautiful and enjoyable than those around him. The inviolate idea of art insulates him against a world of mechanistic formulas and industrial utilitarianism. He was later to explain to Geraint Goodwin: "I have sought and found and taken refuge in art." And in the same conversation: "Art to me is sacred. It is my religion."[20] Without the sanctity of an ideal to sustain him, the artist might lose his creative vision or find himself at the mercy of the crowd's indifference and coarse tastes, forced to earn his survival by slaving over his work like any ordinary factory hand. Industrialization had already swept away traditions and values, even transformed the production of books. Who knew where it might lead? The *Confessions* suggest that "The world is dying of machinery; that is the great disease, that is the plague that will sweep away and destroy civilisation."[21] Such thoughts haunted him most in his early career, when it seemed that civilization might perhaps endure, but not his own standing as an artist.

Between Paris and London, Moore spent a year in Ireland trying to shore up the mismanaged finances of Moore Hall and his own shaken view of the future. The Land War, then at its most intense pitch,

did little to support either effort. He recorded his experiences in *Parnell and His Island* (1887), a collection of impressions and anecdotes that "point to no moral," Moore claims, nor "plead any cause...; they were chosen because they seemed to me typical and picturesque."[22] "Aesthetic schizophrenia," Malcolm Brown snorts.[23] In the *Confessions* a year later, Moore would find "Two dominant notes in my character — an original hatred of my native country, and a brutal loathing of the religion I was brought up in."[24] Although his Catholicism required very little attention before, in *Parnell* he builds violently antireligious harangues around the belief that the Church supported agrarian agitation against the landlords. He ran little risk of harm himself on his return; Joseph Hone claims that he "was kind and indulgent to his tenants"[25] and refrained from any evictions. But he kept his outlandish Paris regalia, and he despised them all, his fellow landlords almost more than the unruly tenants who had forced him back.

The landed class, Moore suggests here, squandered its heritage, allowed its aristocratic way of life to cheapen and decay while it occupied itself with foolish whims. The Big Houses stand "surrounded with a hundred or so of filthy tenements that ... keep the master in affluence and ease" (pp. 69–70). The numbers have now united against him, and for that the master can blame himself. Moore searches out the tomb of Moore Hall's founder and comes across only scattered remains, "the bones of him who created all that has been wasted—by one generation in terraces, by another in race-horses, and by another in dissipation in Paris" (p. 76). As the prodigal armed with quaint French fashions, he readily admits his own contribution to the family spiral of decay, while continuing to support an economic system he recognizes as obsolete and repressive:

> [I]n Ireland the passage direct and brutal of money from the horny hands of the peasant to the delicate hands of the proprietor is terribly suggestive of serfdom.... "I am an Irish landlord, I have done this, I do this, and I shall continue to do this, for it is as impossible for me as for the rest of my class to do otherwise; but that doesn't prevent me from recognising the fact that it is a worn-out system ... whose end is nigh." (p. 7)

Moore would have preferred to extricate himself from the whole sorry mess as neatly as in *Parnell*, where he becomes objectified into yet another scorned and repudiated Irish figure. Yet the prospect of "a country composed exclusively of peasants," with "the entire upper

class . . . deprived of all its worldly goods and turned adrift out on the world to starve" (pp. 92–93), remained too horrible to accept. From this nightmare he retreated into determinism, arguing that the gentry could not possibly avoid or mitigate their destruction. "I foresaw a disaster," he once said to his brother, "and I don't think anything can be done to avert what has to happen."[26] Trapped within the contradictions of his own position, he could only go on collecting rents and hoping for some satisfactory resolution through his art.

Anxiety and guilt about his status as a landlord, however, compounded doubts about his talent as an artist. Moore appreciated the privileges accorded him across the immense distance between landlord and tenant. If he would not rightfully earn those privileges by staying in Ireland to manage the family estate, then the burden fell on him of creating great art, of contributing to the spiritual worth of society as the tenants contributed to the material. His recognition of the injustices in the whole landlord-tenant system, like his fears of personal poverty, only added to anxieties about artistic failure. Dependent upon the tangible financial success of his work, Moore could see constantly before him in these early years the economic connection between his position as unproductive landlord and as the artist who had yet to prove he could produce. The threats of a land-hungry tenantry were not too far removed from those of an unresponsive reading public.

In *Parnell and His Island* Moore repeatedly describes as worse than animals the tenants and laborers who seem on the verge of overrunning Ireland. He observes with vivid, scatological detail the extreme poverty and squalor of their lives but cannot sympathize. The face of the native Irishman "is expressive of meanness, sullenness, stupidity; . . . he reminds me of some low earth-animal. . . . of a degenerate race. . . . they should have died, but . . . are now making headway against superior races" (pp. 95–96). Policies such as land reform, especially when linked to the agrarian crime and rent boycotts of the Land League, produce only more misery and an even faster disintegration of decency within the mind of this primitive people. On the verge of bankruptcy but with heightened expectations, "and headed by Parnell they again come to their landlords and demand large reductions. And this will occur again and again until the landlords are ruined" (p. 246). A new breed of politicians from the middle class encourages this assault on the old manor houses. Having replaced the former patricians at Westminster, they then transform the upper levels of Dublin society into a parody of elegance. Yet an even greater mon-

ster lurks in the countryside. In between their pathetic attempts at fancy dress balls and theatre parties, the new gentry "trembles with sullen fear, and listens to the savage howling of the pack" (p. 34). All of Ireland, from Dublin Castle to the Western bogs, seems nothing but a decaying corpse covered with open sores.

With the Ireland of the present so unacceptable to him, Moore begins in *Parnell* to evoke an imaginative Ireland of the uncorrupted past. His nostalgic dreams, later to draw him into the twilight mood of the Irish Renaissance, at first drifted out of the romantic ruins that marked the world of the ancient Gaelic chieftains. He himself should have lived in those "better and happier" days and "not grown sick with grief in this querulous age" (pp. 165, 166). He also discovers the medieval atmosphere of Lord Ardilaun's huge and wealthy Ashford estate, where one feels "almost shut out of the storm and gloom of crime and poverty that enfolds the land" (p. 182). It is only an island of culture, however, a rare living monument to the past in a dying country whose present lacks all character and distinction. Everywhere else, Moore reads, "as in an epitaph upon a tomb, the history of a vanished civilisation" (p. 10). Within the "country of abandoned dreams" (p. 56) he can rarely escape the nightmare of decay and ruin.

In *Parnell and His Island* Moore reproduces, at times word for word, the entire Irish background of *A Drama in Muslin* (1886). Companion pieces published a year apart, each work lays claim to a position of disinterested objectivity, whether in the *Parnell* sketches pointing to "no moral" or in the scheme, with *A Drama in Muslin*, of a naturalistic novel; and in both the pressures of the Irish question force Moore's own unwilling subjective response into the foreground. If Ireland never seemed to him an island of infinite enchantment, neither could he diminish it in his mind to the size of a pig's back, not from the secluded distance of London, not even with the firm artistic controls acquired from his Parisian masters. Moore Hall constantly held him within the reach of the Joe Blakes of Ireland. His landed class remained the same, unsavory and dissolute, struggling feebly to hold their position against the same threatening and brutish peasantry. In the plot of *A Drama in Muslin*, which Moore superimposes on the Irish sketches, several young women, daughters of gentry from the West, try their luck on the Dublin marriage market. Although most achieve only bitter disappointment, the juxtaposition of narrative line and

Ashford Castle, on the shore of Lough Corrib, County Mayo. In *Parnell and His Island*, George Moore describes this estate, then owned by Lord Ardilaun, as an ideal refuge from Ireland.

social backdrop sets off Moore's attempts to clarify his own situation within such an environment.

Four characters, in particular, represent various responses and solutions to the dilemmas Moore felt. Mr. Barton, a Lewis Seymour grown old, muddles away his life and talent as one more of the many failed artists Moore feared he might have or would become. Barely tolerated by his family and humored by his fellow landlords, he indulges in eccentric dress and behavior, paints massive, heroic scenes in a garishly romantic style, and daydreams about heading an army to put down the savages of the world, particularly those in the Land League. Friends explain him as "genius gone wrong," preferring instead their own more conventional absurdities. When forced on occasion to deal with the practical world, he argues with his unruly tenants in the same clumsy manner as Moore himself in a scene copied nearly exactly in *Parnell*.

The novelist and journalist John Harding, an idealized man of the world, enjoys effortless success in all his literary endeavors. Sophisticated and intelligent, he need only experience what he chooses from Ireland before returning to England to write a book that sounds just like *Parnell*. At the other extreme, the hunchback Cecilia denounces the world as hideous and corrupt. Driven nearly insane by love for her schoolmate Alice Barton, she finally enters a convent, seeking the ethereal and spiritual pleasures of the ascetic, despairing of a world that otherwise excludes her totally. Her combination of religion and sensuality remained one of Moore's most recurrent themes over his career.

Alice, Mr. Barton's daughter, provides the novel with its guiding consciousness. Not as pretty and marketable as the other young women, she turns her sensitive, independent views to account through journalistic pieces such as "Notes and Sensations of a Plain Girl at Dublin Castle." Moore takes pains, however, to emphasize Alice as a product of her times as well as of her nature. She recognizes the shallowness of the social conventions forced on her, especially her mother's jungle tactics in flushing out potential sons-in-law; but Alice's loneliness and isolation can find a resolution in the only social niche available, marriage. Writing provides no secure alternative. Like the young George Moore in her literary tastes, she further labors under the financial pressures attending artistic creation.

Despite his feminist sentiments, Moore can leave her little room to chart a truly independent route through the novel's deterministic universe. Nor does she much want such independence. Ireland appears to her as threatening as to the others of her class. Whether in Dublin or County Galway, the background of poverty and potential violence haunts the consciousness of the entire landed class. They "saw themselves driven out of their ... idleness, and forced into the struggle for life. The prospect appalled them. ... What could they do with their empty brains? What could they do with their feeble hands?"[27] Moore's scorn for them and his criticism of their injustices to the tenantry could not erase his own appalled feelings, and in the extreme conditions of *Esther Waters*, he would seek answers to his own questions. For Alice, exile becomes the answer, a relief from the life of crushing idleness and purposelessness that awaits her in Ireland, a relief as well from the poverty and fermenting revolt. She marries Dr. Reed, a stolid, sensible, plain man who shares with Alice the feeling that "one is disposed to admit in despair the fatality of all human effort" (p. 324). They consequently depart for England and set up a

thoroughly middle-class household, one whose monotonous vulgarity nearly overwhelms Moore. In a final, methodically precise description of their home, however, he mixes his ironic distaste with respect for Alice's solid social position and for the tasteless trappings of her life. In the *Confessions* two years later he laments that "the old world of heroes is over now"[28] but still manages an indignant attack on the artistic philistinism of the Victorian middle class. In the more cautious and prudent mood closing *A Drama in Muslin* he attempts to make his peace with that class. He may have wished to become John Harding but at times feared that Alice Barton's was the kind of life with which he might have to make do.

Parnell and His Island and *A Drama in Muslin* map out Moore's concept of himself in relation to his society, his return, like that of Alice or the "Irish Poet," to an Irish home he has not seen in years, his preparations to re-enter a wholly new world. This society, in Moore's view, had from his beginnings surrounded him with its history and locked him into the universal spiral of decline that swept along the entire landed class. Poetry, like marriage, becomes mere merchandise, property encumbered by mortgages and threatened by rising tenant demands. The Protestant Ascendancy, in *A Drama in Muslin*, can achieve no unity at all, no hope except for still harsher coercion laws from England. An alien populace, aping both English and Irish manners, they live "in a land of echoes and shadows" (p. 159).

With no hope of reversing the decay or of turning human endeavor to worthwhile account, the individual can best seek personal salvation by renouncing the need for action and external success and by turning inward upon an elemental simplicity. The test environment of the naturalistic novel follows various responses to such a universe. Moore's professed respect for Alice Barton's solution, however, remains too strained and artificial. What does endure from Alice Barton is her reliance on an inner level of sustenance, as in her writing:

> Does not the inevitable grossness of those who fight in the outward battle always jar the pensive sadness of others who see life from a distance as a faintly drawn landscape veiled in delicate twilight, and whose victories are won over themselves rather than over circumstances and opponents? (p. 263)

A heroine like Esther Waters would draw even greater strength from internal resources; her defeat on the world's terms would not mean failure but rather a confirmation of her spiritual nature. Moore was

later temporarily to break off his exile and return to Dublin when it seemed that the poets of the Irish Renaissance could transfer such a "landscape veiled in delicate twilight" into the society and maintain it intact. The author of *Esther Waters* holds out no such optimistic hopes.

Alice Barton's departure for England turned all of her artistic ambitions over to the conventional tastes of middle-class Victorianism. George Moore had other ideas, ones that occasionally took on the fervor of a messianic crusade. He spent frequent periods in Ireland during the early 1880s. With Moore Hall looking increasingly shabby, however, and with books like *Parnell and His Island* and *A Drama in Muslin* arousing considerable Irish hostilities, he preferred his London acquaintances, even if they could not quite compete with the high-powered Parisians. And his advocacy of French artistic methods did begin to have an impact on English writing. He wrote several influential articles on French literature, then published *A Mummer's Wife* (1885), an attempt to realize a theory discussed in the *Confessions*:

> The idea of a new art based upon science . . . that should explain all things and embrace modern life in its entirety, . . . be, as it were, a new creed in a new civilisation, filled me with wonder. . . . In my fevered fancy I saw a new race of writers that would arise.[29]

The novel successfully demonstrated the first attempt at French Naturalism in English, and Moore's crusading spirit thrived on the subsequent opposition to the book. Banned by Mudie's vast and influential circulating library, like *A Modern Lover* (1883) earlier, *A Mummer's Wife* nevertheless overcame charges of immorality to become a popular success. Moore followed with a direct attack on censorship and Mudie's "circulating morals" in the pamphlet *Literature at Nurse* (1885). "Even Moore's enemies," claims Malcolm Brown, "praised the novel and [*Literature at Nurse*] as a decisive preparatory step leading to the creation of the twentieth-century novel."[30] The later success of *Esther Waters*, despite a ban by Smith's libraries, further weakened the strait-laced power of Smith and Mudie over English fiction.

Amidst his idealistic demands that authors be granted whatever style they chose, Moore continued in a more practical vein to search for the style that would combine personal gratification with

financial success. Neither Zola nor Pater seemed to offer him solutions. He returned to literary realism in *Esther Waters*, determined to avoid the impersonal naturalism of such works as *Germinie Lacerteux* (1864), Edmund and Jules Goncourt's novel of servant life. Moore's controversial experiments with naturalism, however, were largely confined to the years 1879–1885. Under Pater's influence in the years following, he held to a more widely accepted mode. *Vain Fortune*, under the authorship of "Lady Rhone," was even serialized in the *Lady's Pictorial*, the magazine that carried Somerville and Ross's travel stories at about the same time. Although both naturalism and aestheticism had gained him some financial and critical success, it was not equal to Moore's desires. He maintained his simple and spare life style, complained of the poverty and hard work that accompanied the writing of *Esther Waters*,[31] and suggested his father's influence as the root of his frugality: "[T]he pain that his pecuniary embarrassment caused him seems to have inflicted me with such a fear of money that I am the most economical of men."[32] Moore's naturalistic creed, to "embrace modern life in its entirety," created other difficulties. Modern life consisted of too many things that he simply did not wish to embrace: a repressive publishing business, a lukewarm readership, an Irish landed class in decline, an Irish tenantry with volatile expectations, a further class of people like Esther Waters who could not free themselves from the threat of outright starvation, a growing English complacency about their vast Empire, and materialistic social values that seemed to run everything, including art, over an industrial production line. Following the success of *Esther Waters*, therefore, he determined to abandon naturalism and realism and set off toward what eventually became the artificial and highly wrought style of his final novels.

If naturalism demanded an embrace of reality, this new development promised a refuge from it. The earlier aesthetic novels had described the world Moore knew; he now sought to create the world he desired. Artistic failures and pallid love affairs now gave way to more universal settings. *Evelyn Innes* appeared in 1898, originally planned as one volume, but a second was required, *Sister Teresa* (1901). The miscalculation indicates the artistic problems with the work, its shapeless wealth of detail and exposition that the opulent style never quite organizes into meaning. A decade's work within the Irish Literary Revival intervened, then Moore returned to this style with *The Brook Kerith* (1916) and his later novels. The long, rolling sentences, his characteristic melodic line in these narratives, fuse actions, ideas, and timeless pastoral settings into one continuous web. The work resem-

bles a sensuous but monastic refuge from history, a romantic tapestry of static patterns that develop inward towards greater intricacy and precision rather than outward towards definite goals that must prove futile. He constantly and tirelessly revised earlier books, and similarly extended these attempts at a perfection of form to frequent autobiographical works, as if fearing that posterity would detect, whether in his novels or his life, some evidence of failure.

Moore's participation in the Irish Renaissance began with the hope that the artists could perhaps reconstruct Ireland much as one created a secluded and aloof aesthetic world. The composition of *Evelyn Innes* had progressed swifty and enthusiastically, leaving him totally unprepared for its subsequent critical and financial failure. His discontent with English materialism, partly inspired by his own lack of commercial success, turned to genuine outrage over the war against the Boers. In Ireland, meanwhile, his native country and one not yet ravaged by industry and commercialism, a literary movement was prospering. He decided that "The Englishman that was in me (he that wrote *Esther Waters*) had been overtaken and captured by the Irishman."[33] The *Confessions* had recalled instances in his life of a mystic "echo-augury." Borrowed from Thomas DeQuincey, this concept represented instinctive impulses that periodically guided him out of confused and aimless states and into higher levels of artistic development. Once more these auguries revealed a new calling, this time in Ireland.

As with Moore's previous artistic causes, he embraced the Literary Revival with a messianic exuberance. With Yeats and Martyn, he became codirector of the Irish Literary Theatre in 1899, and in May of that year helped produce Martyn's *The Heather Field* and Yeats's *The Countess Cathleen*. He attacked, rewrote, retitled and finally produced, under his own name, Martyn's unfortunate play *The Bending of the Bough* (1900). A collaboration with Yeats on the play *Diarmuid and Grania* (1901) put similar strain on yet a second friendship. He published two major works during his stay in Dublin, *The Untilled Field* (1903) and *The Lake* (1905). In the first of these, a collection of short stories of which more than half appeared originally in Gaelic translations, Moore sought a definitive statement on the mystic soul of Ireland, its priests and peasants, its gray landscape dotted with ruins. In their thwarted aspirations for happiness, however, the characters continue to resemble earlier figures like the failed artist Hubert Price or the servant heroine Esther Waters. A feeling of pathos also emerges from the melancholy veil of twilight shimmering over many of the stories,

softening the harsher realities of poverty, failure, old age, loneliness, insanity, or death. The main character of *The Lake*, a priest troubled by conscience and doubts, finally seeks escape by leaving Ireland. The avoidance of commitments, the retreat away from a world of sadness and into the security of twilight images, leads naturally into the priest's immersion in the lake that will carry him out of his country.

For by this time Moore himself was becoming disenchanted with Ireland. The Irish Literary Theatre dissolved in 1902, and he felt alienated and excluded from its successor, the Irish National Dramatic Company. When he and Martyn had advocated a more modern psychological drama, Yeats and Lady Gregory took their preferences for peasant and heroic drama over to the new company. Moore later attributed to George Russell the remark that "a literary movement consists of five or six people who live in the same town and hate each other cordially."[34] Fellow writers frustrated his ambitions and plans; "subaltern souls," Moore grumbled. But he had complaints about more than just the five or six. The virginal language that should have given him a revitalized literary style remained inaccessible to him. The enthusiastic audience that should have loyally supported Irish art remained largely hostile or indifferent to the movement. Only the priests seemed to hold any influence, their narrow dogma infecting even movement writers like Martyn.

In one of Moore's frequent anti-Catholic diatribes, he asserted in 1903: "I have utterly renounced my Celtic aspirations."[35] In the same year, his opposition to Catholicism given more shape by George Russell's ideas, he converted to Protestantism. He also took over from the movement the ambition to create Ireland's Sacred Book. In 1906 he began this massive work, and rumors started nervously circulating through Dublin that he was gathering material for a satiric, probably even slanderous, chronicle of the Irish Renaissance. By the time the first volume of this trilogy appeared in 1911, Moore had prudently departed for London, his original vision of becoming Ireland's cultural Messiah transformed into his epic masterpiece of mock-heroic irony, history, and gossip, *Hail and Farewell!*

Joe Blake's startling letter in hand, Moore had returned to Ireland in 1880. In 1901 a mysterious "voice" would call him home, not to a failing manor house this time, but to a flourishing cultural revival that was in part a response by the artists to the perceived decline of

their society. Along with his Irish material in *Parnell and His Island* and *A Drama in Muslin*, the novel *Esther Waters* falls directly between the homecomings. In its concern with the theme of failure, the work points towards both the plight of the Big House and the mystique of the lost cause cultivated by the Renaissance writers. The kind of ambivalence that turned Moore's attitude towards the artistic movement into deflating irony also marked his view of his own class, his alternate repudiation of and then identification with the gentry. In the fictional world of *Esther Waters*, which emerges as a further attempt to answer his own personal Irish question, Moore sought to resolve the uneasy union of aesthete and landlord, to balance his desire to escape from his point of origin against his need to return to it.

Esther Waters is his best-conceived treatment of the experience and emotions of failure, and one of the best nineteenth-century novels by any Irish writer. In this work action becomes irrelevant, success only a transitory illusion, society an unbeatable opponent in a series of wagers destined to come up losers. Unlike the other characters in the novel, however, Esther manages to free herself from a reliance on external supports and from the irrational and desperate hopes for a reversal of fate. Finally outside of the constricting pressures that Moore felt surrounding him, she gains an enviable position through her return to and complete acceptance of simple and fundamental beginnings. And insofar as Esther represents Moore's concept of an idealized self, the novel offers one more form of the autobiography that continually occupied him during his career.

Moore first touched on the subject matter for a novel like *Esther Waters* when he commented on a charwoman, "Poor Emma," in the *Confessions:* "And I used to ask you all sorts of cruel questions, I was curious to know the depth of animalism you had sunk to. . . . I merely recognise you as one of the facts of civilisation."[36] By 1889 the idea of the servant woman had assumed more artistic and economic relevance; he wrote of a forthcoming shift in the tone of his fiction with which he hoped to achieve greater success: "My next novel . . . will be more human. I shall bathe myself in the simplest and most naive emotions, the daily bread of humanity."[37] His attitude of condescending superiority and emotional distance could only sustain itself as long as the novel remained an abstract calculation, and by the time he came to write the final pages, Esther's story had aroused feelings in him far deeper than those aimed solely at the marketplace: "For the first time in my life I cried over my work."[38] In Ginger's hasty and grudging visit to his mother at Woodview in the final chapter, especially when con-

Moore Hall, George Moore's family estate in County Mayo. The interior of the house was burned out during the Civil War by Republican forces.

trasted with Esther's loyalty and devotion to her place of origin, Moore must have recognized his own errant nature.

In drawing on specific features of his Irish experience for *Esther Waters*, Moore had several character models at hand, as well as the details from his father's stable-yard.[39] Mrs. Barfield, the mistress of Woodview, has the same simple morality, piety, and patient kindness that Moore's mother showed. Both women remained on their respective estates, even after their husbands had died, their sons moved away, and their manor houses decayed into shadows of an earlier splendor. Woodview itself resembles in its externals a Sussex home, Buckingham, where Moore occasionally visited the Bridger family during his first ten years in London. What he found attractive about the Bridgers, however, was the same quality of permanence that once graced the landed estates of Ireland. The Bridgers, he felt, "had been on their land, cultivating it, till it had taken on their likeness, or else

they had taken on the likeness of the land."[40] In the Barfield estate at Woodview, Buckingham merges with Moore Hall, whose stable area the novel copies particularly closely.[41] Much of the stable-yard excitement of Moore's youth revolved around the butler, Joseph Applely, and his small, cluttered, but sacrosanct office and press. Like his novelistic counterpart John Randal, also called Mr. Leopold, Applely cultivated an aura suggesting encyclopedic knowledge and secret systems, all guaranteed to identify prospective race winners. Moore later reminisced about "that wonderful press in which all things could be found. It was out of that press that *Esther Waters* came, out of the stable-yard and out of my own heart."[42] Applely aroused considerable admiration in the young George Moore; but what he represented, the horse-racing and the betting, elicited only hostility and resentment from the women of the manor. For Esther, as well, the mysterious press becomes "a symbol of all that was wicked and dangerous."[43]

Although *Esther Waters* describes the life of the large city as well as that of the country house, Janet Dunleavy points out that the details of Esther's experience in London are not as accurate as the accounts of the racing stables and the Woodview estate. Esther's journey on foot to secure a letter recommending her for admission to a lying-in hospital, for instance, would hardly have been possible in the time Moore gives her.[44] He directs his most vivid attention to the world of the stables and the races. What he did not personally observe in his first twenty years he could absorb from the involved reports of the servants. Just as Esther missed "Silver Braid's" race, the nine-year-old Moore did not see the victory of his father's horse Croaghpatrick. Yet the family and servants could talk of little else for weeks, especially as the huge winning purse had signaled an ascent in Moore Hall's unsteady fortunes.

Woodview likewise undergoes periodic shifts in its economic status. The Barfield family three generations before had worked as livery-stable keepers. Under the previous squire, they finally rose to the level of a "county family" and still hold that title, despite the socially questionable marriage of the present Mr. Barfield to the daughter of one of his tenants. The string of racing victories temporarily silences local gossip and, in fact, raises the wealth and esteem of the manor to its greatest height. Yet the personal history of the Barfield's cook, Mrs. Latch, suggests the inevitable reversal of those fortunes dependent on the luck of the races. Her husband, better off than the Barfields at one time, lost heavily through betting; as her son William notes: "The family 'ad been coming down for generations, and mother

thought that I was born to restore it" (p. 41). Within the treacherously shifting cycle of family destinies, however, by the time William can build up a prosperous business, the Barfields have suffered heavy betting losses, and Mr. Barfield has died of a "broken heart."

Esther comes from a much simpler family background. She belongs to the Plymouth Brethren, an ascetically puritan, fundamentalist Christian sect that allows no pictures, ornamentation, or even prayer books into their worship. She and her mother share the same pious religious beliefs within their "narrow, peaceful family life" (p. 21). Although she never learned to read, Esther still carries her mother's books with her throughout the novel. In her first days at Woodview she is awed by the romantic world that emerges from a magazine story read by a fellow servant. Print for her appears mysterious and fascinating but also threatening; her religious instincts win out, and she denounces the story as sinful.

In her dealings with the rest of the world, Esther maintains the perpetual stance of the adversary, and "it was only when she laughed that her face lost its habitual expression, which was somewhat sullen" (p. 1). She must constantly fight to control her quick temper and her open suspicion of other people, seeing anger as a personal weakness as well as a threat to her survival. Throughout the novel Esther feels the need to restrain herself, to shape her conduct and desires through an act of will into those habits she instinctively believes they must take, into "the original convictions and the prejudices of her race" (p. 71). Only when her desires correspond to the simplicity of her instincts, as in her love for her son, can she feel completely happy.

The novel repeatedly contrasts desire with instinct. Desires are capricious and transitory, directed toward external objects or goals, provoked by society, and consequently subject to social disappointment and frustration. Instinct, on the other hand, remains fixed and unchanged, the essential core of a person within the erratic flux of desires. Much like conscience, instinct grows out of ingrained habits of thought that one can trust much more than illusory, worldly desires. Connected to nature, it need not depend for its fulfillment on social gratification or success. Moore believed that "in Esther Waters I represented a woman living in the deepest human instincts."[45] In the Confessions he related the concept of instinct to the semimystical echo-auguries that periodically led him to further stages of his artistic development: "[B]rain instincts have always been, and still are, the initial

and the determining powers of my being."[46] If a person could maintain his awareness of those instinctive powers, Moore suggests, he could more easily recognize what in his life would bring him a measure of happiness and contentment. By giving way to whims and desires, by acting against conscience and instinct, a person separates himself from his internal being and leaves himself at the mercy of external rewards. Implicit and consistent faith in one's instinct offers a much more reliable guide to conduct.

Moore structures the entire novel around such a dichotomy, the opposition of desire and instinct, the external world and the internal self, sense and spirit, complexity and simplicity. One way, the way of the attractions of the world, raises people's hopes and lures them into an active involvement with life. The other, instinctive and religious, seeks through a withdrawal from the world to find contentment in an inner-directed state of mind and a simpler range of human needs. In the course of Moore's novel Esther alternates between these two poles and finally reconciles them into a stable synthesis. She never surrenders to a blind Protestantism; as the novel accurately notes of her, "we are human first, we are religious after" (p. 31). Yet with action leading to nothing but failure and defeat, and outward success offering only fleeting satisfaction, she can find happiness only through a retreat inwards, away from the world and towards her natural instincts. Within the overwhelmingly complex and deterministic social forces around her, desires turn to frustrating illusions. By at last coming to rely on her inner nature, by wanting only a simple existence and no more, she brings desire and instinct into balance. There, Moore would have it, does she win salvation.

Mrs. Barfield experiences the same feeling of opposition between desire and instinct that Esther does. Also a member of the Plymouth Brethren, she becomes Esther's friend and confidante and tries, with meager results, to teach Esther to read. With similar patience and results, she also seeks to win her husband away from the influence of his butler and the world of betting and race horses. The lure of a bet infects almost everyone in the novel, however, including Esther. Only a minor compromise of ethical principles for her, betting for the other characters reassuringly promises an end to insecurity and fear of deprivation, a beginning of pleasure in a life that otherwise seems like a deadening cycle. William justifies their conduct with a recurring philosophy in the novel: "Their only pleasure is a bet. When they've one on they've something to look forward to; whether they win or lose they 'as their money's worth. ... Man can't live without hope"

(p. 293). Nor can he live with hope on a horse. One great stroke of luck could transform a life, or so they irrationally believe. Yet all of them lose, bookies and experts alike, all but for a mysterious Mr. George Buff, who is never seen in the novel nor understood by its characters. Insofar as their own hopes depend on external success, they have no chance of effecting any significant change or of achieving any substantial happiness.

As an analogue to Moore's own experience, betting resembled a gamble on the literary market. His economic dependency on his early writing forced him to try for potential winners by predicting the response of critics and the reading public. At the same time, however, he could paradoxically only regard such a gamble as doomed to failure. If an artist reduced his work to such a calculating and mechanistic level, Moore believed, he would produce inferior art; if he ignored the taste of the marketplace, he would not sell. The dilemma was compounded even further by Moore's own partial success and by his awareness of the economic straits of the landed gentry in Ireland. If decisive action had no influence on such external circumstances, whether as a bet on a horse, or a wager on the literary field, or a responsible attempt to restore the family estate, then Moore could explain to himself his own choice of art, a profession that offered no support to the decaying fortunes of Moore Hall.

For Esther, betting represents only the most obvious side of a whole range of experience she speaks of as the "world." And the world extracts one concession after another from her as she feels alternately attracted to, and then threatened by, contact with the life around her. Since life, in Esther's view, harbors mostly immoral temptations and false rewards, her instincts eventually force her to suspect anything nonspiritual that she finds enjoyable, such as the richness and novelty of her experiences at Woodview. Her seduction by William Latch and resulting pregnancy only confirm to Esther the original premises of her religious outlook. Released from Woodview with very little money and no prospects for further employment during her pregnancy, she believes she can only thank God she has not suffered still more for her sin. Even her feelings for her newborn son Jackie appear to her excessively worldly: "[H]er love for him went to her head like madness. She wondered at herself; it seemed almost unnatural to love anything as she did this child" (p. 169). The pattern repeats itself over and over for Esther: she accepts from the world, then her instincts reassert themselves, and so she rejects what she has desired and taken, sees it as one more temptation leading to moral depravity.

As William Latch can succeed in drawing Esther into more practical attitudes and conduct, Fred Parsons appeals to the traditionally moral and religious side of her personality. Also a member of the Plymouth Brethren, he offers her marriage and spiritual security, a withdrawal into the comforting, childlike simplicity she knew with her mother. But she has lost too much of her earlier innocence to the corporeal world; William and Jackie have both complicated her life with theirs. She accidentally runs into William again, and this time he wants to marry her. Even after nine years of desperate poverty and isolation, she still finds him intensely attractive, partly because he belongs to the Woodview experience, which "had become the most precise and distinct vision she had gathered from life" (p. 205). Against Fred's meager asceticism, William's strong personality and material security prove too attractive.

She spends several happy and prosperous years with William, and together they build up a thriving business from his tavern and an illegal betting operation. Despite this run of good luck, however, Moore depicts almost nothing of her happiness except for a panoramic recreation of a great Derby. For Moore, Esther's character best emerges from her times of hardship and ruin; the material comfort and success seem irrelevant. He thus passes over the good years with tragic accounts of minor characters, especially Sarah, whose life closely parallels Esther's. The similarities between their respective fates suggest that Esther's happiness rests on very fragile ground.

Like a cancer, the betting turns against them. Fred's stern admonishment that the "whole neighbourhood is devoured by it" (p. 289) recalls Mrs. Barfield's despair at her own attempts to achieve good: "[Woodview] has been the ruin of the neighbourhood, and we have dispensed vice instead of righteousness" (p. 85). Moral intentions for the world, like actions, seem irrelevant and unsuccessful. As Esther muses, "Horses had won and horses had lost—a great deal of trouble and fuss and nothing to show for it" (p. 330). The disasters begin to pile up. William contracts tuberculosis, which reduces his gambling to its most elemental level; his life literally rides on each succeeding bet as he desperately tries to raise the money needed to take him to a warmer climate. As he has done throughout his life, he struggles against his fate, attempts to control it himself. But the futile hopes for a winner get played out for the last time in the novel, and William's death leaves Esther at much the same level of poverty as before her marriage.

More than anything else outside her, however, Jackie determines Esther's character in the novel. Even as William lies dying, she realizes that "her boy was what was most real to her in life" (p. 337). Not even her religion ever absorbs as much of her emotions and conscious thoughts, and when she decides on various courses of action, she does so with an eye to what will benefit Jackie most. Moore reserves his most sentimental passages to describe their relationship, but despite the Pre-Raphaelite silliness that occasionally cloys his point, he gives Esther's character the necessary depth through her sacrifices for Jackie. In the realistic context of her hardship and suffering, she does take on the status Moore accords her: "Hers is an heroic adventure if one considers it: a mother's fight for the life of her child against all the forces that civilisation arrays against the lowly and the illegitimate" (p. 163). The claims for universality, romantically overblown in this statement, take on genuinely far-reaching implications in the whole of the novel. There, all human endeavors face the same one-sided struggle, regardless of the limitations of poverty or birth.

Because Jackie exists, Esther must commit herself to action. He, more than anyone or anything else, prevents her from retreating from the external world back into her private, inner nature and self-sufficient isolation. From the time of his birth, he gives her something outside herself to relate to: "Her personal self seemed entirely withdrawn; she existed like an atmosphere about the babe, an impersonal emanation of love. . . . unconscious of herself" (p. 118). As Jackie draws her out into the world, he helps make possible all the other compromises Esther must strike with the instincts that would lead her back to shelter, helps her realize that "One doesn't do the good that one would like to in the world; one has to do the good that comes to one to do" (p. 289). Through Esther, therefore, Jackie provides the novel's ultimate test of the worth of human endeavor. If action is indeed useless, even at its most elemental level, then human life is useless, and birth does little but add to the world's wretchedness. Esther could as well have left her son to die at the hands of the baby farmer.

Moore finally rejects such nihilism, throughout the novel as well as in the closing pages. Yet he cannot entirely control the uncertainties of feeling in the last chapters, the difficulty of withdrawing from a world that remains vital and attractive despite its universal chronicle of failure. When Esther finally returns to Woodview, she feels sensible of nothing but the comfort of a total retreat from the world. While Woodview has changed drastically since she left, she concentrates almost entirely on those things that have remained unchanged,

even obliterating from her consciousness the events of the intervening eighteen years. All that time seems "now a sort of blur in her mind—a dream, the connecting links of which were gone" (p. 365). Mrs. Barfield has stayed on alone at Woodview, just barely able to maintain the estate but still willing to offer Esther the shelter that both women accept as the "final stage" in their lives. Her own family scattered by death or emigration, Esther returns to her permanent beginning and retreats into the comforting reassurance of words she heard from Mrs. Barfield in her first years at Woodview: "[T]ime has passed like a little dream; life is nothing. We must think of what comes after" (p. 318). In the experience of the novel, however, Esther only superficially turns to the redemptive possibilities of Christianity. Moore's own religious skepticism keeps him from a depiction of complete faith in an afterlife and leads him instead to seek a resolution in the context of here and now. Esther's thoughts thus remain primarily with life, though one that has now become internalized and spiritual, insulating her against the world beyond Woodview. She finds contentment by rejecting the complexity and materialism of the external world that so often seems to her like a dream, and by reducing her human needs to a minimal level, a life-sustaining simplicity.

When Esther had to decide whether to marry William or Fred she dreamed of the two men merging into one ideal personality. Woodview for her closely approximates such a combination of their best qualities. She can enjoy the peace and spiritual confidence of her religion without Fred's aggressive dogmatism. And she has the minimal material pleasures and security that William offered her without having to wrench her moral instincts into an acceptance of the tavern and the betting. She also has William's son, who becomes an important concern for Mrs. Barfield now as well. The older woman, too, had to tolerate her husband's betting habits and, with Esther, she now seems happiest with life at Woodview without the interference of husbands. The men of the novel have proven largely unreliable; only women display consistent and unselfish goodness. Even after his heroine marries, Moore continues to refer to her as Esther Waters, never Esther Latch. Nor is it ever clear what last name her son has taken. In the final sanctity of Woodview, the simpler and purer relationship of mother and child resolves the difficult complications of marriage.

In *Parnell and His Island* Moore described two Irish manor houses, both falling into neglect and decay, shabby cast-offs from an earlier brilliance. One of them, Moore Hall itself, was still inhabited by George Moore's mother. In many of the details and in the atmosphere

of melancholy ruin, Woodview closely resembles these estates. Moore also uses recurring notes within the novel itself to add to the dreamlike mistiness of the final pages. In relating Esther's return he repeats almost word for word several sentences that opened the novel with her first arrival at the train station.[47] The cyclic pattern emphasizes what has endured at Woodview, not what has gone, as if to say that the intervening changes did not really matter.

Mrs. Barfield's son Ginger makes one of his rare visits to Woodview soon after Esther's arrival. A gentleman jockey with a small training stable in the north of England, he shuns his home estate while still demanding that it maintain the proper shabby-genteel decorum. He thus becomes enraged to learn that his mother conducts prayer meetings there with people he considers a bunch of petty "shopkeepers." Mrs. Barfield responds, not with argument or protest, but with a patient and simple explanation of her faith. "An expression of great beauty came upon her face, that unconscious resignation which, like the twilight, hallows and transforms. In such moments the humblest hearts are at one with nature, and speak out of the eternal wisdom of things" (p. 369). Shamed by his unfaithful criticism, Ginger leaves the women to their own affairs. In comparison to his mother's transcendent and visionary happiness, his own life suddenly appears to him shallow and crudely businesslike. It does not occur to him to measure his own loyalties against Esther's; yet by resurrecting such a relatively minor character at this crucial final stage in the novel, Moore implicitly compares the two and in the process seeks to resolve some of his own guilt. Much like Ginger in physical appearance, social status, and ambitions of becoming a jockey, he likewise shuns his family home. In many ways Esther is the mirror opposite of Moore. A woman, a servant, poor, illiterate, lower-class, religious, she marries and has a child, has difficulties expressing herself verbally, and she returns home to stay. Moore thus partially absolves himself of his own disloyalty by creating an idealized child like Esther, one who stays on and responsibly cares for the family, who may even miraculously save the estate from sinking further into the general cycle of decline and ruin that depletes the fortunes of the gentry.

Jack's visit at the close of the novel presents Moore with other artistic problems. Seeing her son in his handsome soldier's uniform, Esther feels only pride and affection and quite naturally does not imagine the battlefield dangers he might have to face or remember the hardships he caused her as a child. Given the bleak novelistic universe Moore has presented, we as readers, like Esther, have no logical rea-

sons for supposing that Jack's fortunes will turn out any better than those of the other characters. Each of them, in his or her ambitions and conduct, ended with little but failure and the knowledge that such ambitions and conduct prove ultimately futile. But we do not think Esther blindly optimistic or foolish in her hopes for her son's success in the world. Like a great horse race, the world that Jack has grown into remains an attractive and tempting possibility; even if the bet is irrelevant and hopeless in fact, it does not always seem that way in fancy. The vitality and fascination of the world beyond Woodview continue to raise Esther's hopes for her son; yet Moore puts more artistic commitment into the only other alternative the novel holds out against despair: the kind of retreat Esther chooses for herself.

The final stage in Esther's life does not carry enough conviction, does not ring true enough with what has come before, to carry the universality with which Moore would burden it. Insofar as Esther's solution negates experience, it becomes unacceptable outside her own life, even in a world that irresistibly contaminates action and turns it to failure and ruin. Her happiness on returning to Woodview is too much a negative happiness, the relief one feels when the pain and suffering finally stop. Moore claims much more for it than that in attempting to create a positive ideal. He would have Esther discover a transcendent state of mind in which wisdom and contentment, instinct and desire, merge into one complete whole. And he would locate this discovery in the process of a withdrawal, as thorough as possible, from the external world. The final sentence of the novel retreats even further towards an inner quietness and self-sufficiency, beyond the demands of time and space: "And in silence they walked towards the house" (p. 377). The simple conjunction "and," with its feeling of seamless narrative and continuous gesture, adds the final shadow to the twilight veil of timeless and unchanging beauty. Esther pulls back into her characteristic stoic silence, needing only the presence of the two people she loves in the house of her origins.

It all resembles something too much like death and a denial of the earlier experience. In the vital realism of the stables and the races, Moore created a life that here resists such annihilation. He wishes to refine Esther into an ideal, one who, because of the external limitations of her unique social status, can look at the world out of a deep, elemental simplicity and thus attain a vision of basic and eternal wisdom. She is a person who has "accomplished her woman's work" (p. 377) and a servant who still retains the customary social distinctions with her mistress long after these courtesies have lost their social

meaning. She comes from the lower class and ends in more acute poverty than when she began. And perhaps most important as a recurring motif in the novel, she cannot read. Malcolm Brown believes that her "illiteracy seems to have symbolized for Moore a sort of primordial, almost protoplasmic, strength which would survive all persecutions and outlive her persecutors."[48] Esther has kept her mother's books throughout her life away from home, but shortly before she returns to Woodview even those are stolen from her. Print becomes unnecessary and would, in fact, corrupt her through information, through its exposure of the complex and fatally alluring outside world. But we do not think of Esther as fundamentally different because of her illiteracy or her social status. All of Moore's characters share in the common experience of failure and defeat. Esther's particular response to her disasters may not be as uniquely ideal as Moore claims. Her retreat into peace, silence, and simplicity may rather be very human weakness, an understandable exhaustion with the world, an acceptable desire just to withdraw from it all.

If we as readers cannot take Esther's final stage as a response to emulate, Moore himself had even greater difficulties. Esther is about thirty-eight when her story closes. At that age, Moore was beginning to turn over in his mind the ideas for the novel *Esther Waters*, a book that would bring a solid measure of succes to a career that would last four more decades. His next major heroine, Evelyn Innes, would retire from the world because of too much commercial and artistic success, not because of too little. With his mother's death in 1895, he could more easily accept his decision to leave Moore Hall behind him. While she kept the estate alive, however, and while he still feared he might fail utterly as an artist, Esther Waters, the ideal child, could resolve some of the guilt and insecurity of George Moore, the ungrateful son. Loyal to her beginnings, beyond the need for good fortune, she seemed to Moore truly to have found happiness. He may have wished to become such a person himself, but it was not even remotely possible.

In forming a good part of his view during these years that the world was hostile to human endeavor, Moore projected onto the whole of society the limited experience of his own landed class. The social transition that meant ruin to the Irish gentry meant economic advancement for the tenants and cottiers who could at last purchase their holdings under a more favorable land policy. If a pattern of defeat and failure indeed characterized the status of the gentry, however, it could also warn off those who would materially profit even more from social change. Such attempts to win external success, the novel cautions, can

only bring disappointment. There had been a time in Ireland, as Moore recalled in *Parnell and His Island*, when his class lived in security and elegance. The politicians, the demands for land reform, the agrarian agitation, and the weak and compromising landlords changed all of that. Esther represented a return to the simplicity of an earlier age, a time before the balances in Ireland began to shift. The undeniable loss of that age contributed to Moore's depiction of her within a general environment of defeat and ruin. Yet he also hoped to find that a spiritual return to simple beginnings need not end in ruin, that individual human character might still succeed where history had gone frighteningly wrong. Esther's heroic self-sufficiency seemed to offer Moore an answer to his personal and class anxieties, an internal peace beyond the need for social gains. Not finally able to follow her example of material poverty, he still sought to retreat from the world into the artificial monastery of his work. If success did not lie within society, he would seek it through the ideal constructs of art, led on by the hope of salvation within the self.

edward martyn

To a degree that George Moore in the early 1890s could not manage, his friend Edward Martyn did succeed in establishing a correspondence between his own life style and that of his major literary characters. With an extensive family fortune behind him, Martyn could more securely afford the luxury of personal ideals that clashed with social conventions. And he further differed from Moore in his desire to shield his sensibilities from the imperfect company of people. What attracted him belonged to the world of ideas: his Catholicism, his library and his study of art and music, his frequent pilgrimages to cultural centers on the European continent, his dabblings in Home Rule politics. More the monk than the urbane man of letters, he thrived on the same kind of spiritual isolation and simplicity that inspires the idealistic heroes of his best plays. Such idealism, he thought, demanded an uncompromising dedication. For his plays, therefore, Martyn created characters who follow their visions of perfection even into madness or death; and for himself, in nearly all aspects of his personal life, he disdained compromise.

Martyn's career came to assume a curious mixture of attitudes, and his literary characters, set apart within their experiences of freezing or drowning, visionary madness or ecstatic death, act out the isolation and disconnection he himself surely felt. He became a central figure in the Irish Literary Revival, and his biographer Denis Gwynn agrees with an early reviewer that "Without Edward Martyn, the modern Irish drama might never have been born."[1] Ernest Boyd credits him with a nearly complete dominance of the Irish Literary Theatre, since "the three most successful plays produced, and those wholly congruous with the professed aims of the Theatre, were the work of the one man who has been constant to the first principles of the Movement."[2] In spite of Martyn's ideals and principles, however, the

113

most tangible assistance he could offer at the birth of the theatre came from the resources he scorned most of all—his own material wealth. From writers like Yeats and Moore his plays received more criticism than respect, and his dogmatic Catholicism occasionally became an annoying inconvenience for a theatre that produced modern versions of pre-Christian Irish legends. In Martyn's almost exclusively Protestant landlord class, as well, Catholicism marked him as a social rarity, just as his Home Rule stance singled him out as a political maverick. And his homosexuality, whether latent or overt, could find no place in his religion nor in a society even more puritanical than that of England, then hounding another Irish exile of sorts, Oscar Wilde.

Martyn's role as the Irish landlord is the easiest to locate within a broad social spectrum, and it created many of the pressures that drove him into a garrison mentality in which specific problems, such as demands for land reform, could then be translated into more metaphysical and thus, for him, more comprehensible equations. He assumed his place in 1879 as the young, wealthy lord of the manor and also accepted the almost automatic invitation to join the Kildare Street Club, the Dublin social headquarters for the Irish landholders and a bastion of conservative Protestant Ascendancy. Yet the upper levels of Irish society failed to measure up to his ideal of an aristocracy. He saw his class as a weak and degraded realization of its true potential, contented with the mere trappings of nobility while in the Viceregal Court of Dublin Castle, and even more contented with the materialistic values of the lower classes while on the estates. In the face of mounting pressures from their tenants and from an urban middle class, the landlords seemed paralyzed by indecision and fear. And they seemed only too willing to compromise: with Westminster, in the hope that the British connection would supply enough military force to protect them from their own people; and with the tenants themselves, in the hope that minor concessions like rent reductions and fixed tenure could head off a major revolution. Martyn felt that such tactics would only encourage and finally unleash a wave of barbarism in Ireland. Against this threat he settled into his own extreme position as both the harsh and unyielding landlord and the radical Home Ruler and in so doing, simultaneously alienated himself from his tenants, who tried unsuccessfully to assassinate his land agent, and from the Kildare Street Club, which tried, also without success, to expel him.

Spurred by contempt for the society he found both in England and Ireland, Martyn turned his attention from that world to the aloof self-sufficiency of his own mind. There, unencumbered by the

limitations of an imperfect humanity, he could construct models of a timeless, utopian civilization and the visionary geniuses inhabiting it, all dedicated to the highest ideals of beauty and knowledge. The dramatic tension of his best plays arises from the diametrical opposition between these two worlds: the one, ordinary, finite, flawed, superficial, physical, and mundane; the other, exotic, infinite, ideal, visionary, and spiritual. His literary characters, imprisoned in an all too oppressive and common existence, long for an ideal they only rarely and dimly perceive. In their efforts to unite the two worlds, they inevitably fall back between two irreconcilable opposites, left with little but ecstatic, visionary madness or death as the only possible resolution.

By as early as 1902 Martyn had begun a cautious retreat from such an uncompromising position that so relentlessly decreed the self-destruction of his characters. But in his two major plays, *The Heather Field* and *Maeve*, both written in the 1890s, he defines an ideal of heroism that demands complete sacrifice to its principles. Aloof from and superior to the world around them, his heroes commit themselves totally to their private visions. For these, in the language of the plays, are "real." The world of the senses, that perceived by ordinary human faculties, is the "dream," the veil that separates humanity from and conceals its higher reality. In the visionary realm ideal beauty transcends all being and experience, unites it within one perfect whole. The hero, marked by his superior vision and genius, can recognize this higher reality; ordinary humans are left with the vague terms of the preceding sentences, terms that Martyn's plays clarify only dimly.

In the novel he published in 1890 under the ponderous title of *Morgante the Lesser: His Notorious Life and Wonderful Deeds*, Martyn describes an island-city called Agathopolis, a "majestic iceberg which soars aloft in its cold purity amid the abominable seas of the world... the ideal commonwealth for uncloistered monks of all time."[3] In a satirical style imperfectly modelled on Rabelais and Swift, the novel begins with a grandiloquent dedication to the genius of error and a belittlement of all other modern writers, who, the narrator claims, concern themselves solely with superficial fads of the moment. Before introducing Morgante, the grotesque "hero" of the work, the narrator sketches in the highlights of Morgante's ancestral line. The extended genealogy gives Martyn the opportunity to range beyond contempo-

rary society into an attack on any historical figure whose ideas he considers erroneous. There once was, for instance, "a poet named Jelly, who at the beginning of the nineteenth century shook, melted, stiffened, shrieked, squirted, and blasphemed with prodigious versatility and vigour" (p. 20). All of the worst traits of such ancestors come together in the last of his line, the notorious Morgante.

In balancing out the various equations in his allegory, Martyn intends his creature to represent skepticism, materialism, individualism, and error. Morgante degrades both spirit and reason, denies the existence of any spiritual authorities, and preaches instead a worship of the individual in particular and humanity in general. Given Martyn's dim view of humanity, this is damnable heresy. Morgante advises his followers to "assert your humanity by gratifying in every manner your various whims and instincts.... The more notorious your deeds, the more will admiration be accorded to you" (p. 89). His influence on society advances it still further into mechanized and industrialized conformity and a boring dullness. Through his concern for appearance over substance, he leads his followers into superficiality and error, although this makes no difference to such a smart society crowd. Only the truly aristocratic "gentlemen" refuse to accept his amoral and selfish philosophy. In a barbed thrust at George Moore, Martyn notes that Morgante's teachings excite the most admiration in Paris, especially among the artists who frequent the Café de la Nouvelle Athènes.

Morgante's philosophy of deeds is finally refuted by one of ideas, the common sense and reason of a God-loving man named Theophilus. A citizen of Agathopolis, the city of ultimate good, Theophilus describes his home as an alternative to the gloom and confusion rampant everywhere outside that utopia. In Agathopolis people emulate the ancient Greeks in devoting their attention to knowledge, a sense of beauty, and an appreciation of the arts. A rigid Catholicism underlies their natural goodness and morality and keeps their first thoughts always fixed on God as the true center of existence. A dictator, a latter-day philosopher-king chosen for his superior learning and wisdom, rules over the island in complete isolation from his community, while those citizens who occasionally leave for a time, like Theophilus, recruit new members from men sufficiently pure in spirit to enter the city. Women, he explains without hesitation, are not allowed. The embodiment of everything emotional, unreasonable, and inferior, they would quickly reduce the city to the miserable level of the outside.

In devising his own personal strategies for living in the world beyond Agathopolis, Martyn often simply retreated from those experiences that violated his ideals. His mother had devoted herself entirely to her children with rigid, cold discipline and inadvertently helped foster Edward's horror of women and the unlikelihood that the family line would survive him. A "frail, pinched figure" in Yeats's memory, she may have told her two sons stories of John Martyn's peasant mistresses; Yeats does report this widespread Tulira gossip, not without a tinge of horror himself: "I have heard of his getting from his horse to chase a girl for a kiss."[4] The father of one such peasant woman, a man named Smith, had bought land under the Encumbered Estates Act and managed it with such astute business skill that when his daughter married into one of the best county families in 1857, the Martyns of Tulira, he provided her with a dowry of £10,000. Then, only three years later, John Martyn was dead, leaving the young widow to raise their two sons.[5]

Aside from his brother John, Edward Martyn saw almost no other children until his mother moved the family to Dublin to begin the boys' education. Edward attended a Jesuit preparatory school, Belvedere College, where he was nearly expelled for rebellious behavior. His mother, determined to create as many social opportunities as possible for her children, soon afterward hustled them off to better schools in London. Edward entered another Jesuit school in 1870, Beaumont College, and in 1876 his relentless mother managed to procure him a place at Oxford and a chance at even better social credentials. Except that Edward failed to cooperate. Lonely, awkward, and miserable, one of Oxford's few Catholic undergraduates, he showed no promise as a scholar, and in 1879, with no degree of any kind and with a bitter resentment of English education, he returned to his family home in Tulira and took up his position as landlord.[6] George Moore served for a time as his tutor in 1880, and their careers remained closely intertwined for many years afterwards. Yeats, his friendship with the two having undergone severe strain, later wrote: "They were cousins and inseparable friends, bound one to the other by mutual contempt."[7] Moore's own views were not radically different: "We have gone through life together, myself charging windmills, Edward holding up his hands in amazement."[8] Their tour of Greece and Bayreuth at this time indulged Martyn's early passion for art and music; it also offered him a welcome, albeit temporary, escape, not only from his repressive and ambitious mother, but also from the dangers of the Land War.

He believed that common people would destroy what they did not understand, and that the upper class therefore occupied a vital position in the defense of the old way of life. Along with the Catholic religious leaders, the aristocracy had a duty to safeguard the highest values of their society. At the height of the Land War, however, the Irish gentry needed some extra protection themselves. Martyn's unsympathetic treatment of his own tenants led to a predictable climax when they shot at his land agent near Tulira. One could think of many reasons during such times for taking in Bayreuth or remaining isolated within a medieval tower. The considerable personal risks Martyn faced provided him a solid framework for the polarized forces in his later plays. There, the peasants would merge with weak and compromising landlords and parasitical Englishmen under the amorphous banner of materialism, which they then advanced against the solitary, idealistic hero. From the peasants' standpoint, of course, the rich landlords represented materialism at its most extreme. In Martyn's view the peasants threatened what was rightfully his: his estate, his status as an Irish landlord, his freedom to indulge his tastes in art, literature, philosophy, and music. He found it a simple and convenient matter to characterize these possessions, in his plays, as inherently ideal, appreciated only by a few men of vision and genius, not to mention wealth and position.

Even though he refused publicly to support Home Rule as late as 1887, Martyn's interest in politics began during the Land War. Local judicial functions offered him one defense against the tenants; as his Nationalist friend R. J. Kelly later wrote, "he was most extreme in his landlord views, and no man on the Galway Grand Jury . . . was more severe, strict and hard on the popular class, in measuring out compensation for malicious injuries."[9] From still another quarter, his mother continued to pose her own threats and to provoke Edward's characteristic defenses. Especially after the death of her second son at the age of twenty-three, she repeatedly invited eligible young women to Tulira. In 1882 she replaced the old family house, itself once a beautiful building, with a massive stone mansion. "[A]mong the worst inventions of the Gothic revival," in Yeats's opinion, it combined everything that wealth and Victorian taste could resurrect from medieval romances. And, Yeats added, Martyn "hated that house in all its detail."[10] The original Norman tower of the estate, a separate building from about the twelfth century, stayed put, and the two adjoining structures vividly demonstrate the clash between Edward's desires and those of his mother. He not only refused to provide the opulent

Tulira Castle, Edward Martyn's family estate in County Galway. Martyn's Norman tower is on the right, the late nineteenth-century mansion built by his mother on the left.

new mansion with a bride, he scorned to live in it at all. George Moore saw that the modern house lacked the aesthetic qualities Martyn demanded and explained: "[Edward] prefers that his hinder-parts should suffer rather than his spirit. Every drawing-room is, in the first glance, a woman's room ... and his instinct is to get away from women."[11] He kept as his bedroom a bare, ascetic cell over the stables, and he wrote standing up before a plain wooden desk that looks out through two stained glass windows depicting Shakespeare and Chaucer. Dated 1883, they appear to be his mother's, or perhaps Edward's, only concession toward remodeling the old tower. The only concession toward the new was the installation of a pipe organ in the chapellike entry hall of the mansion. Arthur Symons, after one of his visits at Tulira, described his awed inspections of first the tower and then the mansion:

> It is a castle of dreams, where, in the morning, I climb the winding
> staircase in the tower, creep through the secret passage, and find
> myself in the vast deserted room above the chapel. . . . In the evening
> my host plays Vittoria and Palestrina on the organ, in the half dark-
> ness of the hall, and I wander between the two pillars of black marble,
> hearing the many voices rising into the dome. [12]

With its marble pillars, stately rooms hung with tapestries, and magnif-
icent library, the mansion served as a chilling reminder of how much
Edward's mother wanted to do for him. Symons, finding himself "in
some danger of loosening the tightness of my hold upon external
things,"[13] felt the chill in the tower as well, with its deliberate distance
from all pleasures or humanity.

Just as he shunned the mansion, Martyn felt alienated from all
the social activities expected of a wealthy landlord. Recoiling from his
mother's schemes to work him into such circles, he began to fashion his
own ascetic refuges and small groups of friends. Yeats, who along with
Symons visited Tulira for the first time in about 1895, wrote:

> [H]e had read Saint Chrysostom, Ibsen, Swift, because they made
> abstinence easy by making life hateful in his eyes. He drank little, ate
> enormously, but thought himself an ascetic because he had but one
> meal a day, and suffered, though a courteous man, from a subcon-
> scious hatred of women.[14]

During the 1880s, Martyn invited many famous English and Irish
artists and intellectuals to his estate for both learned discussions and
lavish banquets. In this select company at Tulira and at his London and
Dublin clubs, or alone in his tower study, he could imagine some of the
happiness that Agathopolis seemed to promise.

In his plays Martyn consistently sets male-female love rela-
tionships in direct conflict with such happiness; the friendship of two
men, by comparison, might foster it. Martyn for a time shared rooms in
London with Sir William Geary, who also visited Tulira on occasion
and shared Martyn's feelings about women and marriage. Yeats addressed the issue directly: "[Martyn] once said the majority of lost
souls are lost through sexuality, had his father's instincts through
repression or through some accident of birth turned, as Moore
thought, into an always resisted homo-sexuality."[15] He was tireless in
his criticism of women; in 1900 he granted only that they "have always

been unrivalled at depicting the violent emotions of life" and hence find their proper place in the stage.[16] In dance too, "her unideal and somewhat absurd figure assumes a beauty of outline never to be imagined in any other circumstances."[17] Martyn's literary characters also demonstrate the futility of seeking happiness or success in a love relationship. Only within their private visions do they triumph over the inevitable failures in the outside world.

Martyn's depiction of heroic failure in the world of action, and his own isolation from the socially conventional activities of the landed class, must be set against his energetic involvement in areas like politics, Irish and liturgical music, and the Literary Revival. *Morgante the Lesser* received extensive reviews in 1890 and gave him enough self-confidence to enter local government as a county magistrate. The death of his mother in 1898 removed even more of the private obstacles. Yet this emergence from his cloistered existence of the 1880s into the public life of the 1890s maintained the character of a lonely religious crusade. Martyn entertained few illusions about the practical success of his ideals. It is rather as though the failure of the ideal in the public arenas would demonstrate its spiritual worth and thus serve to inspire a select few who might then keep these values alive. Without such inspiration, the ideal, like the Martyn family line, might well end with Edward himself.

In his final memoirs Martyn referred to liturgical music as "the chief interest of my life."[18] He tried to initiate a revival of Palestrina in Ireland and England and, to that end, paid out £10,000 in 1902 toward the establishment of a Palestrina choir in Dublin. Despite the considerable respect he commanded from the clergy and bishops in artistic matters, the negotiations through Archbishop Walsh of Dublin proved difficult and time consuming. In 1898 he also publicized a traditional form of Irish music still current among the peasantry and became one of the strongest supporters of the revival of Irish music in such annual festivals as the Féis Céoil. First started in May 1897, the Féis seemed to Martyn to embody "a complete absence of all vulgarity."[19] This cultural heritage, he felt, was being rapidly destroyed by public education, which gave the lower classes ideas above their station. In 1902 he wrote that

> the Irish people were once musical and artistic in the best sense, although they are now probably the most unartistic people in Europe.

> ... A pernicious unnatural education alien from the native genius was forced on the nation by alien doctrinaires ... until it brought the country to educational barrenness.[20]

While opposing the presence of women in the church choirs, he discovered and supported several young Dublin artists, women among them, who specialized in church design, stained glass, sculpture, and architecture.

By the time of the Boer War Martyn had become radically anti-British, a position that increased in vehemence throughout his life. With Yeats and Maud Gonne, he took part in the nationalist demonstrations in 1898 and, in protest against England, resigned his county magistrate's post. This brought several requests that he enter national politics, but he settled instead on an active executive position in the Gaelic League. More than any other force, the language movement seemed capable of eliminating the English-Irish mixture at the heart of Ireland's problem:

> It is to this mongrel condition ... that may be attributed such loss of character and enterprise as causes the general inefficiency pervading all effort in Ireland, and the fatalistic doctrine that nothing Irish can succeed. ... Now the foundation of de-anglicisation and of Irish nationalism is the Irish language.[21]

In an attempt to bring more nationalism into the movement, he contributed a steady flow of propaganda to the newspapers and to the official Gaelic League publication. Then, in 1904, he accepted the presidency of the ultra-nationalist organization Sinn Fein and finally provoked the Kildare Street Club into trying to expel him. Predictably, Martyn refused to leave. The resulting lawsuit sapped much of his energy from 1906 to 1908. Even though he eventually won, his retreat back into a less strenuous way of life led him in 1908 to resign from Sinn Fein.

He made an early will with provisions for the relief of all his tenants, on the condition that he had not been murdered by them. He wasn't, and the four-thousand-acre estate was subsequently divided according to his wishes. The will further stipulated the dissection of his corpse to determine the cause of death, and then its burial in a pauper's grave. Inspired by his trip to Greece in the early 1880s and in the hope of achieving literary fame, he labored over a long poem in a classical style that he repeatedly polished and revised. In 1885, stricken with

religious qualms about such work, he burned the manuscript. A year later his work on *Morgante the Lesser* began to turn some of the early bitterness back on the world. Many of his early lyrics were published in 1911 in several issues of D. P. Moran's weekly paper, the *Leader*. Clumsy and strained, burdened by archaic diction, they attempt to describe his youthful love of beauty and his visionary experiences of ecstasy and passion. What also emerges is his feeling that his youth was most frequently characterized by sadness and disillusionment. He published *Morgante the Lesser* under a pseudonym, "Sirius;" for his next and greatest work he had nothing more to conceal. Dedicated to Yeats, Moore, and Symons, *The Heather Field* was performed in Dublin on 9 May 1899; with Yeats's *The Countess Cathleen*, it signalled the beginning of a spectacular period in Irish drama.

Along with Yeats and Moore, Martyn became co-founder of the Irish Literary Theatre in 1899, a step he called "the most significant action" of his life.[22] For the first time he could unite all of his talents on a public project commensurate with his private ideals. He imagined the theatre, just as in Agathopolis, as a cultural center that could possibly even begin the long process of restoring the genius of the Celtic past. His hopes for a revival of the soul of Ireland started with theories about possible similarities and connections between ancient Greek and Celtic civilizations. Such a relationship, he speculated, could be transmitted through a world spirit of creative and intellectual energy. Transcending time and space, this spirit would unite two cultures within the same ideal, mystical character. If a "native genius" could be reawakened in Ireland through such means as a national theatre and literature, then the Irish people would share their appreciation of beauty and knowledge at the spiritual level of Martyn's utopian civilization. Furthermore, those men of vision and genius who had initiated their nation into its true heritage would receive their just recognition as cultural leaders.

Even during the triumphant celebration after the Literary Theatre's opening performance, Martyn could not have expected either his own reputation or the Irish society to reach such airy heights. The obstacles within Ireland had become too many and powerful. The intended social function of Martyn's plays rather lay in his attempts to keep alive the ideals he associated with Ireland, the values Maeve represents as the "fairy lamp of Celtic Beauty." Maeve herself may die, yet the enactment of her death on stage could turn her personal defeat at the hands of the world into the triumph of a spirit ultimately stronger than the world. As pure spirit, Martyn's ideals could, he felt, remain

indifferent to and uncorrupted by any historically limited social conditions. The person of vision had only to inspire further guardians of the lamp, who would of necessity always remain a select few. The broad mass of society, although welcome to support artistic ventures like a national theatre, could best serve by keeping a respectful distance.

Although he consistently advocated Irish artists over the importation of foreign models and styles, Martyn did draw considerable attention to Richard Wagner and Henrik Ibsen, the two figures who, more than any other non-Irish artists, exercised a shaping influence on the Irish Literary Theatre. Wagner had demonstrated the symbolic power latent in a culture's legendary heroes and epic themes and, at a time when artists were seeking a greater autonomy for their work, significantly expanded the previous boundaries of art. After Wagner's visionary aestheticism and such concepts as the *Gesamtkunstwerk*, artists could better define the unique place of their work in society, a place that need not serve morality or politics. Henrik Ibsen seemed to Martyn in the late 1890s "the most original as well as the greatest of dramatists."[23] Distinctly Norwegian in his work, Ibsen, like Wagner, also appealed to the hope that art might reflect a specific national character. But the Irish writers learned much more, about technique as well as emphasis, from his precise and tightly organized realism. For Martyn, just as later for James Joyce, Ibsen cleared much of the way toward a treatment of psychological themes and social criticism in literature.[24]

Martyn could therefore bring to the Irish Literary Theatre not only extensive financial backing but also his knowledge of Continental drama. As one of the Theatre's directors, he tried to transfer Ibsenesque techniques to the Irish stage. From the beginning, however, he felt dissatisfied with the local company and its stage facilities. His impatience with the actors, his recurrent fears about possible religious heresy in anyone's play, his reluctance to improve one of his weaker scripts, and his resistance to peasant drama all strained the theatrical venture. A second play, *Maeve*, was successfully produced in 1900, but two years later the talented acting brothers, William and Frank Fay, split off along with Yeats and Lady Gregory to form the Irish National Theatre. Martyn felt incapable of creating the peasant plays asked of him because "the peasant's primitive mind is too crude for any sort of interesting complexity in treatment." If Yeats and Lady Gregory chose folk drama as their mode, they would have to settle for nothing more than a "folk theatre."[25] Dissociated from the new organization, Martyn was left to carry on with only amateur actors.

He soon got two more of his plays produced in Dublin, *An Enchanted Sea* in 1904 and *The Tale of a Town* in 1905. As a pivotal work in Martyn's career, *An Enchanted Sea* points forward to his later rejection of unworldly aestheticism but also backward to the essence of the Irish Renaissance and his two major plays. Lord Mask, a scholar and connoisseur of art, imagines himself the spokesman of an Irish spiritual awakening. His young friend Guy Font brings to Mask's intellect a childlike, visionary quality, one directly in touch with the elemental spiritual forces of Ireland and its mythology. With Guy's imagination to sustain him, Mask can endure the "shadows," the mundane external world he finds so repressive, but finally follows Guy into "a vision of eternal art in the antique glory of the sea!"[26] Mask once imagined that in the depths of the ocean he saw the young boys in the court of Mananaan, the Irish god of the sea. After Guy's death by drowning, therefore, vision in the appearance of Guy beneath the waves beckons Mask to his own death. The final words of the play, a marriage proposal offered by a practical naval commander who knows the sensible way to deal with oceans, lead back to the world of society and the living. Yet Martyn has put more conviction behind Mask's speeches and his wistful adoration of the dead.

Martyn's later work clearly repudiates much of the aesthete's role. In terming this development a "progression towards realism,"[27] however, Courtney tends to obscure its negative side. Martyn's final memoirs, bitter and satiric in tone, returned to the style of *Morgante the Lesser* in describing the Literary Revival. Martyn borrowed a phrase from the novelist Samuel Lover, "Handy Andyism," which he repeatedly used for all the bumbling, narrow-minded, bureaucratic, materialistic forces in Ireland. Yet in this self-serving chronicle, entitled "Paragraphs for the Perverse," even Yeats and Lady Gregory received only ironic praise. In turning away from aestheticism, the flailing irony of the memoirs, as in his play *The Dream Physician* (1914), progresses not so much toward realism as toward bitterness and disappointment. During the last decade before his death in 1923, arthritis and general poor health kept Martyn confined to his tower study, frequently in pain, never able to put the records of his career into publishable form.

In Martyn's play *The Heather Field*, completed sometime before 1894 and first published and performed in 1899, many of the major themes and character types resemble those of *An Enchanted Sea*. As he

did in the later play, Martyn here develops the same pattern of the composite personality to define his heroes. Two characters, one a realist and the other an idealist, would, if merged, yield a personality able both to recognize the ideal in vision and to tolerate the mundane in everyday routine. Barry Ussher, the realist, possesses an intellectual understanding of beauty and genius as absolute qualities. Through his scholarship and love of art he can learn about and believe in a higher reality without ever having any direct experience of it. The idealistic Carden Tyrrell, on the other hand, the central figure of the play, brings to this distanced recognition the immediate vision that inspires and transforms knowledge, charges it with a transcendent energy. He acts as a prophet who can initiate the realist into the possibility of vision; and Ussher, through his learning, can explain and clarify the meaning of that ecstatic experience, not only for Tyrrell, but for the audience of the play as well.

Society perceives the realist as the better adjusted of the two personalities, and Ussher's fortuitous personal circumstances render him even more immune from many social conventions. He has to endure the plague common to many of Martyn's bachelors, the suspicions directed at the man who chooses not to marry. Still, he is notoriously successful at everything he undertakes, whether as a landlord or as a philosopher and scholar. In life style he closely resembles Martyn himself, the wealthy, aristocratic sage sequestered among his books, ideas, and works of art. Yet he scorns all his accomplishments as too tenuous and mutable, prey to reversal in the next round of luck. His refusal to rely on any external, material values comes, not from his nature as the hardened and cynical philosopher, but rather, as Tyrrell explains, because "he can see the truly beautiful, and so is heedless of shams."[28] Pure happiness for Ussher does not depend on external conditions, the superficial and irrelevant prose of life. He seeks it rather in such poetry as he once enjoyed in the company of Carden Tyrrell, in the days before Tyrrell married.

Tyrrell's youthful optimism in those days made the world seem infinitely fascinating to the imagination, and his visionary ideals also appealed to Ussher's longing for something spiritual and perfect. Ussher describes the younger Tyrrell as one "so ideal, so imaginative, as engaging as some beautiful child who saw nothing real in the world outside his own fairy dreams" (p. 7). In Tyrrell's ability spiritually to transcend the limits of the senses, Ussher found his link to the ideal and a release from the frustrating restrictions, materialism, and banality of the common world. Both men could share in Tyrrell's energy and

inspiration, approach life with hopeful expectations. When Tyrrell therefore, "like one bewitched," decided to marry the beautiful Grace Desmond, Ussher tried to dissuade him, not only to prevent the abatement of their friendship, but also because he recognized how unfit Tyrrell was for marriage to any woman.

Lacking Ussher's worldly cynicism and experience, Tyrrell often plunges headlong into situations he cannot possibly manage with any success. Always confident about his own talents, he readily trusts in a benevolent and appreciative society to support him. But society shows itself less kind to the idealist than to the realist. Against one such as Tyrrell, who values before all else his private visions, the society masses powerful and implacable pressures. Marriage becomes only the most obvious and constant example of the conventions hemming him in. At the point where the play begins, ten years after his marriage to Grace, Tyrrell has come to realize that Ussher was right. With increasing frustration he feels the awful discrepancy between his experience in the world of society, to which his wife would adapt him, and the world of vision, which she would close off from him. But he still has Ussher to listen to his wistful complaints: "[H]ave you ever seen on earth something beautiful beyond earth — that great beauty which appears in divers ways? And then have you known what it is to go back to the world again?" (p. 68). His ideal of beauty haunts him all his life and leads him constantly on in search of it. Throughout the play, however, the distance grows between that beauty, the only true reality for Tyrrell, and the world he finds so painfully tedious and limited.

As Ussher says of Grace, she "would probably have made an excellent wife for almost any other man" (p. 6). Efficient, intelligent, and sensible, she still alienates her husband as much through her manner as through her values. She complains of time and money wasted on Tyrrell's eccentric projects or on his conversations with Ussher about art and philosophy. His study of medieval architecture simply bores her, while his collection of books and art objects around the house annoys her with its clutter. Disregarding all the social events attendant upon his status as a landlord, Tyrrell soon drives her from mere boredom into poorly concealed hatred. But although Grace discusses her husband as though he were some strange and inferior animal, she still understands him as well as anyone does, realizes that "I became as nothing to him — that what he loved was something mysterious — beyond me" (p. 33). Her confidante, Lady Shrule, a shallow aristocrat who married strictly for convenience and station, has managed to endure her own husband all these years and hence

thinks Grace might have done better in manipulating Tyrrell: "Most men have notions before they marry: but they are soon brought to their senses, if their wives are clever" (p. 30). But Grace has run out of cleverness and patience; she reveals to her friend a plan to have Tyrrell declared legally insane.

The immediate occasion for this step is the heather field. On the side of a mountain that constantly dominates the background scenery of the play, the field is the first stage in a massive plan Tyrrell has devised for reclaiming untillable acreage. He envisions his work expanding into an eventual reclamation of all the waste land in Ireland, and as a further goal in an already extravagant project, he hopes that through his foresight and genius he will win recognition as his country's true benefactor. Impatient with the halfway gestures of the politicians, he measures his own efforts against ultimate standards: "When from the ideal world of my books those people forced me to such a business, I was bound to find the extreme of its idealisation" (p. 48). He consequently turned the humdrum, routine methods of farming into a scientific exercise, one that allowed him to ignore the landlord's usual day-to-day problems of managing an estate and that will, he hopes, transform ineffable vision into concrete reality. Preferring a detached, scholarly method over the dull drudgery of field work, he conducts the entire operation from his study. Thus isolated from the men who actually carry out his theories, Tyrrell decides that the work could begin progressing much faster.

From the beginning of the play, the collapse of the enterprise appears inevitable to everyone but Tyrrell himself. And in analyzing the breakdown of his friend's marriage, Ussher expands the image of the field into a symbolic parallel that controls the play's entire structure:

> There are some dispositions too eerie, too ethereal, too untamable for good, steady, domestic cultivation, and if so domesticated they avenge themselves in after time. Ah, foolishly his wife and her friends thought they were going to change Carden to their model of a young man, but the latent, untamable nature was not to be subdued. Its first sign of revolt against suppression was when he began this vast work in the heather field (p. 8).

In returning to his "old, wild nature," Tyrrell paradoxically adopts his wife's methods for dealing with external problems. He tries to wipe out the heather and turn the field to more productive use, ignoring that

individuality and love of freedom within himself that abhors such restrictions.

The metaphor leaves him no escape; if Tyrrell succeeds in eradicating the natural growth of wild heather and converting the field into manageable farmland, he will signal the victory of forces he has always resisted and the degeneration of spirit to the level of ordinary matter. His claim that he has raised common farming practices to an idealistic and visionary level does not convince Ussher, despite Ussher's reassuring, if ponderously symbolic, pronouncements about agriculture: "If heather lands are brought into cultivation for domestic use, they must be watched, they must have generous and loving treatment, else their old wild nature may avenge itself" (p. 9). Tyrrell himself, at the hands of his wife and his society, has not received sufficiently gentle treatment; that has made some difference, but not much. The fatal mistake, as Ussher realizes, grows out of Tyrrell's attempt to unite real and ideal, and his subsequent inability to distinguish one from the other. He defends his theories on a material level, arguing that increased rents for the property will more than compensate for the expenditures threatening to ruin the estate. Yet he is motivated far more by the desire to get his ideals recognized and accepted outside himself. Ussher knows his society too well to entertain such illusions, knows that Tyrrell's visions and idealistic principles maintain their fragile existence only so long as they are protected from the outside world. When Tyrrell seeks to transfer them outward into the realm of material action and practical endeavor, when he tries to realize the ideal in the real, he can end up with nothing but failure.

Marriage has taught him nothing about the limits of his abilities and expectations within society. He has become as bitter and cynical about women as his friend Ussher, scorning them all as little more than insufferable burdens: "[I]nstead of inspiring they more often prevent us from doing anything" (p. 43). Mired in his wife's plans to make a social being out of him, tormented by what he calls the "simple barren prose" of her mind, he becomes even more determined and insistent on his plans for the heather field. He sees Grace as the chief cause of his own failures in the marriage and hence can maintain a show of confidence in his other projects, for "your true idealist can only be a man" (p. 16). In the rarefied idealism he applies to the heather field, Tyrrell lapses into the same mistake that doomed his marriage; once again he demands that earth-born matter transform itself into his ideal of spirit.

Tyrrell governs his tenants according to similarly absolute

principles. In refusing to compromise with them, he bases their rents on his theoretical assessment of the land's worth rather than on their actual ability to pay. His harsh policies finally provoke the tenants into assassination threats and make Tyrrell a virtual prisoner in his own house, a situation not unlike Martyn's own at the height of the Land War. The external pressures grow increasingly stronger throughout the play. Tyrrell's creditors, refusing to gamble any further on the heather field, begin to insist on repayment. And always there is Grace, her hostile criticism driving him ever deeper into frustration and panic. Tyrrell has locked himself into such total commitment to his personal ideals that he cannot afford to admit the importance of mere external circumstances. Rather, "the only remedy must be something which would make me forgetful that I am myself" (p. 67). He finds that remedy, the obliteration of self and surroundings, within his personal visions.

The moments of visionary "wakefulness" become more important as the long periods between those moments grow more oppressive. Circumstances so painful and unmanageable, Tyrrell feels, must be fragments of an insubstantial nightmare: "[P]ersons and objects are receding from me and becoming more unreal in these later times. . . . I often think that my life of pain and unrest here is only a dream after all" (p. 19). Voices on the wind, "Choristers singing of youth in an eternal sunrise!" (p. 49), call him back to the "real life" he once enjoyed. He denies that "imagination" has anything to do with his visions; the ideal exists, an absolute and superior reality, independent of other people's failure to perceive. Ironically inspired by the very wild nature he now seeks to tame, however, he finds the "ideal domain" for his visions in the heather field.

In Tyrrell's breathless attempts to describe his visions, Martyn unintentionally but repeatedly threatens to plunge the entire play into silliness. He avoids that through the realistic psychology of nostalgia. Tyrrell's younger brother Miles helps revive in him the remembrance of a happier youth, the days when "the marvelous seemed real." In an image that Lord Mask will later inherit and transfer to the court of the sea god, Tyrrell recalls a tour of Europe he once made with Miles and "that Sunday morning in Cologne Cathedral when all the boys sang Palestrina so divinely" (p. 19). Ten years later, burdened more and more by the present and "haunted by those departed joys of my youth" (p. 20), Tyrrell understandably seeks refuge in a happier time. He himself recognizes the psychological motives that lead him to romanticize the past, explaining that "memory has idealised those past

scenes, till only their beauty remains, wafted back to me like an aroma from some lost paradise" (pp. 17–18). The play claims much more immediate substance for the present visions than for mere nostalgic ramblings. But with an eye to Ibsen and the demands of the well-wrought play, Martyn holds his character to a degree of psychological realism that can withstand the assaults of the ethereal choristers.

Tyrrell's son Kit, already much like his father, also revives in Tyrrell the memories of youthful energy and inspiration. And it is Kit, the "wildflower elf," the "dream child," who finally and naively leads his father into madness. Tyrrell himself, frightened by his wife's accusations, has earlier begun to doubt his own sanity and to wonder, "which is the reality and which is the dream?" (p. 29). But Ussher's words, well reasoned and moderate throughout the play, again forecast most accurately the dangers Tyrrell faces. Ussher urges Kit to forget his childish ambitions of becoming a sailor in the world of men and to remain instead a child forever, for "down under the sea grow numberless fair flowers whose leaves close softly around many a poor sailor" (p. 39). Already so like his father, if Kit also sought to transfer his sheltered, private visions into the public world of action, that world would destroy him just as surely as it does Tyrrell. Driven insane by his son's report that the wild heather has again broken out on the mountain, Tyrrell slips permanently into his youth. In his fantasies of ten years ago, Kit has become a "field-fairy" playing in the depths of the Rhine with the sirens of Lorelei. Beneath the sea of his visions, Tyrrell has lingered too long.

In madness Tyrrell finds ecstatic, untroubled happiness and a release from a world that left no place for him. The visionary rainbow that he points out to Kit, the "mystic highway of man's speechless longings!" (p. 83), leads him to the ideal he has always longed for. He has finally burst through the "dream" into his perfect, immortal reality. Just as Tyrrell failed to destroy the heather, the attempts to civilize and contain his nature have failed. Of course we, as audience or readers of the play, must regret insanity and deplore the impossibility of ever uniting real with ideal. Ussher's behavior at the end of the play satisfies these social obligations. Confronted with Tyrrell's madness, he sadly wonders if beauty and happiness are, after all, only the illusions of lunacy, and then he and Miles set to work busily restoring the estate to financial solvency. Martyn thus conveniently removes all practical barriers to a vicarious identification with Tyrrell. For his is a romantic tragedy, the heroic downfall of a man totally committed to his personal ideals. Like many heroes, Tyrrell fails only by the mundane standards

of the society that refuses to tolerate such genius. Measured by his own more superior and inviolate values, his spirit has risen into triumph.

In his introduction to the 1899 edition of *The Heather Field and Maeve*, George Moore wrote that "to triumph thus over common instincts and infect the reader with sympathies and longing which lie beyond the world is surely to succeed" (p. xxvii). For Moore, Martyn's dramatic success hung on Carden Tyrrell's spiritual triumph. Yet a large part of Tyrrell's "victory" depends, not on the superiority of the man of vision and genius over the common herd, but on reasons that have little to do with any heroic ideals. If one perceives something lacking, as in the treatment Tyrrell endures from his wife or from society, then one can more easily imagine a wholeness, a wish-fulfilling opposite of finite experience. Only by first paying the visible world its due can Martyn construct a dramatically viable conception of an invisible one. To placate a world that demands psychological realism and comprehensible dramatic characters, Barry Ussher, the rational and sober intermediary, brings an aura of nostalgia as a motive for Tyrrell's idealistic longings. Part of Tyrrell's success as a dramatic character lies in his response to a mundane and stifling society, his idealism that, while mad, is made sympathetic as a response. But the success of the character also depends in part on Ussher's understanding of Tyrrell; as a sane, decent man, Ussher lends an air of authenticity to his friend that does not vanish with the madness and the defeat. If the real, practical world as represented by Ussher can approve of Tyrrell, we as audience then have more on which to base our acceptance than simply the spiritual visions. Through Tyrrell, Martyn claims as an idealist philosopher to disdain any compromise with such a world and to rely instead solely on his absolute principles. As a practical dramatist he takes care to recognize both sides.

Ussher could have become much more than a dramatic convenience in the play, a foil to support and define Tyrrell's visionary idealism. He suggests a more attractive philosophy that might successfully balance the demands of the real against the fascination of the ideal. Especially within the setting of a national theatre, the strength of a realist like Ussher could greatly expand the influence of an idealist like Tyrrell. The dream survives as dream, even though Tyrrell himself can finally only maintain it in madness; but Ussher offers a more definite possibility that it could survive as concrete substance, because he suggests how vision may work upon and transform lived experience within a more practical and, for a nationalist literary movement, political arena. Except that Martyn fails, perhaps willingly, to bring

Ussher beyond the limits of faint suggestion. He remains an engaging character, in part because he most closely resembles Martyn himself. Yet Martyn chose instead to give the idealist Tyrrell nearly total domination over the play. When Tyrrell is on stage, all attention and conversation turn around him; and when he is absent, he is constantly discussed by characters who attempt to understand and explain him and to define their own roles in relation to his. The few lines in the opening scene that leave Ussher an opportunity to establish his own philosophy in the play fade quickly into the circumstances surrounding Tyrrell. As Ussher consciously decides uncritically and totally to support his friend, so too does Martyn decide not to qualify and dilute his ideal. He builds his play entirely around the visionary idealist and portrays Ussher's accomplishments as minor in comparison. The main concrete achievement within the play is not the survival of the estate, which concerns the realist Ussher, but which Martyn could have parcelled out as ruthlessly as he decreed the division of his own land in his family will; it is rather the survival of the heather field.

The concessions to Ibsenesque realism and the tight structure of the play gained further strength from the opening performance of Thomas Kingston in the role of Tyrrell. The *Daily Express* felt that, despite Tyrrell's "insane idealism," Kingston "did not for a moment lose his hold upon his audience." After serious reservations about Yeats's *The Countess Cathleen* the previous evening, the paper now had unqualified praise: "Mr. Martyn has in this work . . . proved himself to be the greatest living dramatist who writes in the English tongue" (10 May 1899). This was heady stuff, and Yeats felt miffed. He later explained, somewhat condescendingly, that *The Heather Field* was "in the manner of Ibsen, the manner of the moment."[29] Ignoring his usual skepticism about Moore, he accepted Moore's story that the "masterly construction"[30] had been his: Moore "had constructed *The Heather Field*, he said, telling Martyn what was to go into every speech but writing nothing, had partly constructed *Maeve*."[31] Arthur Symons too, Yeats continued, had a hand in *Maeve*. Moore was not finished with Martyn yet either: "He is thinking that his dreams are coming to pass, and believes himself to be the Messiah — he who will give Ireland literature and her political freedom."[32] Of all the messianic hopefuls in the aftermath of the theatre's inauguration, Moore regarded himself as the most qualified.

The initial popularity of Martyn's play came almost in spite of his wish to inspire only a prophetic few, the select geniuses who would keep alive the spirit of Tyrrell's vision. The play remains limited by its

focusing so completely on the character of Tyrrell and on the intangible and remote ideals he represents. Regarding *Maeve*, Yeats's review of Martyn's artistic debts points towards a related question: if experienced critics like Moore and Symons did in fact influence Martyn's work to any degree, why is *Maeve* so bad, especially since it was written with a definite theatre and audience in mind? At the time of his work on *The Heather Field*, Martyn was only dimly aware of the possibility for an Irish national theatre. In *Maeve*, a piece expressly intended for such a theatre, he greatly diminishes the character of the realist and accentuates that of the idealist, as though scornfully resisting the opportunity to reach a broader audience. Once given an actual, popular forum where his ideas could have had political results, Martyn instead made his position even less accessible by seeking the extreme of its expression and by resorting to vague and oversimplified rhetoric. The few men of vision could still find inspiration in *Maeve*; the broad mass could make do with the play's slogans.

Maeve was published in 1899 and performed a year later. Closely adhering to the themes of *The Heather Field* while sacrificing much of the earlier realism, Martyn here undertakes a more direct definition of his spiritual ideals within the dense atmosphere of Irish nationalism and mythology; in that shift in emphasis lies much of *Maeve*'s failure as a dramatic work. Many of the themes and ideas in *The Heather Field* remain ambiguous, even questions as fundamental as whether the play ends in pessimism or optimism. *Maeve*, with its often trite and pretentious oversimplifications, moves to clarify such ambiguities. In consciously writing a showpiece for the nationalistic literary movement, Martyn had to redesign much of his earlier scenery. He locates the play in a rundown castle and in the ruins of an ancient abbey rather than in an aristocratic manor house, and he takes as the central problem the question, will Maeve O'Heynes sacrifice her spiritual ideals to her father's ambitious materialism and marry the wealthy Englishman, Hugh Fitz Walter? Hugh represents an end to the string of misfortunes that have plagued The O'Heynes[33] and reduced him to near poverty. If Hugh marries Maeve, his money and position can restore the O'Heynes family line to its once proud status. Now more the peasant than the aristocrat in his manner, The O'Heynes cannot conceal his anxieties about his daughter's marriage: "Oh child, if you could only realise how I have waited and waited for this—for the time

when fortune would enable our family to resume its fitting position in the county!" (p. 92). Obsessed with his own bad luck and Maeve's unconventional behavior, he rightly fears that she may upset his plans.

In her devotion to a philosophy of mystical and intellectual idealism and in her visionary imagination, Maeve closely resembles Carden Tyrrell. As with Tyrrell, people wonderingly speak of her strange and ethereal youth, the years when she immersed herself in visions of Irish antiquity. Inspired by the legends and poetry of the ancient Irish bards, she claimed a spiritual kinship to the past that she never felt to the modern world. Her happiness arose from her visions, in which her idealization of the "immortal beauty of form" came alive in the aspect of Tir-nan-ogue, the "Celtic dreamland of ideal beauty." All that seemed to end two months ago, with Hugh's proposal of marriage. But now, on the eve of the wedding, people fear that Maeve is returning to her "old self."

With his plot and characters already overburdened with abstract philosophy, Martyn makes the play even more top-heavy with his theories about ancient Greece. Maeve owns an old manuscript, "The Influence of Greek Art on Celtic Ornament," which reveals to her the spiritual unity of the Greek and Celtic races as well as "a curious unreal beauty besides, which she says the Greeks invented" (p. 94). Martyn first attributed this theory to Agathopolis and later would put it in Lord Mask's mouth. Here it remains a clumsy and artificial imposition on the play, despite the patient efforts of Maeve's sister Finola to explain it.

Finola is the only character capable of explaining Maeve and spends most of her time on stage doing just that. She thus performs a function similar to that of Barry Ussher in mediating between the main character and the audience. Since Maeve so completely dominates the action, however, and since Finola's personality remains so conventional and submissive, the play fails to cross the gap from common world into vision. Finola can agree with her father that Maeve "seems to me quite regardless of realities" and adds: "Those feelings and impulses which are in our hearts and which govern our affections, with her are all in the head" (p. 93). As an explanation, this does more to isolate us from Maeve than to win any identification. More concerned with the abstract glorification of his heroine than with a concrete delineation of personality, Martyn dispenses with the interpretation and psychological realism that might have rendered her believable.

He further isolates Maeve within the recurring image of ice. Wanting to suggest her exalted purity, as he once praised the "majestic

"The action takes place ... among the Burren Mountains of County Clare in Ireland." — from *Maeve*

iceberg" Agathopolis, Martyn instead surrounds her with connotations of death. She wanders through the abbey ruins on a freezing night exclaiming, "How beautiful to be like the ice!" (p. 111) and feeling nothing but the lure of the moonlight. Ice represents to her a state of timeless, unchanging perfection and a union with her beloved ideal of beauty, personified as a prince of Tir-nan-ogue. Although she longs for him as the hero who will "deliver me from bondage" (p. 119), Maeve's lover never appears except as pure idea. She shrinks from any contact with him, believing that "the beauty of love would come to an end in the lover" (p. 101), and instead seeks an infinitely expanding love of the imagination and intellect, one frozen in a transcendent state outside the limits of time and space and consummation of desire. The play thus postulates an ideal and all-encompassing equation in which ice equals Maeve's feelings of love and her beloved ("My love is so divinely cold,"

p. 117), equals beauty ("a beauty which is transcendently cold," p. 123), equals the spirit of ancient Greece ("The greatest beauty like the old Greek sculpture is always cold!" p. 119), equals the spirit of ancient Ireland. Within the vague and shadowy depths of this formula, Martyn finds no obstructions to a further equation of the Irish spirit with Maeve herself.

The popular success of the play depended heavily on the nationalistic rhetoric of this final symbol. Maeve, apotheosized as the "fairy lamp of Celtic Beauty" and the "Last Princess of Erin," becomes a representative of anything in Ireland the audience might ever choose to commemorate. And Hugh, guilty only of loving Maeve, finds himself the hated culmination of centuries of British banditry: "I say a bandit," declares Maeve, "like his English predecessors who ruined every beautiful thing we ever had" (p. 113). He brings material prosperity, which Maeve's avaricious father and the rest of the dull, common herd may find attractive, but he ignorantly rapes the country of its spirit and beauty. Maeve's spiritual mentor, the mysterious and sinister beggar woman Peg Inerny, confronts Hugh head on: "You think I am only an old woman; but I tell you that Erin can never be subdued" (p. 127). Peg, a spiritual relative of Yeats's Cathleen ni Houlihan, carries on the Irish tradition of the Shan Van Vocht, the "poor old woman" who symbolizes Ireland itself. She appears to true Irish patriots as the beautiful young woman Maeve sees in her final vision; to ordinary mortals like Hugh, she conceals herself behind the guise of old age. And in her final, defiant rallying cry that brought an immediate response from the nationalist audience, she insured for Martyn the popular success of his play. Enraptured by her vision of Peg Inerny's true kingdom and insensible to the cold around her, Maeve freezes to death at her castle window. Her fate recalls Carden Tyrrell's; in death or in madness, they merge completely with the spiritual perfection they have longed for. Even more than with Tyrrell, Maeve's fate must be regarded as her triumph.

In his introduction to *The Heather Field and Maeve* Moore offers this summation of the two plays:

> The idea of both plays is that silvery beauty which survives in the human heart, which we see shimmering to the horizon, leading our longings beyond the world. ... The morning light, the hoar frost, the moonlight ... are the natural symbols of this divine beauty. (p. xxvi)

In locating beauty within the silvery, romantic mists of the Celtic Twilight, however, Martyn renders it both inaccessible and deathlike.

Deliberately vague and indistinct, he tries to suggest the infinite ex-
panses and pervasive but immaterial spirit of his ideals; they instead
vanish completely, smothered by the all too apparent muddle and
confusion of human language. In the final scenes of *Maeve*, seeking
to verbalize the essence of his heroine's visions and ideals, Martyn
again and again falls back on the inadequate term "beauty." Especially
when recited aloud, its incessant repetition quickly transforms the
word into little more than nonsense syllables. Carden Tyrrell's ideals
take on a somewhat greater clarity than Maeve's because of their
realistic and material context. But shorn of those limits, which merely
define where the ideal does not extend, they have the same tendency
to drift apart into confusion or the verbal absurdities of choristers and
mystic highways.

    Although it controls much of the vagueness that spoils *Maeve*,
the realism of *The Heather Field* also obscures the full extent of what
Martyn rejects in these two plays. He ultimately reduces his ideal of
heroism to a choice of death over life. In death, or madness for Tyrrell,
the hero finds the essence of the immortal ecstasy and perfection he
has longed for but only fleetingly glimpsed. His ideals have failed
within the external world of action and practical success, but they, and
he, can better exist outside that world. Martyn's hero thus annihilates
experience to retreat into vision; since experience seems so limited and
oppressive and miserable, the end of experience seems to promise
ultimate vision.
    The failure of Martyn's work lies in his inability to return from
such a vision back to the world of experience. Yet the failure has its
personal dimension as well. Martyn felt himself in headlong flight
from an Irish society that he could not tolerate and that he saw turning
increasingly worse. His depiction of Ireland's heroic past became more
idealized as his view of the relentless future became more horrified,
and his retreat points toward a paralyzed desire to stop those changes
in his society. Yeats described Martyn as a man "always on the brink of
the world in a half-unwilling virginity of the feelings."[34] In his frozen
isolation on the brink, incapable of abandoning his sanctuary, he could
only claim for his personal dilemma an ideal, visionary status that
resisted contact with the society that had spawned it. Only the select
few could share in the dream. So that when it seemed he might gain a
measure of political influence through his art, he made his position

even more extreme and inaccessible. His own terms left him at an impasse: only a pure ideal could transform the world, yet an ideal touched by the world could not remain pure. Maeve consequently faces even higher odds than Tyrrell, and her defeat demands even more sacrifice and perfection from those visionaries who would follow her inspiration and example. Her path leads away from experience; somehow, in ways Martyn could never discover, that path also needed to return to and redeem a changing society. For the Irish landlords such a redemption had hopelessly vanished within the shuffle of new economic and political structures. Like Tyrrell or Maeve, they could triumph, could define their inner nature, only by rejecting their external surroundings or being defeated by them. Martyn may have had definite goals in mind to which Irish society, he hoped, might one day aspire. But these more specific views became completely overwhelmed by his feelings that his society left him only defeat and despair.

In 1899 Moore could accept such a denial of life. He admired the spiritual purity and idealism of Martyn's heroes and the insignificance they attach to real things and people: "Maeve's love ... shrinks from all contact or even thought of contact of flesh" (p. xxvii). In just a little over a decade, however, Moore was capable of suggesting, although he stopped short of it, that such love shrinks from flesh much as a middle-aged man might flee the clinging, demanding embrace of his own mother. Moore's "dear Edward" becomes much more real, and sympathetic, than either Maeve or Carden Tyrrell:

> He is an amateur; that is to say, a man of many interests, one of which is literature. Edward is interested in his soul, deeply interested; he is interested in Palestrina and in his property in Galway, and the sartorial reformation of the clergy.... He wants Home Rule, and when he is thinking of none of these things he writes plays.[35]

Moore to the contrary, Martyn very likely was thinking about "these things" when writing plays. Strict Catholicism, radical Home Rule politics, the Kildare Street Club and its conservative Protestant Ascendancy membership, the spiritual idealism of *The Heather Field* and *Maeve*—all these come together within a feeling of profound dissatisfaction over the changing course of Irish history. Perhaps the faithless British government could be discarded, the weak aristocracy inspired with a new standard of heroism, and the materialistic lower and middle classes confronted with the superficiality of their values. One can imagine Martyn thinking of all these things while writing plays

about visionary dreamers fated for defeat at the hands of society. For in the conflict between ideal dream and degenerate circumstance, the ideal could only survive by retreating, by refusing finally to compromise its spiritual nature and preferring instead an icy, deathlike perfection.

GEORGE RUSSELL

L|ike Edward Martyn, George Russell exercised a strong, directing influence on the early Irish Renaissance while having almost no impact on subsequent generations of writers or readers. Lacking Martyn's material resources, Russell served the younger artists more as spiritual father than financial backer. Yet Stephen Dedalus notes that "A.E.I.O.U.," recalling another of his many small loans; more importantly for Joyce, Russell enabled him to print part of *Dubliners* in the *Irish Homestead*, stories the more established Dublin publishers would reject as too hot to handle. For other writers Russell could offer support of a more aesthetic nature. In his poetry from the 1890s, the metrical effects, recurring phrases, and poetic attitudes and atmospheres often closely resemble those in work Yeats was doing at the same time. Russell admired Yeats's prose pieces such as *Rosa Alchemica*, while cautioning that he should "never forget that poetry is their proper language."[1] He criticized *The Wind Among the Reeds* for "Your detestable symbols" that take on "a reflected light from the general twilight luminousness and beauty which does not belong to them by right."[2] Such remarks will not explain Yeats's abandoning of a prose work like *The Speckled Bird* or the subsequently sharper outlines to his poetic symbols, but neither could he ignore Russell's critical accuracy.

The two writers had become close friends in 1883 or 1884, when both were enrolled at the Metropolitan School of Art in Dublin. There, Yeats admired Russell's ability to paint ethereal, symbolic scenes that floated free of any reliance on an actual model. As Jack B. Yeats would later capture the natural realism of peasants, beggars, and tinkers, Russell continued to depict Ireland's supernatural interests. His dreamlike atmospheres overhung with mist and twilight contain the same visionary power W. B. Yeats found in Russell's poetry:

A. E.'s "Homeward: Songs by the Way" embody . . . a continual desire
for union with the spirit, a continual warfare with the world. . . . No
voice in modern Ireland is to me as beautiful as his; and this may well
be because the thoughts about the visible and invisible, and the
passionate sincerity, of the essays and stories, had long held me under
their spell.[3]

Later in the decade, after several years of the two exchanging comments on each other's work, he assured Russell: "I think you will yet
out-sing us all. . . . Absorb Ireland and her tragedy and you will be the
poet of a people, perhaps the poet of a new insurrection."[4] With such
comments closely applicable to his own aspirations as a writer, Yeats
could ill afford to overlook the influence of a potential "poet of a
people."

But "the poet of a new insurrection"? The hope must have
seemed totally futile to Russell at the time, depressed as he felt by
scenes of desperate poverty in Ireland. In 1897 he had begun work for
Plunkett's Irish Agricultural Organisation Society (IAOS) and set
about establishing cooperative credit banks in the Congested Districts
in the West. He recognized the strangeness of his position. On the one
hand, he felt inspired by the peasants' tales of faeries and folk beliefs,
yet his job was to turn them away from this supernatural heritage
toward more advanced economic ideas and greater material benefits. If
he doubted the survival of their beliefs, even more oppressive were his
doubts that the peasants could survive at all. "I explain to starved
looking peasants," he wrote to Yeats, "how advantageously they could
buy pigs under the benign influences of a rural bank!"[5] Often he could
bring himself to write nothing at all, not even letters to his friends:
"This wild country here has imposed such a melancholy into my blood.
. . . I had nothing to say except accounts of the distress here which is
a disgrace to humanity."[6] His belief in the ability of the human spirit
to transcend its material bounds had been changed into a near crisis
of faith.

Russell's travels in the West came after the publication of his
major poetic works in the 1890s, *Homeward Songs by the Way* (1894) and
The Earth Breath and Other Poems (1897). Yet the poverty and suffering he
witnessed did not profoundly alter his earlier poetic philosophy. Best
known for his poems of vision, he had also recorded in verse a melancholy sense of real life as an oppressive material barrier to unity with
the ideal. And as a clerk for Pim Brothers from 1890 to 1897, he had
ample time to brood upon the long periods between his visions. "I had

heard how, when earning forty pounds a year in an accountant's office," wrote George Moore, "he used to look at his boots, wondering whether they would carry him to the sacred places."[7] Burdened by an impersonal urban life style and his separation from his ecstatic experiences, Russell often felt "trapped in some obscure hell."[8]

Born in 1867, Russell spent his first years in County Armagh until his father, an Ulster Protestant businessman, moved the family to Dublin in 1878. George's visionary experiences began in the early 1880s and influenced his ambition to become a painter. Even more directly, however, they led him to an interest in theosophy that began in 1885 and remained a major concern throughout his life. He joined the Dublin lodge of the Theosophical Society in 1888 and two years later became a member of the Esoteric Section. The theosophists occupied all his attention during these years, and John Eglinton recalled: "The event of 1891 was not, for Russell, the death of Parnell, but that of Madame Blavatsky."[9] As Russell later phrased it himself, he preferred to look toward "the politics of eternity."[10] The Household, a resident community of theosophists in Dublin, became his home for most of the decade and provided him with a group of companions in which his imagination could thrive.

Traditional religion offered little as a spiritual alternative. Russell's father had been attracted to the evangelical strain of Irish Protestantism, and the rhythms of church hymns run through a number of George's poems. In his years in Armagh, however, Russell had seen enough sectarian rivalry to distance him from both Protestantism and Catholicism. He turned instead to theosophy and read widely in Indian philosophy, Hindu scripture, Hermetic writings, Plato, and Madame Blavatsky. His personal visions impressed him as an annihilation of selfhood, a splitting off of his spirit from its alien body, and this came to seem a necessary process by which the universal spirit could manifest itself. He scorned fame and personal success and began to write as "A.E.," a name identifying the immortal part of the mortal body known as George Russell. Our "real personality," he explained in an early letter, had nothing to do with "our intellects and bodies." At a higher level of visionary consciousness, "there being but one spirit through us all, we could not distinguish between ourselves and anyone else."[11] Whatever seemed to impede the development of this true, inner personality, whether material success or politics or the Church, even alcohol or physical love, was strictly to be resisted. Despite his opposition to so much of common life and his adherence to small theosophical groups, Russell still emphasized a democracy of spirit

that ran counter to the elitist ideas held by many in his group and by writers like Yeats and Moore. Genius was not a quality peculiar to the few.

To prepare oneself to tap this available spiritual resource, one must escape from personality, which meant, to Russell, an escape from all desires, for "Desire is hidden identity."[12] From Madame Blavatsky he learned of the necessity to remain celibate and avoid love if one wished to maintain an awareness of the infinite. An 1893 story, "A Talk by the Euphrates," warns against romantic love as one of humanity's most difficult temptations, and one that always turns out badly. It was therefore with painful doubts and regret that he found himself falling in love with Violet North, a young English theosophist who had joined the Household in 1895 and become one of Russell's spiritual disciples. The year 1897 thus marked several major changes in his life; he decided to leave the Household, resign from Pims', take on the task of Plunkett's organization, and accept his feelings about North. Their marriage took place early the next year. The group's inevitable shock reaction did not last long, and soon evening gatherings at Russell's new home became a lively center for intellectual discussion, both among his theosophical friends and the emerging literary circles.

The first evidence of Russell's interest in the Celtic past dates from an 1895 article, "The Legends of Ancient Eire," and he soon came to hail the spiritual nature of the Renaissance as a major revolutionary force.[13] Like many others in the literary movement, he drew on O'Grady's *History of Ireland* for inspiration, finding striking affinities between his own visions of gods and those heroic figures O'Grady described. His belief in an ancestral memory suggested that his idealization of the Earth Mother was a religious feeling directly descended from the ancient beliefs of his ancestors. What he could now offer Ireland was a coherent system of transcendental idealism based on the Irish past. He joined the Irish Literary Society in Dublin in 1895, and subsequent visions led him to await the imminent appearance of the Celtic Avatar who would effect immediate revolutionary change. He wrote to Yeats in June 1896: "The gods have returned to Erin and have centred themselves in the sacred mountains. . . . they will awaken the magical instinct everywhere, and the universal heart of the people will turn to the old druidic beliefs." What others had sensed about this return was corroborated by his own visions, and "the revival of ancient

mysteries" in Ireland would have a transforming effect of worldwide proportions. "By the way," Russell added, "can you tell me some moderate priced hotel to put up at" in the Sligo area?[14]

Although the actual search for the Avatar remained, by necessity, a low-budget operation, Russell's imagination felt no such restrictions. *The Candle of Vision* (1918), his spiritual autobiography, recounts several visions from the 1890s, all in a fairly calm, matter-of-fact manner, yet all imbued with an apocalyptic significance. In one, the Avatar seemed like a "young Napoleon," the center of light for all of Ireland. The figure of British empire grew weary and faded, then fell completely as "a gigantic figure, wild and distraught, beating a drum, stalked up and down, and wherever its feet fell there were sparks and the swirling of flame and black smoke upward as from burning cities." Russell identifies the figure as the "Red Swineherd" of Irish legend, who drives humankind into an "insane frenzy." The image recalls Yeats's apocalyptic Black Pig, and the destructive violence likewise combines both terror and longing — in the wake of Russell's Swineherd, Ireland becomes beatified.[15] In 1918 Russell still hoped to see the Avatar before he died; in 1896 he believed him actually to be living in the West and set out to find him.

Yeats agreed that the time was right and by August of 1896 was able to report from Tulira Castle, in a letter to William Sharp: "I have had some singular experiences myself."[16] By the following summer, Russell had narrowed the search to "a little whitewashed cottage....in Donegal or Sligo." Again he needed Yeats's advice on hotels, this time one with two bedrooms, as "Miss North is coming with me to hunt the astral splendours."[17] The splendors gave way later that year to much lonelier hotels from which Russell carried on his work for the IAOS; but an increasing awareness of Miss North also played a part in focusing his thoughts on less astral matters.

Although he was unable to sustain his vision of the Avatar at such a level of hopeful immediacy, Russell did publish two pamphlets in 1897 that gave more precise indications of what Ireland might become. *The Future of Ireland and the Awakening of the Fires* contrasted Irish idealism with English industrialism and materialism. Since they had maintained their spiritual links with nature, the Irish would bring about the rebirth of a new and enlightened phase in history. The dichotomies were brought closer to home in *Ideals in Ireland: Priest or Hero?* The assistance and companionship he would soon receive from priests in the West had not yet softened Russell's opinions of them, and he here attacked the clergy for hampering the national movement with

their overly strict influence on politics and individual freedom. Opposed to them were the idealists who looked toward the old Celtic
heroes as the true Irish spiritual guides, for "whatever is not heroic is
not Irish."[18] These young idealists, "who throng the literary societies,"
would bring about the new "intellectual future of Ireland," a rebirth of
genius and heroic idealism.[19]

Alongside the Promethean figures of the Irish past, who
typified for Russell the redeeming spirit of heroism in humankind,
stood Parnell: "What Finn or Cuchullin were to the generations which
heard their story, Parnell was yesterday to us, a magnetic personality
. . . his image has sunk deeper into the Irish heart than any other in our
time."[20] Russell's article went on to discuss other contemporary politicians and their policies, and his detailed awareness in this field contrasted sharply with a series of stories he published in the same paper
several months later. Set in timeless, exotic lands, the stories described
hermits, visionaries, Greek gods, or Indian wise men, their concerns
for the spirituality of nature far removed from the mundane world of
Irish politics. Such contrasts become blended in Russell's later prose
works. *The National Being* (1916) combines both history and prophecy,
hard work and vision, and *The Candle of Vision* contains lengthy speculations on science, modern psychology, philosophy, language, and
physiology. *The Interpreters* (1922) consists of a dialogue between several characters typifying various positions in the Irish revolutionary
movement, those of the heretic, the poet, the socialist, the historian,
the aesthete, even the industrialist. Russell's prose of this kind, his
editorials and open letters, made him a major public figure during his
last thirty years. Once the father-inspirer to younger poets, he became
a voice of the national conscience and won attention even in Westminster and Washington. So often consulted on public matters, so willing
to argue his moderating proposals against the prejudices of religion or
politics, he found little time to develop his poetry beyond its crude
beginnings. Yeats's prediction, intended to reassure Russell with the
thought that "you will yet out-sing us all," remained little more than an
early, nagging doubt as to who was the better poet.

In both *Homeward* and *The Earth Breath* a general, inconsistent
progression emerges within the separate volumes. The earlier collection, by example, begins with the "Prelude," a caution against the
visionary losing sight of the divine because of the attractions of the

"sun-rich day"; by the final poem, however, real and ideal have merged into a stable union, the divine made manifest in common things. As in *The Earth Breath*, this movement from pure vision to inclusion of the real world passes through poems of pain in which the narrator is separated both from his vision and from other people. Yet the awareness of pain and suffering rarely becomes more explicit than as a loss of vision and a separation from the divine. In recording what he regarded as his most intense experiences, therefore, his ecstatic visions, Russell produced his most notable work.

The most successful poems of vision in *Homeward*[21] are "By the Margin of the Great Deep" (p. 2), "The Great Breath" (p. 12), and the sequence "Dusk," "Night," "Dawn," and "Day" (pp. 13–16). The first of these begins in sunset, the typical occasion for Russell's poetic visions, and the spirit of unity running through all of nature and humankind brings him feelings of "peace and sleep and dreams." Yet the vision, at this early part of the volume, also draws him apart from domestic life and even human contact in his longings for the "primeval being." Sunset likewise introduces "The Great Breath," the fading sky suggesting both a cosmic flower and an awareness that the death of beauty occasions its most complete fulfillment. This unstable insight, like the paradox of spiritual union through physical separation in the above poem, becomes more nearly resolved in the four-poem sequence. Instead of sunset, the mingling of chimney fires from a village signifies the merging of humanity within "the vast of God." Night, for Russell, usually brings on despair and loss of vision, as in "The Dawn of Darkness" (p. 25); in "Waiting" (p. 27) he can only hope that dawn will shake off this sadness and reawaken humanity to its former joy. The above sequence reverses this process, however. "Night" brings on a rebirth of spirit and beauty, a complete union of "living souls," while "Dawn" begins to fragment the unity. In the light of common day, vision is lost but not entirely forgotten, for a dim awareness of "a thread divine" keeps humankind still yearning for the "dim heights" and recalling, in dream, the "Light of Lights." This last phrase, echoing *The Countess Cathleen*, or the "hair of the twilight" ("Mystery," p. 9) that shields the visionary in ways similar to *The Wind Among the Reeds*, or the characteristic combination of "sad and gay" feelings ("Inheritance," p. 40) — all these directly link Russell's work with Yeats's.

The range of vision that Russell sketches out in the above sequence and the unity of the four poems succeed far better than his attempts elsewhere to link mortal pain with immortal vision. "Self-

Discipline" (p. 5) argues the necessity of realizing "our lofty doom" through a combination of the world's pain with the beauty of the divine. The Christ figure of "To One Consecrated" (p. 11) draws wisdom from the "Mighty Mother" along with a "crown of thorns." To have a human spirit is to know sorrow, Russell argues, and to be burdened by the world, for that is the path to wisdom. No one would argue the point; the difficulty lies in Russell's failure to integrate one into the other beyond the level of unconvincing abstraction. The intense feelings he brings to the poems of vision here disperse into assertion ("I have made a god of Pain," p. 22) or hollow comfort ([O]nly/Gods could feel such pain," p. 21).

More successful are the poems that simply present occasions of sorrow. "Pity" (p. 7) oppresses the visionary with the sight of the "monstrous fabric of the town," its "cries of pain" drifting up from dimly lighted streets. A poem from *The Earth Breath*, "The Dark Age,"[22] presents a similar scene with more precise details of the city as dirty, cold, metallic, and impersonal: "[T]he iron time/Manacles us in night." These two poems are separated in time by Russell's discovery of the Irish legends and his more historical awareness of the Irish present. At first a personal hell from which he longed to escape through vision, the city came to represent a historical period imprisoning all of humanity. He wrote of his own feelings of "despair in the Iron Age;"[23] but believing it to be an Age and hence subject to time and change, he could envision a Golden Age as well, history transformed for an entire people. An 1896 story, "On an Irish Hill," has already begun to expand his personal situation: "I would bring to my mountain the weary spirits who are obscured in the foetid city where life decays into rottenness."[24] In that year Russell and Yeats began planning the Castle of Heroes, the island sanctuary to which Irish visionaries could temporarily retreat and renew their spiritual energies. Between *Homeward* and *The Earth Breath* the city thus becomes part of the world that will be swept aside in the apocalyptic revolution, to be replaced by a more agrarian and natural society. The earlier poems have not yet found this faith in spiritual rebirth.

Human love in the *Homeward* poems also fails to overcome the pain of the world or the loss of vision. Beauty, as with Yeats, is sometimes identified with the timeless woman of romance, a similarity of vision Russell makes more explicit in *The Candle of Vision*: "The beauty for which men perished is still shining; Helen is there in her Troy, and Deirdre wears the beauty which blasted the Red Branch."[25] Yeats's poems, however, despair of winning Maud Gonne, whereas

Russell here regards the entire principle of human love as a diversion from the divine. In "Divided" (p. 46), the two, as children, "were not apart" but united in their common awareness of the spirit of "ancient magic." Now adults, they have come to love and thus come to lose this spiritual unity: "We know no more of the superhuman:/I am a man and you are a woman." Their kisses, in "Echoes" (p. 17), seem but an "echo of a deeper being." The woman's palpable sexual presence in "Parting" (p. 20) is apparent only after their vision has "died away"; she becomes a mere part of "the outer things," separating him from the "Mother's heart." As in "Warning" (p. 45), Russell sees no "middle way" for love to follow. If the two fail to unite their spirits in vision, then they face, as physical lovers, only "sadness and decay." One of the most striking poems on this theme, "The Symbol Seduces" (p. 42), creates the image of the poet rushing headlong from the lures of a prostitute, all the while exclaiming how "the great life calls." The "symbol of the world's desire" would seduce him with her wiles and bind his soul to earth. Suddenly, "The robe of Beauty falls away," a vision, Russell claims, although he doesn't hang around to watch. "I think I would break any woman's heart whoever happened to love me," he wrote to Yeats. "She would find me as elusive as the spirit itself."[26]

"The Veils of Maya" (p. 47) deals with an idea similar to "The Symbol Seduces" but without the unintended humor. Maya represents the illusion of beauty, the "lesser glow" of life that, if accepted, separates the visionary from the divine. The poem immediately following, "Symbolism" (p. 48), abruptly reverses the poet's flight from earth. The imagery turns to rural, domestic scenes, the lighted cottage to which the laborer returns, the "loved earth things" that have a new symbolic function. No longer "delusion," they acquire a "seal celestial" and lead him to love in its complete, spiritual form. "The Secret" (p. 51), the final poem in the collection, makes a similar claim. He learns to see "the mystic vision" in all of nature and humanity, and the "dream of life" finally merges with his "own dreams." As an ending to *Homeward*, the sentiments are admirable but not entirely convincing, confined to but two poems, neither of them written out of the imaginary power Russell invests in the accounts of his visions. *The Earth Breath* will deal more fully with the belief that common things also manifest the divine; *Homeward* has not yet reached that goal.

Yeats's initial admiration notwithstanding (and he too came to change his opinion), the limitations of *Homeward* are immediately apparent. Russell's metrical effects are too mechanical, his rhymes too predictable, his diction too conventional and artificial, his ideas too

vague, his range of themes too narrow, his voice either too breathless or too philosophically preachy. There are good poems here, but many are deeply flawed by a naivete of vocabulary. Clouds become "veils of pearly fleece" (p. 8), the moon a "wizard glow" (p. 9) or a "pale primrose" (p. 34), the wind "tremulous lips of air" (p. 9), the stars "the tiny planet folk" (p. 36). Even more serious is the paucity of clear images around which Russell's spiritual concepts might conceivably take shape. The village scene in "Dusk," with the chimney smoke "like a thin grey rod,/Mounting aloft through miles of quietness," is a rare success, one the reader fastens onto with something akin to desperation. Another good effect: "O'er the waters creeping the pearl dust of the eve/Hides the silver of the long wave rippling through" (p. 49). The opening phrase, its participle delayed, further delays the subject and the final movement of the water. The word order re-enacts the natural process, motion that is present but barely perceptible, becoming suspended in time.

The image will not bear too much pressure; "pearl" is precious, "o'er" and "eve" archaic. Like the chimney smoke, these lines define both the strengths and weaknesses of Russell's imagery, which he locates, almost without exception, in scenes of twilight, semidarkness, mist: "At dusk the window panes grew grey" (p. 6); "Dark head by the fireside brooding" (p. 21); "Shadowy petalled ... loom the mountains" (p. 36). Among the fifty-one poems of *Homeward*, there are only about a dozen clear images like the above, and even these tend to dissipate in the shadows. And there are many shadows; well over half of the poems contain references to dawn or twilight.

Russell defended himself against Edward Dowden's criticism of this same lack of observed detail in *Homeward*:

> I think that facts and details with many of us hardly subserve the purposes of soul. We are for the most part overpowered by material forms; whereas we ought to be free and to be able to oppose as vivid and rich a consciousness welling up within ourselves to that which day and sunlight give projected on us from without.[27]

What *Homeward* lacks, however, is a consciousness sufficiently vivid and rich to communicate itself as clearly as impressions from without. The work remains too intent on serving the purposes of soul and neglects the purposes of poetry.

The Earth Breath, although it suffers from many of the same problems that dog *Homeward*, represents a significant advance in Russell's poetic range. The poems are generally longer, including several extended pieces, and they rely much more on a clearer imagery as Russell expands his earlier idea of the divine made manifest in the world around him. A new, more specifically Irish note also runs through many of the works, extending from an identification of personal vision with Irish legend to poems celebrating an awakening national spirit. One of the first of Russell's Irish poems, "The Dream of the Children" (p. 30), recounts a visionary journey into faeryland on a haunted hillside. The faeries offer the children the kind of world that is so alluring in works like Yeats's *The Land of Heart's Desire*: "And this was a cure for sadness,/And that the ease of desire." Identified with Ireland, the faeries differ from Yeats's in that nothing about them suggests evil or danger. As in "Song" (p. 33), their call promises a "land more fair" with none of the attendant threats to mortals.

Russell's best poems in *The Earth Breath* remain those like "A Vision of Beauty" (p. 14), a classic poem of vision in its broadest sense. Dawn again provides the cosmic backdrop to the ecstasy in which all of time and space unites within "the mystic heart of beauty." Russell's vision of the whole simultaneously allows him attention to the particulars of nature, as in the striking sense of winds being shaken loose from the forest leaves. The long, fifteen-foot lines with their heavy trochaic meter and the long sentences that blur subjects and verbs all combine in an appropriate obliteration of outlines. The "Alter Ego" (p. 13), Russell explains, is the spiritual part of him that leads him into the timeless, joyous, visionary world of the faeries. "The Fountain of Shadowy Beauty" (p. 34) reveals more about this spirit. He is a "Brother-Self," a "Dream Bird," godlike in his eternal youth, the Pilot who leads the poet on an elaborate boat journey suggesting Yeats's *The Shadowy Waters*. The dream city, located on the usual "mystic isles," consists of many parts, including some attractive sidestreets the poet wishes to explore. These, his Pilot cautions, offer simply a temporary ease to care and desire, a drowsy magic that leads to a consumption of the self. Instead, they pass on to a higher plane of the "Ancient One divine," the Father from whom everything originates and who is the "end of all desire."

Russell is on somewhat firmer poetic ground in writing about the Mother, the spirit of the earth in contrast to the universal spirit represented by the Father. "The Earth Breath" (p. 11) is a hymn to the force permeating all of nature, transforming the world and those who

perceive that transformation into a visionary divinity. In poems like this one, "A New World" (p. 55), "Brotherhood" (p. 57), "The Seer" (p. 58), or "In the Womb" (p. 88), Russell more effectively develops the ideas only beginning to take shape at the close of *Homeward*. Nature becomes "dense with revelation" (p. 11), and divinity emerges beneath the surface of common humanity rather than in far-off worlds. The visionary suffers his inevitable return to "the human/Vestiture of pain," yet he retains the memory of what lies beyond the veil. The "Star Teachers" (p. 89), symbolizing the divine, inspire him to find the "God-root within men."

The inspiration did not always work for Russell. He wrote to Yeats that he thought "sadly" of *The Earth Breath*; "It is too melancholy."[28] Poems like "Tragedy" (p. 87) come to mind, with their ironic pain at humanity's separation from the gods. The human subject of the poem, not unlike a clerk at the end of a "long day's toil," draws from the stars only the knowledge of his exile from past glory: "He turned him homeward sick and slow." The speaker in "Weariness" (p. 44) similarly mourns the absence of vision, the "petty tasks" that imprison him within time. "Blindness" (p. 47) expands Russell's sense of suffering to include the inadequacy of human love, a theme that has changed little from its *Homeward* treatment. The lovers meet only in pain, their longing and loneliness unremedied because of their visionary need for a higher life that cannot be satisfied by human love.

The Earth Breath is dedicated to Yeats, and the opening "Prelude" (p. 9) captures a distinctly Yeatsian style and diction. Instead of "quietness and ease and peace," the poet proposes to give to his "beloved" what he has learned from pain and sorrow. The growing internal conflict in Russell's feelings about Violet North here transforms the beloved in ways similar to *The Wind Among the Reeds*. As in "A Woman's Voice" (p. 24), "Heroic Love" (p. 25), or "Illusion" (p. 49), the realization of love can only come about through vision, through an obliteration of the actual beloved in a unity with the more attractive ideal. North, as deeply committed to theosophy as Russell, was not dismayed by these notions. He had written in "Dream Love" (p. 28): "I shall not on thy beauty rest,/But Beauty's ray in you." But he had also written "Love" (p. 18), which expresses the hope that he may not entirely lose himself in vision, that he may always return from his experience of the divine back to that of the human. This idea, only suggested in *Homeward*, becomes a much stronger integral part of *The Earth Breath*. "Duality" (p. 71) asserts the need to unite pain with glory, peace with strife, the divine with the human. "The Tide of Sorrow"

(p. 86) likewise asks for acceptance of the passage of pain. Through that knowledge alone may life and death become as one and dark unite with light. The poem closes, however, by wondering what voice exists "for the world of men" before such universal harmony can be achieved.

Russell answers that question with his new theme of the messianic seer, a theme derived from his belief that Ireland was about to awaken into a new spiritual age, one free of the old confines of Church and England and inspired by the ancient Celtic past. "The Hour of the King" (p. 80) and "A Leader" (p. 81) both suggest that a spiritual leader will arise, and "The Message of John" (p. 74) explores this idea more fully. St. John, one of those seers who "arise as Gods from men," prepares the way for God's revelation to the world. Inspired by his vision, he knows the elemental unity of this world with the divine, its origins in a universal spirit that will again become manifest. The poem offers an interpretation of St. John, 1:1–33, but Russell's opening trinity of the Mother, the Father, and the Wise makes clear that the poem is far outside traditional Christianity. John is a mystic poet, a seer who has experienced the presence of God in the world. The Biblical hierarchy of Christ above John, however, has broken down by the final stanza of this poem. Russell distinguishes those who "know God in man," the inspired visionaries, from those who recognize the visionaries as "Sons of the Divine." John himself here becomes the Son, as could any truly inspired visionary, George Russell, say, distinguished by the glory of a "hero's head." Russell rejects, reluctantly, the status of such a prophet in "A New Theme" (p. 59); but not entirely. He will no longer sing the "tender songs" he once offered to his readers, for now there is a new message:

> I think that in the coming time
> The hearts and hopes of men
> The mountain tops of life shall climb,
> The gods return again.

When that happens, when the right poet announces the apocalypse, Ireland will be transformed. Russell tries but fails "to blow the magic horn"; another poet must "Kindle the magic flame."

Although Yeats had aspirations to such a role, Russell was more likely thinking of his Celtic Avatar in the mountains of the West, where the "gods have returned to Erin." Russell could not himself

"awaken the magical instinct" in Ireland, but as one voice he could help prepare the way. Yeats is again instructive in his description of himself as "a voice of . . . the revolt of the soul against the intellect."[29] Russell considered himself a similar voice, one of many prophets of Armageddon and the Messiah; on his friend's compelling personal manner, Moore wrote: "[W]hile speaking on a subject that interests him, nothing of himself remains behind, the revelation is continuous, and the belief imminent that he comes of Divine stock, and has been sent into the world on an errand."[30] Ireland beatified appeared only dimly in Russell's visionary scheme of things, yet the actual shape of the Golden Age seemed unimportant. For Russell, more than for any other writer in this period, the material benefits to be realized through revolution, whether the preservation of the Big House, an improved standard of living for the tenants, the advantages of national freedom, or the increased stature of art, held little attraction. He saw economic stability as necessary, for without it people would be forced into economic competition and spiritual separation from each other as well as from the divine. Yet his main goal remained the awakening of humanity to its spiritual potential, a revolution more mystical than social, a movement from intellect into soul. There is an irony to his work for Plunkett's IAOS, in which Russell achieved more direct material gains for the peasantry than did any of his fellow writers. He himself was conscious of the irony, fearing at times that the prosperity he promised the farmers would also serve to diminish their faith in and reliance on the primitive world of faeries, folklore, and spirit. He could partially resolve that irony by alternating, in the *Irish Homestead*, visionary poems with articles on improved farming practices and ag-ricultural cooperatives. The poems themselves, however, the ones Yeats termed in 1898 "perhaps the most beautiful and delicate that any Irishman of our time has written,"[31] retreat finally from the conflict of matter with spirit. Relying too much on vision to do the work of intellect, on the spirit within to replace the world without, they fail adequately to communicate that spirit or to transform the world. Rus-sell's deeply personal qualities resisted dramatic expression, and he gave his energies to others rather than to his work. His vision remains religious without ever becoming, as he wanted, a religion, one that could free the Irish to become as gods as it did free George Russell to become A.E.

W. B. YEATS

Prose Works and *The Countess Cathleen*

So all the Irish movement rose out of Yeats and returns to Yeats,"[1] said George Moore, recalling the achievement of the Abbey Theatre and its debt to the writer whose influence extended over the whole of the 1890s. Yeats's tireless activities in public affairs, in the Literary Revival and the national theatre, in theosophy and spiritualism, and in nationalist politics appear even more energetic when set against the unfailing quality and wide range of his own work. He wrote essays, reviews, diaries, short fiction, verse plays, long narrative poems, lyrics, and an autobiographical novel, and followed many of these with repeated and substantial revisions. And he wrote just as he conducted his public affairs and private life — with a view towards the all-encompassing system that would unite each of these activities within one unified whole. His love for Maud Gonne provides only the best-known example: they worked together on many of the same projects within both the literary and the political movements, they joined the same theosophical circles, and she inspired much of his writing. Yeats's relationship with Gonne also exhibits a tone that recurs throughout his work during this decade. In failing to win her assent to his repeated marriage proposals, Yeats not only accepted but also cultivated a feeling of ultimate defeat and despair typifying so many of his 1890s projects.

His dreams of what he or his art or his country might become remained clear enough; but his awareness of the Ireland of the waking present menaced those dreams with the inevitability of their own destruction. The half-way state suited him best, an indefinite middle ground where suggestion replaced overt assertion and where action could be suspended in a condition of impending failure. Dismayed at the changing course of Irish history, he felt compelled to alter its direction. Perhaps the poet could keep certain ideals alive within his

nation or even lead it back into a golden age that would nourish its noblest qualities. Yet at the same time Yeats felt himself withdrawing from the historical processes he found so repugnant. In *Yeats: The Man and the Masks* Richard Ellmann provides one of the best analyses of the conflict in which dreams provide no escape and action no results, concluding that "Success in action, therefore, can never be more than ephemerally rewarding,"[2] and thereby suggesting one strategy for poetry to follow: the dreamer must fail.

As strategies go, ones that end in failure generally don't fare as well as Yeats's did, and so it is not surprising that this one also offers him the opportunity to keep his ideals intact and untarnished. Defeat allows the dreamer to withhold his vision from the world that has rejected him; isolated from the demands of society and made even stronger by his experience of defeat, he can protect his spiritual ideals from being dispersed and diluted by the materialist crowd. In *Yeats and the Heroic Ideal* Alex Zwerdling explains this circuitous victory in relation to Yeats's concept of the hero:

> There are at least three heroic attributes which can be taken as constants: intensity, solitude, defeat. The hero's intensity is a product both of his absolute conviction and of the need to defend it against a hostile environment.... The failure which Yeats's hero experiences is primarily external. His defeat in the world of circumstances prepares for his triumph in the internal world of the self.[3]

The conflict generates much of the energy making Yeats's work so effective. It inspires a re-examination of Ireland's traditional culture and an idealization of the past as a means of measuring the present. It creates a place for standards of perfection within a society that might choose to overlook them. But in his early work, Yeats fails finally to balance and unify the real and the ideal. In a society he saw as degraded and getting worse as he watched, his feelings of hopelessness and despair lead him over and over to retreat at some crucial point from a literary expression of real reconciled with ideal. One character after another demonstrates the futility of action, fails at precisely the level where he attempts, through action, to transfer his heroic dreams and ideals into the commonplace world of social processes and disappointing changes.

The later work manages to unite previously irreconcilable opposites within a single whole. In the 1890s, however, whether in his writing or his many enterprises, Yeats tends rather towards a simple

alternation between poles. The man of contemplation exchanges his role for that of action, but only temporarily, and always with an eye to the next reversal and new adversaries. Yeats planned theatre groups that would tour the countryside and bring cultural enlightenment to even remote rural areas. At the same time, he was designing rituals for the select Castle of Heroes and increasingly complex symbols for the verse play *The Shadowy Waters*. He wished to offer Ireland better guidance than its politicians could deliver. Yet even before the national theatre opened to jeers of protest against *The Countess Cathleen*, he had taken the precaution of calling in an element of crowd control more persuasive than intellectual guidance — the Royal Irish Constabulary. Real and ideal remained in a state of persistently unsettled contraries.

In his early work the reliance on mechanical contrasts is nowhere more apparent than in the short novel *John Sherman* (1888). Two characters, Sherman and John Howard, form the central dichotomy of an autobiographical and imaginative projection of the self. Sherman, the one Yeats thought he more closely resembled, seeks only rest and peace. He leads a pastoral, meditative existence in the West Irish town of Ballah and finds his escapist life completely satisfying until society demands that he go off to London to make something of himself. The theme of the novel, Yeats felt, was "hatred of London,"[4] and his letters to Katharine Tynan from this period describe an unhappiness there much like Sherman's. Yeat's family was constantly poor during this time in London, and his mother especially detested the city they had been driven to by meager finances. In 1888 under the recent Ashbourne Act, the last of his father's Kildare property had to be sold to the tenants. Sligo meant a settled existence in a small agrarian community where material possessions had never assumed much conscious importance before because one could always count on them. The pragmatic materialism of London, so rarely a solution to his own family's poverty, seemed to crush life into something shapeless and tenuous.

Sherman's friend and counterpart John Howard, by contrast, feels much more at ease in London than in what he sees as a crude and ignorant countryside. Worldly and sophisticated, he can bring genuine energy and insight to his various public projects. But as a model of the man Yeats thought he might himself become, Howard quickly loses out to Sherman. Of course, Sherman requires a few modifications first. He

returns to Ballah, decides to take up farming, and proposes to the loyal Mary Barton. Despite Yeats's assistance, however, Sherman still approaches life as a moody escapist, seeing farming as an assumption of adult responsibility that necessitates no struggle to get ahead in life, and also as an enterprise that will somehow run itself with a minimal amount of vaguely pleasant puttering on his part. With Mary Barton, too, his relationship is that of an idealized love of the mother for the child, a preference to linger within purified, comforting dreams. In the London environment that seemed totally chaotic and out of his control, Yeats could at least create order within the serene world of his own art. The rigid texture of *John Sherman*, like a literary version of a William Morris tapestry, relies heavily on repeated motifs, paired opposites, precise and intricate decorum, and a timeless pastoral atmosphere.

By the mid-1890s Yeats had moved beyond such mechanical techniques. His work on a three-volume edition of William Blake had refined his ideas about mysticism, ideas further reinforced by what Arthur Symons had to say about French symbolism. In 1894 Yeats saw Villiers de l'Isle-Adam's play *Axël* and wrote of it that the two lovers enact

> the fourfold renunciation — of the cloister, of the active life of the world, of the labouring life of the intellect, of the passionate life of love. The infinite is alone worth attaining, and the infinite is the possession of the dead. Such appears to be the moral. Seldom has utmost pessimism found a more magnificent expression.[5]

Yeats had come to evoke the invisible, symbolic life of eternal beauty and to claim that life as the true subject of his art. His literary characters yearn for an ideal, spiritual beauty; but just as they fail to find anything satisfying in the mortal world, so are they unsuccessful in their visionary attempts to achieve the immortal. As a "possession of the dead," the infinite would lead him increasingly throughout the decade toward the apocalyptic impulses of *The Wind Among the Reeds*.

Early in the decade, however, he still sought a resolution of his material-spiritual dichotomy in the other direction, toward utmost optimism. The answer seemed to lie in the Irish peasantry, a culture Yeats saw as having a unified view of the world. While modern life had become increasingly complex and fragmented, the peasantry had clung to a primitive, traditional past in which a sense of mystery infused all of nature. Shaped by poverty and simplicity as well as by

legends and religion, the peasants had avoided materialist corruption and sustained a fresh and instinctive awareness of the supernatural and the symbolic. In the direct, simple style of *The Celtic Twilight* (1893), Yeats set about creating such a world.

It was not to be his own. Peasant culture offered the Irish Renaissance a rich and genuine literary source; for Yeats, however, grown intellectually complex and fragmented himself, the peasants of *The Celtic Twilight* could provide only a standard, and an artificially literary one at that, against which to measure his own far different world. If any bonds still remained to link the peasant with his Gaelic legends, faeries, and spiritual traditions, the Parnellite split seemed to sever them, the last act in a historical process beginning with O'Connell and Catholic Emancipation and surging on through land bills and agrarian turmoil. The infinite, as Yeats conceived it in the cultural breadth of *The Celtic Twilight*, indeed lay in the possession of the dead.

He gradually turned to a more intricate style and more occult subject matter, to a literature for the elect. The old dichotomy of Sherman and Howard re-emerged with fresh intensity and a far more sophisticated literary complexity in such characters as Owen Aherne of *The Tables of the Law* (1896).[6] Aherne combines Sherman's poetic sensuousness with Howard's intellectual mysticism into an uneasy union: "He had the nature, which is half monk, half soldier of fortune, and must needs turn action into dreaming, and dreaming into action; and for such there is no order, no finality, no contentment in this world" (pp. 8–9). Caught between the ineffectual longings of dream and the perfect coherence of vision, Aherne can do little but despise the material world and await its destruction, meanwhile surrounding himself with art. He possesses a sacred book of prophecy that foretells the coming age, the "Kingdom of the Spirit." To that end, a select few must begin to reveal the hidden world of spirit and to practice "that supreme art which is to win us from life and gather us into eternity" (p. 20). In some respects Aherne resembles Yeats's friend Lionel Johnson; in others he represents the most revolutionary spiritual ambitions of the Irish Renaissance. He sees the awakening Celtic imagination as the beginning of the new revelation, and art as the means to advance it: "[T]he beautiful arts were sent into the world to overthrow nations, and finally life herself, by sowing everywhere unlimited desires." (p. 9). Aherne himself, sending forth visionary prophets and planning a final unleashing of the apocalypse, plays the role of the Messiah.

He fails in his quest, largely because of his own awareness of sin and of his separation from divinity. Mere longing for the immortal

does not suffice as long as humanity remains part of the mortal world. The narrator of the story warns against the evil and danger of such aspirations and himself returns to his original orthodoxy. What remains in the mind, however, is the glimpse of the promised new world, a vision similar to that held by the entire Literary Revival. Cut off from its realization, Yeats could not regard himself as part of either the mundane or the spiritual order. Vacillating between the arcane rituals of theosophy and the committee meetings of a national literary movement, between exotic French symbolists and romantic Irish balladeers, between hope and despair in his love for Gonne, between the economic miseries he could not escape and the half-sensed visions he could not attain, he often felt himself stranded on some ill-defined and constantly shifting margin of his society.

In his stories from this period, many of them collected in *The Secret Rose* (1897),[7] Yeats's heroes typically fare badly at the hands of their societies. Michael Robartes is set upon by a witch-hunting mob in "Rosa Alchemica" (1896). In "The Crucifixion of the Outcast" (1894), the title already tells the outcome. In the original for that story, an eleventh-century romance, the outcast eludes his fate and gains the king's favor.[8] Such fortune may have been possible once, but Yeats suggests that the modern artist has a different time of it. "The Wisdom of the King" (1895) demonstrates the impossibility of a poet-visionary living in harmony with his society even when it tries to accept and understand him. Yeats chose as an epigraph a line from Villiers de l'Isle-Adam to sum up, from the stories in *The Secret Rose*, his sense of proud loneliness, aloof superiority, and contempt for the common herd, and his belief that this world has no acceptable place for the person of vision and genius: "As for living, our servants will do that for us."

The servants would presumably discharge the necessary debts to politics as well, for these literary heroes remain too distant from such matters to have any practical effectiveness at all. Their attitudes belie Yeats's own activities of the time, such as his membership in the Irish Republican Brotherhood, but they indicate the strategy he was constantly refining over the decade: his hero would encounter the world of action and mundane social conventions, and that world would defeat him. The defeat occasions both sadness and joy; the hero withdraws reluctantly from material reality, even though he has kept his ideal intact. Yeats himself continued to linger somewhere between the two poles, seeking both to make his ideals politically meaningful and to drain actual events of their historical immediacy.

To guide him in the definition of his heroes, he could rely on the character and career of Parnell. He had taken surprisingly little notice of Parnell before the divorce scandal and paid him only occasional attention after Parnell's death. But from the figure of the fallen leader he could extract almost every aspect of his own earliest poet-heroes: the aloof pride, the superiority, the emotional intensity masked by a disciplined reserve, the relationship of love to failure, and above all, the sacrifice of the hero by his own mediocre followers. The same identification with the hunted quarry ironically led Yeats to an early sympathy with Richard Pigott, who unsuccessfully tried to use forged letters to implicate Parnell in the Phoenix Park murders. In a casual expression of pity for "Poor Pigott," Yeats remarked in 1889, "One really got to like him, there was something so frank about his lies. They were so completely matters of business, not malice. There was something pathetic too in the hopeless way the squalid latter-day Erinyes ran him down."[9] The reference to the Erinyes gains its bite from its application to present-day politics in England and Ireland — squalid. Yet it is not clear whom Yeats means. Pigott had participated in a conspiracy with the London *Times* to discredit Parnell, and much of England wished it success. Wade dates Yeats's letter prior to the police action in tracking Pigott to Madrid. The Erinyes thus come to resemble those who methodically broke down Pigott's story on the witness stand.

One spectator's account of the trial is revealing. Mrs. Sydney Buxton, wife of an English Liberal, wrote: "In the end we came away simply astonished that a fellow-creature could be such a liar as Pigott. ... but I could not help thinking ... 'It's so easy to be virtuous on £5,000 a year;' and to see that old man ... driven into a corner at last ... was somewhat pathetic."[10] She accurately recognized the trial as "a tremendous triumph for the Home Rulers," something Yeats must have seen as well. Yet her sympathies were Unionist, and Yeats's, at a time when Parnell seemingly stood to gain the most for Ireland, were either unbelievably naive and ill informed or else not on the side of Parnell. Ireland's road to salvation was not to lead through the squalid muck of politics.

After Parnell's death poetry could safely begin to interpret. Yeats wrote: "During the quarrel over Parnell's grave a quotation from Goethe ran through the papers, describing our Irish jealousy: 'The Irish seem to me like a pack of hounds, always dragging down some noble stag.'"[11] This was in 1922; but the Erinyes had become firmly entrenched in modern Erin before this. Yeats had used Goethe on the

Irish in 1909 in defending William Smith O'Brien,[12] and would use him again in 1926, this time for Synge as well as O'Brien.[13] The myth seemed applicable everywhere, with history only a minor backdrop, necessary perhaps, but readily malleable within the poet's vision and will. When "Parnell's Funeral" suggests that "popular rage,/Hysterica passio dragged this quarry down,"[14] Yeats is submitting his subject to historical processes similar to those that reshaped Pigott in such curious disregard for Ireland.

The outcast who deliberately provokes his society into attack or who shakes people out of their habits and complacency had always appealed to Yeats, and this was one of the first sides of Parnell to draw his attention. Excited over the divorce scandal and doubtless enjoying the awkward position of the Catholic hierarchy, he wrote that Parnell "has driven up into dust & vacuum no end of insincerities."[15] In death, however, Parnell soon came to symbolize much grander ideas and values. Yeats located much of Parnell's nobility in the isolated and besieged position he came to occupy in Irish politics, and the myth grew as his regard for the Irish who had supposedly martyred Parnell lessened. The specific details of Parnell's career did not particularly interest Yeats, but as a devotee of historical subjectivity he could recognize in Parnell an archetypal hero. The day before Parnell's funeral he published a poem on the dead leader, "Mourn — And Then Onward!"[16] He himself would not mourn since the large funeral crowds discouraged him from attending. Nor was he very clear about where the nation should go next, for his discovery of the myth of the sacrificed Messiah now occupied all his attention: "His memory now is a tall pillar, burning/Before us in the gloom!" Parnell had been reduced to the level of an external stimulus, requiring only subjective fidelity from the poet and offering an evasively symbolic literary product in return.

By remaking Parnell to suit his own literary needs, Yeats depleted the Irish leader of much of his political and economic significance. Parnell can appear as the revolutionary prophet actively committed to Ireland's service or as the reserved, aristocratic genius who abhors the mob. Yeats theorized that the perfect symbol would restore a lost unity between man and nature, between intellect and imagination. In an 1895 essay, "The Moods," he explained how the material world could serve to reveal the spiritual: "Everything that can be seen, touched, measured, explained, understood, argued over, is to the imaginative artist nothing more than a means, for he belongs to the invisible life, and delivers its ever new and ever ancient revelation."[17]

Parnell as poetic stimulus resembled Parnell as poetic revelation. In striving for such a unity of substance and idea, however, Yeats stripped away those substantive qualities of the external world defining Parnell as the politically effective leader. If Yeats saw the artist's function as that of delivering revelation, then he still, as an Irish poet, had to deal with a further question—revelation to what social purpose?

Yeats offered one kind of answer in a statement in October 1901: "Moses was little good to his people until he had killed an Egyptian; and for the most part a writer or public man of the upper classes is useless to this country till he has done something that separates him from his class."[18] His statement appears to favor strong, decisive action, perhaps even violence, if necessary, from the "writer or public man," and it further suggests that the upper class stifles such action and hence needs to be thrown off. The metaphor does not wholly support this reading, however. Parnell had long been compared to Moses, by his followers and by the writers, and in October 1901, on the tenth anniversary of Parnell's death, Yeats was reminding his readers of that myth. The Egyptians, according to the myth, were, of course, the English. But in turning Parnell into the figure of the Messiah, the myth, contrary to Yeats's metaphor, presented him as the slain victim sacrificed by his followers, who came neither from England nor from the Irish upper class. The fact that Parnell discouraged violence throughout his career further confuses and weakens the metaphor's support for determined action.

To push the metaphor harder: Yeats's statement would therefore have Parnell (Moses) separating himself from the English (Egyptians). Parnell did alienate his fellow upper-class Irishmen by his politics of separation from England, and Moses separated himself from the Egyptian upper class to join his own people; but the metaphor has shuffled class and nation so as to make them indistinguishable. Yeats, connecting himself with Parnell in the phrase "writer or public man," also separated himself from his class, but he left the middle class to identify his interests with the upper class. The metaphor by this point is slipping almost out of control; but out of our control as readers, not Yeats's as the author of a very careful statement. The metaphor calls for action, then dampens it, takes from the upper class, then from the middle, then gives to both of them. The second-rate politician would like to have it both ways on an issue; the first-rate writer can simultaneously have it at least half a dozen ways. The author of this statement does indeed resemble Parnell, the first-rate politician and pragmatist, in ways the metaphor does not stress. Yeats had mastered the

public posture that said different things to different people; he could
construct metaphors that left him finally uncommitted, suspended
between action and contemplation, between political realities and
mythic ideals, evoking the memory of a heroic Messiah who had failed
to see his people into the Promised Land.

The place where the Yeatsian artist ideally merged with his
society was the aristocratic Big House. The great estates seemed the
very essence of a unified culture, permanent and organic, hierarchical
yet symbiotic. The aristocratic family, conscious of its part in a historical
continuum, carried on a long tradition of nobility and excellence. It also
served to focus the values of a whole people and, in its reciprocal
relationship with the peasantry, had earned devotion and support. A
certain training was necessary, plus continuity, wealth, and leisure,
whereas an aristocracy forced to labor for itself in a world of commerce
would leave all of society the poorer. Rent reductions, for instance,
threatened not only the Big House but also its ability to perform service
to its tenants. Reacting to such circumstances in 1909, Yeats wrote of
Coole Park: "How should the world gain if this house failed, even
though a hundred little houses were the better for it...." The Gregory
family had provided "energy, precision ... beneficent rule ... living
intellect."[19] In the careers of Lady Gregory herself, her son Robert, and
her nephews Sir Hugh Lane and John Shawe-Taylor, Yeats had a
living, aristocratic model for his ideas of heroism.

The model did not come easily, however. Devotion to the
tenants was not always pleasant, as George Moore noticed about
Yeats's cautiously aesthetic attempts to gather dialect and folklore:

> I don't think that one can acquire the dialect by going out to walk with
> Lady Gregory. She goes into the cottage and listens to the story, takes
> it down while you wait outside, sitting on a bit of a wall, Yeats, like an
> old jackdaw, and then filching her manuscript to put style upon it.[20]

More concerned with a better standard of living than with faery beliefs,
the tenants, too, in Yeats's ideal, required a fresh layer of style. Furthermore, the aristocrats themselves seemed to have degenerated
throughout the nineteenth century into an irresponsible gentry, no
longer aware of their roots, their land, or the tenants. As a Protestant

Ascendancy, they represented a religion Yeats saw as abstract and commercial, and as Anglo-Irish, they represented a literary tradition that had restricted that of the native Irish and even helped create the abhorrent stage-Irishman. Their willingness to sell off beleaguered estates and retreat to England only verified a steady process of corruption.

These early views required time to overcome and modify. It was not until well into the twentieth century that Yeats began to construct a systematic ideal of the aristocracy, ignoring even the Gregory family in his earlier writing. In *W. B. Yeats and Georgian Ireland* Donald Torchiana discusses the last two decades of Yeats's life as a period of close identification with the eighteenth-century Ascendancy.[21] Yeats himself lacked any connections to the old, established families and thus had to remedy this imagined deficiency by cultivating patrician sympathies and attempting to locate, somewhere in his ancestry, some strands of noble blood. George Moore recounted Russell's rebuff when Yeats told them of his aristocratic lineage: "In any case, Willie, you are overlooking your father." This was poor taste on Russell's part, Moore added piously, because "AE knew that there were spoons in the Yeats family bearing the Butler crest, ... and he should have remembered that certain passages in *The Countess Cathleen* are clearly derivative from the spoons."[22] More mischief from a slanderous mouth, perhaps, but the story inevitably inspires a textual search for the Butler spoons.

Even before *The Countess Cathleen*, however, Yeats's notion of an ideal Irish aristocracy had been taking shape. The nineteenth-century gentry may have reached a debased stage, but they still manifested the past and thus held out promise for the future. In 1891 Yeats wrote of the Georgian period:

> I find nothing but fortunate prophesies in that dead century. I see there the Celtic intensity, the Celtic fire, the Celtic daring wasting themselves, ... [and yet] ... The vast energy that filled Ireland with bullies and swashbucklers will some day give us great poets and thinkers.[23]

Yeats sought out such hopeful prophesies to counter the absence of any visible context for the ideal in present-day Ireland. The actual decline of the Big Houses, rather than posing a threat to the ideal, contributed in part to its lure. As with his literary heroes, Yeats associated the physical ruin of the Big Houses with their spiritual nature. Anachronis-

tic and doomed, they still preserved the ideal within the imagination and would not devalue it within the modern world. As long as a heroic conception of life remained for the poet or an elite few, it was possible to evoke utopian visions.

The conscious nostalgia of the aristocratic vision, the association of heroism with sacrifice, the renunciation of ease and peace for a life of social responsibility—all these elements went into Yeats's play *The Countess Cathleen*. So, too, did his cultivation of controversy, although he did not immediately perceive that. Yeats wrote his play in large part for Maud Gonne and dedicated it to her through all its separate revisions. Begun in 1889 within a month or two of their first meeting, it was first published in 1892. Yeats then produced *The Land of Heart's Desire* in 1894 and, with added stage experience, returned to *The Countess Cathleen*. Four more major versions were to appear, the last in 1919, making this play as difficult to collate as his other verse drama from this period, *The Shadowy Waters*.

The composition difficulties in both works grew in part out of Yeats's attempt to create a theatre at once uniquely Irish and completely different from Irish drama of the past. The Irish stage up to this time had been dominated by the musicals and light comedies of English touring groups and by the popular plays of Dion Boucicault and his imitators, with their stage-Irish melodrama, comedy, sensation, and patriotism. For the new theatre, foreign models seemed more appropriate, like Antoine's Théâtre Libre and Lugné-Poë's Théâtre de l'Oeuvre in Paris, or Ole Bull's national theatre in Norway. In London the Elizabethan Stage Society had experimented with a chanted recitation of dramatic verse, an effect Yeats desired for *The Countess Cathleen*. The dance style of Loie Fuller had its counterpart in *The Land of Heart's Desire*. Richard Wagner's work suggested theatre as the richest combination of dance, song, mime, background music, elaborate scenery, and verse within a total artistic effect, the *Gesamtkunstwerk*. When Yeats grafted the further complexities of Irish mythology or occult symbolism onto this new tradition, as in *The Shadowy Waters*, he imposed nearly impossible demands on both audiences and performers.

Arthur Symons had introduced Yeats to Continental theatre and the possibilities of a symbolic drama in which misty outlines and suggestive imagery seemed more important than the ungainly vulgarity of action. The foreign models stressed a drama of the interior and of

mysterious stillness, a dreamlike mode that left little room for ordinary expressions of personality. Even a character's sexuality became ambiguous, like the figures of Millais or Burne-Jones, or Rosetti's "guys," or the beautiful Florence Farr cast as Cathleen's lover. Yet in revising *The Countess Cathleen*, Yeats managed to turn his vision outward, away from the atmosphere of self-conscious communion that dominates *The Shadowy Waters*. As Peter Ure notes in his discussion of the revisions, the most striking feature is the development of the poet Aleel. His appearances in the play increase in number and importance, so that by the final version, he is present in every scene:

> Aleel now speaks for Yeats himself and is the chief means by which the element of "personal thought and feeling" achieves progressively fuller expression. What was, in the versions of 1892 and 1895, simply the Countess's vain longing for a peace breathed forth by Oona's tales ... becomes in the third version objectified in the relation with Aleel.[24]

In offering a more visible and theatrically more effective model for the subjective life, Aleel's personality better represents that half of the debate between the internal world of dreams and ideals and the realistic, practical world.

In *The Countess Cathleen* Yeats connects his ideal of heroism to an acceptance of social commitment. In her dedication to her people, Cathleen recognizes the demands placed on her by her station and the world. Duty forces her out of Aleel's seductive life of dreams and love and into the nightmare of famine and suffering. For Cathleen, who sells her soul to demons to save her people, action has definite rewards. Her heroism does not end in failure, for she wins both spiritual and material release for her people; nor does heroism bring her personal defeat, for her deed wins her a place in heaven despite her contract with hell. Yet the personal difficulties that Yeats had with the play and the artistic problems that remain in the various texts bear out deeper feelings he could not overcome: the world of easeful peace and dreams might be preferable after all. His attempt to show the contrary demonstrates just as great a sympathy for those values Cathleen claims to reject. Yeats intended the play in part as a flattering idealization of Maud Gonne's service to Ireland. Alongside that genuine admiration, however, and like Aleel, Yeats himself also wished his beloved to leave behind the world of action and linger with him in the poetic dream: "I came to hate her politics, my one visible rival."[25] His uneasiness about Gonne's work prevents him finally from a wholly convincing portrayal of Cathleen's motives and actions.

The play opened under charges that it was anti-Catholic and anti-Irish. The doctrinal questions first led Edward Martyn to consider withdrawing both *The Heather Field* and his financial backing from the enterprise, and a pamphlet by Frank Hugh O'Donnell, *Souls for Gold! Pseudo-Celtic Drama in Dublin*, then helped fire the controversy. O'Donnell accused Yeats of blasphemy for letting the Countess escape damnation; but the more serious charge was lack of patriotism — the pure and noble Irish simply would not traffic with demons. Yeats could easily deal with such dogmatic hysteria and, in connection with the uproar, preferred to recall the attacks from O'Donnell and from Cardinal Logue, who condemned the play even before reading it. Other critics had taken shots at his play, however, and with much greater accuracy. Stephen Gwynn wrote in 1901 that "this was not a very hopeful beginning for an enterprise that was to rest upon popular sympathy and support in Ireland. . . . No normal Irishman would have expected an Irish audience to regard with equanimity an Irish peasant kicking about. . . an image of the Virgin."[26] Compared to his usual skill at artistic debate, Yeats's later reply seems lame indeed: "In using what I considered traditional symbols I forgot that in Ireland they are not symbols but realities."[27] Yeats was hardly a normal Irishman; but neither could he afford, for the sake of his theatre, to misread Irish sentiments and then dismiss them when they rose against him, all in the name of symbolism.

T. P. Gill's *Daily Express*, reprinting *Literary Ideals in Ireland* at the same time, offered the expectedly enthusiastic praise for the founding and initial efforts of the Irish Literary Theatre: "Mr. Yeats is a king in fairyland — in the world of imaginative symbol and spiritual thought"; and he possesses a "genuine dramatic faculty" as well. The reviewer, however, for all his desire to promote the theatre, still felt that Yeats "does not know the Irish peasant and what he believes and feels, and the Irish peasantry in this play are, and always were, totally incapable of the acts and sayings attributed to them." Now mindful of O'Donnell, the reviewer went on: "We do not say that [the peasantry] are too good or too wise or too religious, but merely that their minds are not made that way." They would not, for instance, accept "the central conception of the excessive value of a beautiful Countess's soul" (9 May 1899). The born aristocrats among the Celts seemed to have withdrawn into the ancient past or into the lectures of the literary societies.

A protest action by about thirty University College students raised the needs of national freedom against those of artistic freedom.

Like the *Daily Express*, they took care to distance their views from O'Donnell's, although the rhetoric was similar: "[Yeats] represents the Irish peasant as a crooning barbarian, crazed with morbid superstition." A national theatre, their letter argued, should not create yet another version of the stage-Irishman, a caricature that would only reinforce English ignorance about Ireland's religion and nationality: "We do not seek the goodwill of England, but we object to be made the butt of her bitter contempt."[28] The O'Donnells and the Logues, basing their attacks on narrowly religious doctrines or chauvinistic conceptions of the Irish peasantry, obscured the more pertinent question: amidst widespread interest in national unity and independence, should Ireland's foremost poet inaugurate a national theatre with a play that many Irish regarded as antidemocratic, anti-Catholic, ignorant of the peasantry, suggestive of proselytizing, and a confirmation to the English of their continued dominance over Ireland?

Yeats saw the symbolism of his play as its saving virtue and, on that, based his major defense against his critics:

> The play is symbolic: the two demons . . . are the world, and their gold is the pride of the eye. The Countess herself is a soul which is always, in all laborious and self-denying persons, selling herself into captivity and unrest that it may redeem "God's children," and finding the peace it has not sought because all high motives are of the substance of peace.[29]

The argument is a familiar one: happiness comes to those who devote themselves to the happiness of others. A further implication, although Yeats does not state this nor does the play demonstrate it, sees this kind of happiness, the exultation of redemptive self-sacrifice, as more complete than any other. Through her charity Cathleen transforms the crass materialism of the demons into a means to salvation, both for herself and for her people. Within the terms of the play, that transformation would ultimately relegate the life that Aleel offers, the subjective world of poetic beauty, love, and ideal spirit, to the level of a dream that would prove hollow and meaningless. Yet neither the letter nor the play insists on such a reading. Aleel's poetic world also remains compatible with "high motives" and becomes just as clearly drawn and palpable as the realistic world Cathleen accepts.

She has initially decided to protect herself from the brutalizing conditions in her kingdom and so returns with her nurse Oona and a group of musicians to an isolated castle to wait for the famine to subside: "I was bid fly the terror of the times/And wrap me round with music and sweet song/Or else pine to my grave."[30] Aleel at first helps divert her and, with his poetry and music, can seemingly halt the ravages of time and change: "For though the world drift from us like a sigh,/Music is master of all under the moon" (p. 16). His love, as yet only implicit, is foreshadowed in his first lyric song to his "impetuous heart." Since its "sorrowful love may never be told" (p. 17), he must remain separated from the "infinite fold" of heaven and his ideal of divine love.

The lyric adds another aspect to the play's most complex motif, that of sleep. Because God is asleep, Aleel cannot attain his ideal love, nor can the peasants find a respite from the famine. In the wine offered by the demons, though, the peasants gain sleep of a different kind:

> Wine that can hush asleep the petty war
> Of good and evil, and awake instead
> A scented flame flickering above that peace
> The bird of prey knows well in his deep heart. (p. 24)

The demons, in the guise of traveling merchants, offer to buy the souls of the peasants and thus save them from the famine; their deeper appeal, however, is to the "impetuous heart" in everyone wishing to find an end to turmoil. The souls that renounce all further necessity of moral choice, the demons claim, "Have gained an end, a peace, while you but toss/And swing upon a moving balance beam" (p. 87). Yeats casts the demons as merchants to emphasize the materialism he sees as the primary evil in the play. The peasants' traditional and humble religion, Aleel's life of art and beauty, or Cathleen's devotion and self-sacrifice are all spiritual values preferable to the greedy materialism marketed by the demons. Frequently identified with the birds of prey, they contrast with the gentle birds of Aengus, the god of poetry and beauty,who represents a retreat from the world of practical responsibilities into the realm of eternal youth. Yeats asserts, through Cathleen, that her choice is the best one; yet the sympathies of the play do not exclude Aengus and his kingdom.

One reason for the poor reception of the play lay in the staging difficulties. In later versions Yeats removed many of the references to

Celtic gods, complaining that his audience had no knowledge of Irish mythology. He further simplified things by eliminating various minor spirits who, in some scenes, simply could not all fit comfortably on the stage. The scenery became progressively simpler and more abstract, while the speeches of the peasants took on a greater realism. In 1899, however, the adjustments to fit the audience's needs only made Cathleen's final choice more difficult to accept, more uncertain and indefinite, as a representation of Yeats's own choice. The need for resolution also led him, through the various drafts of the 1890s, into the theatrical fireworks of the ending.

The symbolism of sleep functions most effectively in the play as a promise of escape from responsibility and sacrifice. In his own sympathy with the lure of such a retreat, and in his own hesitancy about the world of action that Cathleen chooses, Yeats could fully explore the various complexities sleep held. It suggests the indifference of God and also the release from moral choice; but for Cathleen it takes on a more personal dimension tempting her away from the world. She tries to inspire herself as well as her people when she explains to them the resistance the world offers to God's goodness:

> Be silent; He does not forsake the world,
> But stands before it modelling in the clay
> And moulding there His image. Age by age
> The clay wars with His fingers and pleads hard
> For its old, heavy, dull, and shapeless ease. (p. 78)

The desire for ease and rest may temporarily upset the world's order, but God's order will reassert itself in the end. People therefore should shake off their desire for the escape of sleep, she counsels, and instead waken to the image of God. Oona advises her that the only refuge from love or loneliness or famine is "growing old and full of sleep" (p. 34), and so youth should be merry while it can. Yet the merriment of music, rather than distracting Cathleen, begins to annoy her with its superficial dulling of consciousness: "I am tired of tympan and harp,/And tired of music that but cries sleep, sleep,/Till joy and sorrow and hope and terror are gone" (p. 33). She longs for a world in which her spiritual ideals can find a more heightened and complete expression, and not just an anaesthetized languor.

More appealing to her is the world of Fergus, the ancient Red Branch poet-king who renounced his throne for a life of peace deep in

the woods. When music evokes this kingdom, whether through Oona's or Aleel's song, then for Cathleen, "Tympan and harp awaken wandering dreams" (p. 35). The song of Fergus calls upon humankind to "no more turn aside and brood/Upon Love's bitter mystery" (p. 39). In Fergus' kingdom the disappointment of love turns to a carefree enjoyment of life. Then, burdened by still more news of the famine, Cathleen desires an even "deeper peace" than Fergus knew:

> Would that like Adene my first forebear's daughter
> Who followed once a twilight's piercing tune,
> I could go down and dwell among the Shee
> In their old ever-busy honeyed land.   (p. 42)

The world of the Celtic faeries and gods, the world of Aengus, promises a fulfillment of spiritual ideals, a land of beauty and poetry and lasting peace. It is this world of eternal spirit that Aleel finally comprehends in his vision at the end of the play.

Cathleen almost immediately renounces the temptation of the Shee. Her duty to her people and her sorrow at their fate compel devotion to their salvation, rather than to the personal salvation Aleel offers her. She first decides to keep her thoughts fixed solely on heaven and prayer to win redemption for the peasants: "This heart shall never waken on earth" (p. 56). Yet Cathleen must recognize and renounce prayer as one more ineffectual form of sleep, and she finally bids farewell to Mary and the saints: "A sad resolve wakes in me. I have heard/A sound of wailing in unnumbered hovels,/And I must go down, down, I know not where" (p. 79). To save her people both from starvation and hell, she must sell her own soul and enter into the turmoil of the world, even to the ultimate reality of death: "The storm is in my hair and I must go" (p. 101). She resolves to face the life outside herself, her responsibilities to her people and her share in their misery and suffering. Turmoil is also a characteristic of the demons, who have sold a false peace and who really bring only the hollowness of materialism. Aleel's final vision identifies them with the forces of evil in Celtic legend who have always warred on goodness and beauty and peace.

The vision is crucial to a final clarification of the opposing forces in the play, not only the material against the spiritual, but also the different kinds of each. The material world is not all to be rejected, as Cathleen's descent into the experience of famine-stricken hovels

makes clear. Nor are the different forms of the spiritual world equally preferable, for she rejects the dream world of Aengus. Aleel mediates between sense and spirit and thus holds out the dramatic possibility of uniting the two into a comprehensible whole. The play is his story as well as Cathleen's, for he changes over the course of it from a common singer and poet into an inspired visionary. One of the demons, who knows people better than they wish, reports that Aleel previously concerned himself only with the tales of the Fenian and the Red Branch kings, "And he cared nothing for the life of man" (p. 88). That changes because of Cathleen and "The sadness of the world upon her brow" (p. 88). When she commits herself to her people, Aleel tears out the strings of his harp in mourning, and after her death he calls for his own destruction, "for she whose mournful words/Made you a living spirit has passed away/And left you but a ball of passionate dust" (pp. 102–103). Aleel does not draw from Cathleen the inspiration likewise to dedicate himself to "the life of man," however. He pleads with her to keep her soul, forget the peasants, and "Leave all things to the builder of the heavens" (p. 94). The spiritual value of her sacrifice does not survive in him, only his despair and his bitterness at the world that killed her.

Aleel turns away from humanity and material concerns to immerse himself in the world of eternal spirit. Cathleen's inspiration gives him the power to demand of the angels, "speak to me, whose mind is smitten of God/That it may be no more with mortal things" (p. 104). He learns that Cathleen has become triumphantly glorified in heaven, but what he sees is a vision of the demons, the Celtic figures of evil, who "when they lived they warred on beauty and peace/With obstinate, crafty, sidelong bitterness" (p. 97). Because of their further success in that war, Aleel can take comfort only in his thoughts of revenge. The demons are beaten back into hell, and as for the other representatives of matter and sense, he bitterly calls down "curses on you, Time and Fate and Change,/And [I] have no excellent hope but the great hour/When you shall plunge headlong through bottomless space" (p. 103). Although he lashes out in despair, what remains for the play as his most compelling ideal is not Cathleen's commitment to social responsibility, nor her traditional religious faith; it is his heightened awareness that the spiritual world of "beauty and peace" can be sought by annihilating experience. Like Yeats, he is ultimately unable to accept the loss of his beloved, no matter how socially heroic her motives and deeds may have been.

The difficulties of the play, as well as its complexity, grow out

of this unresolved state. Yeats claims that Cathleen heals the split between sense and spirit by accepting the visible reality outside herself and transforming it through the heroism of her choice. Yet her inner, spiritual nature remains more important than her external union with the world. The symbolic nature of the play lends itself to such an emphasis on spirit and to a diminished interest in the material world in itself. One of the final lines, held through all the different versions, explains Cathleen's apotheosis in heaven because "the Light of Lights/Looks always on the motive, not the deed,/The Shadow of Shadows on the deed alone" (p. 105). What she has actually done, her deed of rescuing the peasants from starvation and misery, appears insignificant in comparison to her spiritual heroism. Her choice is not between good and evil, but between Aleel's world of beauty, peace, and dreams, and the material world of pain, unrest, change, and death. Even though Cathleen chooses, the play does not finally follow her in rejecting Aleel. In different ways they both triumph over the material world, Cathleen through heroic motives and social duty, Aleel through a vision that is ultimately just as heroic.

Yeats's personal identification with Aleel gives to the poet an attractiveness and strength that do not finally fade before Cathleen's nobility and sacrifice. Cathleen may empathize totally with the misery of the peasants, but Yeats qualifies his own sympathy — one of the peasants merely feigns hunger in order to get a handout from the Countess. Aleel, by contrast with Cathleen, acts much more like Yeats himself, and partly for that reason does not realize his vision as Cathleen does. In leaving Aleel finally separated from his dream world and from Cathleen, Yeats depicts his own feelings of isolation from the ideal. And like Aleel, he looks forward towards the same experience of apocalypse as a way of resolving the half-way state.

Yeats once explained this play to Gonne by telling her that "I had come to understand the tale . . . as a symbol of all souls who lose their peace, or their fineness, or any beauty of the spirit in political service, but chiefly of her soul that had seemed so incapable of rest."[31] As with his adjective "pity-crazed" to describe Cathleen in "The Circus Animals' Desertion," the problem with this explanation is that it does not account for the play. Cathleen is not "pity-crazed," and even less does she lose her "fineness, or any beauty of the spirit." The confusion grows out of Yeats's own mixed feelings about his play, an ambivalence that leads him into its artistic problems. He wished to idealize Gonne's work for Ireland, wished even more that he himself could achieve the same level of heroic social service. But even more than that, he wished

for her "rest," wished for her to accompany him into a life removed from political and economic sacrifices and personal hardship, a world much like the one Aleel promises to Cathleen. His inability to resolve that ambivalence gives *The Countess Cathleen* a powerful complexity and at the same time produces its artistic weaknesses.

W. B. Yeats

The Rose and *The Wind Among the Reeds*

I n the early poems of *The Rose*, Yeats begins to develop what became his most complex and adaptable symbol for the 1890s. The rose represents a mystical and eternal state of perfection, peace, and beauty; the poet, trapped in time and the saddening limitations of change and decay, longs for the divine rapture that will unite his soul with the rose and enable him to transcend his material existence. Not entirely, however, for the rose joins real and ideal into a perfect unity, at once participating in the sorrows of time and containing the essence of eternity. These poems work toward a visionary awareness of the ideal, or they express the poet's sorrowful disappointment with a real world that separates him from vision and promises only old age and death. Similar to these two themes are poems relating the man of action to the spiritual ideal and those pointing towards *The Wind Among the Reeds* in their consideration of love as a means of attaining the rose. Beauty seems the one value both eternal and capable of infusing the specific historical experience of Ireland with a transforming ecstasy. The same conviction runs throughout *The Wind Among the Reeds*; but Yeats's increased experience with love, both for Maud Gonne and Olivia Shakespear, directs the symbolism in the later work toward a deeper interpretation of that experience. Moreover, the transformation of Irish history comes to assume a far more apocalyptic immediacy.

Yeats took all of *The Rose* poems from his 1892 volume, *The Countess Kathleen and Various Legends and Lyrics*, and grouped them under one heading to make up a section of his first collected edition, *Poems* (1895).[1] Dedicated to Lionel Johnson, the section shows the influence Johnson had on Yeats over the first half of the decade. All the members of the Rhymers' Club took Rossetti's poetry as one model; Johnson, however, combined the vague, narcotic religiosity of the Pre-Raphaelites with a distanced asceticism and emotional neutrality.

The poems of *The Rose* thus lack the narrative voices Yeats sought to identify in *The Wind Among the Reeds*, and they idealize the beloved in more generalized and impersonal language. Those poems that do contain a definite speaker function more as drama than as poetry. One such poem, "The Death of Cuhoollin" (p. 202), lent its theme to a much more ambitious and complex work, the play *On Baile's Strand* (1903), and Yeats repeated the title again in his last play, *The Death of Cuchulain* (1939). The warrior-king of the Red Branch legends exemplified a heroic stature that Yeats sought all his life to define. The dark, sad man had suffered a final, Promethean defeat in battle, yet the defeat verified the spirit of his heroism by proving his absolute dedication. Like many writers of the Literary Revival, Yeats too followed O'Grady's lead in seeing Cuchulain as a model for the aristocrat fighting a doomed rearguard action against the changing social forces in modern Ireland.

In this poem, and unlike the play *On Baile's Strand*, Yeats focuses on the figure of Cuhoollin himself and disregards those characters who later dramatize a conflicting social order. Cuhoollin's wife Emer, betrayed and nearly forgotten after his years away from home, turns on him with vengeance and sends their son out to challenge Cuhoollin in battle. Only when his son lies dying does Cuhoollin learn his identity, and although the father remains the mightier warrior, he unwittingly proves the truth of Emer's charge that "he is old and sad with many wars,/And weary of the crash of battle cars." He had wished to avoid the combat, but compelled to fight because of his own heroic past, he can only brood in misery upon his victory. Fearing that Cuhoollin will sink into madness and "raving slay us all," his Red Branch companions place a spell on him:

> In three days time, Cuhoollin with a moan
> Stood up, and came to the long sands alone:
> For four days warred he with the bitter tide;
> And the waves flowed above him, and he died.

His sorrowful isolation, the futility of his action, his inevitable defeat and madness, but also his indomitable heroism all combine in this final stanza. The poem compounds the tragedy by emphasizing the inability of love to avert defeat. Emer's passion turns from love to hate, leaving Cuhoollin inseparably linked to his past; his new mistress is helpless to win him from his grief; and the potential love between father and son becomes entirely lost in the treacherous world of action and conflict.

On Baile's Strand will add yet another affliction: the son he kills is Cuhoollin's only child.

The Red Branch king Fergus, in "Fergus and the Druid" (p. 199), turns away from action before it can destroy him. He had first sought happiness apart from civilization, devoting himself only to hunting, feasting, and freedom from all his old cares and responsibilities: "A wild and foolish labourer is a king,/To do and do and do, and never dream." But this, too, has turned hollow, and now he wishes for the "dreaming wisdom" the Druid can provide him. Yet as the Druid warns, "Because I be not of the things I dream," such total wisdom separates Fergus from the world of experience. He becomes concerned with the sorrow and pain of the whole world, powerless to act, incapable of love. Like the Druid who flows "from shape to shape," he finds himself "grown nothing, being all." Apart from the life of common humanity, he can gain no unifying vision to give coherence to his wisdom.

For Cuhoollin, the man of action, wisdom brings sorrow; Fergus, who renounces action for dream, suffers the same fate. The mystical rose likewise shares in human suffering, but Yeats seeks in this collection to locate a balance of sense and spirit, wisdom and rapture. Unlike Cuhoollin or Fergus, the rose seems to promise that unity, as the title of the first poem in this collection suggests. "To the Rose upon the Rood of Time" (p. 197) combines defeat with victory. Crucified by the sorrow of time and change, the beauty of the rose nevertheless remains eternal. From the opening images of ruin and loneliness, the poet invokes the power of the rose to help him find Eternal Beauty "In all poor foolish things that live a day." He recognizes the need to accept the painful side of human experience, to find a spiritual ideal amidst common things, and the poem enacts this search for an appropriate balance: "Come near, come near, come near—Ah, leave me still/A little space for the rose-breath to fill!" If he becomes totally engulfed by the ideal aspect of the rose, he will, like Fergus, fall outside the world of humanity. The rose can overpower the visionary, lure him into wishing only "to hear the strange things said/By God," or "to chaunt a tongue, men do not know." But "Eternal Beauty" manifests itself only within history, and the poet must speak to real readers. Just as the rose can transform experience, language can have an effect on Ireland.

"The Rose of the World" (p. 208) likewise asserts the appearance of universal beauty throughout time, now in Helen of Troy, now in a woman like Maud Gonne. What the inspired visionary must

follow, Yeats suggests, is a delicate line between seeking and finding, between dim awareness of the ideal and full, shattering immersion in it. The balancing act becomes clearer insofar as Yeats identifies the rose with Gonne. On the one side, he desires her love and the translation of disembodied emotion into physical experience; the failure of love, the separation of the ideal from its real manifestation, occasions genuine sadness and longing. The separation also preserves the ideal, however; Gonne's acceptance of him would cut limitless imagination down to the level of verifiable reality. The repeated insistence in the poem on the loneliness and sorrow of the rose does not hold out much hope of a happy resolution. Even "The Rose of Peace" (p. 209), an elaborate compliment to a woman's beauty, qualifies its proposed marriage of heaven and hell by remaining always in a conditional tense.

To leave the opening poem in the collection, therefore, is to enter the fallen world. Rather than uniting real and ideal in a harmonious balance, Yeats pursues each in turn into its separate camp. "The Rose of Battle" (p. 210) traces out this dilemma of the quest. Those who find peace and refuge in the conventionalities of domestic love contrast with "The sad, the lonely, the insatiable" who long for more than the world of senses can give. Initially separated from them, the narrator finally becomes entangled in their half-world, a timeless blur of Old Night, God's bell, God's battles, the dim gray sea, and the Rose herself. Much of this scenery, even the battle, is not portrayed. The course of action leads first to mere waiting and then to a defeat that brings no resolution, no release from the intermediate state between life and death. Even language fails finally; the "sad hearts" become silent, the poem ends.

The central philosophical problem of *The Rose* collection, as set forth in the opening poem, abruptly vanishes here. The quest for a harmony of beauty and change dissolves in the symbolic flood of "The Rose of Battle," and in the poems that follow Yeats focuses instead either on his disappointment with the limits of the human world or his longing to escape from it entirely. In "The Two Trees" (p. 232), a poem written for Gonne, the narrator begs her to "gaze in thine own heart," to linger within the joy, innocence, harmony, and peace of love. This state, however, bears little resemblance to the world of "common things," nor does it shield her from the threatening "outer weariness" that, in the face of time, laments the passing of beauty into "barrenness." In other poems Yeats's own narrator falls prey to a similar sadness. He can take little pleasure in the immediate presence of his beloved, for he feels constantly oppressed by the specter of her aging

or even death. He imagines her dead and buried in a foreign country, or grown old and weary, dwelling on the loss of love. "The Pity of Love" (p. 216) catalogs several everyday images, all of which "Threaten the head that I love." In a reversal of disquieting forces, "The Sorrow of Love" (p. 217) recounts how the tenuous natural order is upset by the image of the beloved and her accompanying burden of earth's sorrows and weariness. In part, Yeats depicts love as fleeting, intangible, or disquieting because of his own failure in courting Gonne. More than that, however, the poetry subjects love to the limitations of all human experience. If love does not outreach the real in striving for the ideal of its expression, it must suffer the sadness of time and change.

Yeats offers his simplest solution in proposing that the poet and his beloved escape into the secluded, otherworldly happiness of faeryland. The best-known poem of this kind, "The Lake Isle of Innisfree" (p. 213), describes such a retreat as an island hideaway for the poet alone. The peaceful beauty of nature falling like a veil from the sky contrasts with the "pavements gray" of a large city. In London in 1890, Yeats longed for the Sligo landscape that offered him his own place in nature. Innisfree thus represents a refuge, but more than that, a perfect state in which the poet can gain complete self-sufficiency, even if only to build his own mud cabin and raise beans and bees. "The Man who Dreamed of Faeryland" (p. 223) feels himself drawn beyond even these material needs. Money, reputation, human love, none of these escape the shadow of mortality that recurs in each stanza. Even in the grave, his spirit yearns for a faery world of eternal peace, a "dim, green, well-beloved isle." The same landscape lures the narrator of "The White Birds" (p. 219). Again, human love proves unsatisfactory, burdened with the "weariness" of change and decay; the lily and the rose, which Yeats associated with his two lovers in *The Shadowy Waters*, would remain behind in a faery search for the "numberless islands" outside of Time and Sorrow. One easily forgets that Yeats wrote all these poems before he had reached the age of thirty, and that far from dulling with time, his love for Gonne had not progressed beyond her refusal of his earliest marriage proposals.

The final poems in *The Rose* turn to the theme of Ireland. "The Dedication to a Book of Stories selected from the Irish Novelists" (p. 226) states Yeats's intention, as an Irish poet, to give his country the sense of peace and community that existed in the more completely agrarian past. Ireland is now weary and sorrowful, its people exiled, but through the medium of poetry they can still remember and love "the cause that never dies." Such words, in 1890, evoked a specific

political framework of Parnellism, English domination, and parliamentary maneuvering towards Home Rule. Yet despite the closing line, the poem directs its reader into a dim and languid past. The "cause" remains part of what unites the soul of Ireland; the question, what should one actually do in its immediate behalf, is never raised.

"To Ireland in the Coming Times" (p. 234) seeks more directly to define the place of poetry in a nationalist movement, a poetry written out of a yearning for the rose rather than for any definite political gains. Yeats opens with an apologia for the symbolic nature of his work, his devotion to the rose as a perfect unity, and claims his place in the Irish tradition of "Davis, Mangan, Ferguson" because of his dedication to Ireland's spirit, which transcends any temporary nationalist causes or political expediencies. As the closing work in *The Rose* collection, this poem also points back to the opening statement in "To the Rose upon the Rood of Time." Poetry, like the rose, like Ireland, embodies eternal values made manifest in time. In their best balance, they combine an awareness of both ideal and real, spiritual beauty and human suffering. The sequence of Davis, Mangan, and Ferguson sketches out a related configuration. In 1886 Yeats had associated Davis with the nation's "battle call" and Mangan with "its cry of despair." But Ferguson alone "could give us immortal companions still wet with the dew of their primal world."[2] The battle call of the man of action, like the dreamer's despairing separation from the world, does not achieve the balance of the rose. Neither Cuhoollin nor Fergus, Davis nor Mangan, discovers the means to that balance. Only Ferguson's epic unity brings heroic figures into harmony with their world. In 1892, when this poem first appeared, Yeats dedicated himself to the same task.

That same year found Yeats battling with Duffy for control of the New Irish Library and the broadest platform then available for literary expression. "To Ireland in the Coming Times" relies on the same arguments he used against Duffy and the overly rhetorical poetry of Young Ireland that had served patriotism first and art hardly at all. The poem thus challenges Duffy for possession of those names, Davis, Mangan, and Ferguson, closely associated with Young Ireland's poetry. Just as he would later invoke the authority of Berkeley, Swift, or Burke, Yeats here gives notice that his kind of art will triumph in the eye of posterity. Yet he turns away from the real present, whether it be the library editorship, immediate political effectiveness, or Gonne's acceptance of his love, only with hesitation and reluctance. The rose, because it forever eludes his grasp even as it divides him from the real world, causes a similar wavering in his commitment. His argument,

directed at establishing his freedom as a poet, leaves him without the ideal whose attainment would justify his seeming neglect of the real.

The rose in these poems symbolizes Gonne as well as Ireland, and Yeats closely associates his love for her with love of country. Like an inattentive readership, she refuses his attempts to possess her, yet out of that failure he wins an imaginative richness and idealism for poetry. The cost of gaining the ideal is the sorrow at losing the real—or rather, would be the sorrow, since Yeats does not accept his loss as total, nor does he wholly commit himself to the ideal. Like the narrator of "The Lake Isle of Innisfree," who imagines the shore of an island while standing on the pathways of the city, he remains cut off from both worlds with nowhere to go. The rose he hopes will unite the two fails to transform the real with its presence, rather lures him by its absence towards an unattainable goal. To settle the dilemma of the irresolute middle ground he must appeal, in "To Ireland in the Coming Times," to the authority of a vague and distant future. The limitations of these poems lie partly in their failure to achieve, as vision, and control, as poetry, the perfect rose-like balance; but they suffer even more from Yeats's own evasive, see-saw movement between two contraries, with the rose tending to obscure the real more than it reveals the ideal.

The publication of Yeats's 1895 *Poems* added valuable credentials to an artistic status that he had previously based in large part on his journalism. He had begun publishing articles and reviews in 1886, and for the next ten years these provided him with much of his income. They also offered him one outlet for his frustration with the urban life of Dublin and especially London, where he often felt out of place among the more knowledgeable and sophisticated British artists. Although he could not maintain the role of the aloof and superior man of genius, he could emphasize his Irish background. In his art it distinguished him from his British counterparts with their own set of traditions and conventions. And in his articles, he could couple Irish nationalism to an exacting critical sense and thus claim an even stronger personal position. But the years of journalism and gradually deteriorating health had wearied him. Not until Lady Gregory came to his aid in 1897, offering him the summer sanctuary of her estate at Coole, did he regain his energy and what he felt was adequate time to work on his poetry.

Coole provided Yeats with the personal equivalent of a more ambitious project first conceived around 1896. His earlier involvement with theosophy had included three years as an active member of

Madame Blavatsky's London branch, and he developed a close association throughout the 1890s with MacGregor Mathers, who dominated an organization of Christian cabalists called the Hermetic Society of the Golden Dawn. The various blends of psychic research, mystical and Eastern philosophy, ancient and secret lore, and arcane ritual gave Yeats a general system that both opposed scientific materialism and seemed to invest his own poetic dreams and values with a larger philosophy. If such a system could be transplanted to Ireland and linked to folklore and legend, it could begin to serve nationalist ends. The overtones of worldwide revolution, forecast by Blavatsky as well as Mathers, had particularly immediate significance for Ireland. Yeats, along with Gonne and George Russell, hoped to obtain an isolated castle on an island in Lough Key, conveniently close to Sligo, and then establish a cult headquarters, complete with a system of mystical rites and meditations to evoke the collective visions. The Castle of Heroes, as it was to be called, would unite all the people of genius in Ireland within one common group. Besides tapping many spiritual forces, the order would also give a more unified center to the literary movement. For the next ten years, Yeats wrote, "my most impassioned thought was a vain attempt to find philosophy and to create ritual for that Order."[3] The writers could merge their awareness of ideal, immortal spirit with the visible, natural beauty of Lough Key. In London Yeats's own unhappiness and sense of the city's ugliness made such a visionary union impossible. By characterizing the city as commercialized and materialistic, he could then postulate that a life devoted to an almost pagan worship of beauty would bring him closer to his sanctified ideals.

Even better than the magic rituals, the Castle of Heroes allowed its members to combine social and political influence with a life style detached from both politics and society. As with Yeats's association with O'Leary, the path to the ideal led away from direct involvement with any overly active, and potentially violent, political organizations. Yeats joined the Irish Republican Brotherhood in 1896 at a time when the IRB seemed capable of gaining control of the Irish parliamentary party and thus of tempering its revolutionary past with constitutional concerns. He did, on occasion, passionately extol the role of the hero and the value of heroic deeds, as in the 1886 article on Ferguson. He appealed there to those "whom the emotion of Patriotism has lifted into that world of selfless passion in which heroic deeds are possible and heroic poetry credible."[4] Yet the choice of adjectives is a cautious one. Deeds need only be possible, not commit-

ted, and poetry need only be credible, not a reflection of the totality of a poet's beliefs. Yeats never had to face the practical consequences of such sentiments, nor did he allow his rhetoric to trap him into a well-defined hero's role.

Throughout these early nationalist years, he constantly vacillated between the positions of man of action and man of contemplation. The solution seemed to lie in the fragile, indefinite quality of the contemplated ideal. The hero could embody that ideal in the public world of action and events, but there the world would inevitably defeat him. As his father's vague artistic goals had led the Yeats family into a steady decline towards poverty, it seemed natural enough to his oldest son to expect, and accept, that intangible ideals would inevitably fail by the standards of the practical, commercial world. And in the defeat of the ideal, the hero could demonstrate, to himself and to the world, how superior it really was.

The formula applied to Ireland, as well, saved from the corruption of success by its spiritual virtues of simplicity and poverty. Yeats envisioned an impossibly grandiose union of Irish political factions to emerge out of the Wolfe Tone centenary celebration in 1898. Armed with his IRB credentials, he became president of the London branch of the centenary planning association and began working toward what his speech to a Wolfe Tone banquet called "the union of the Gael." The preceding era of politics, Yeats explained, was "utilitarian, and the Celt, never having been meant for utilitarianism, has made a poor business of it."[5] The main concrete achievement of the Parnell years had been land reform, not Home Rule, a reversal of Parnell's own priorities and one that Yeats found disturbing. Tenants with property at their disposal would take on the materialist values of the middle class, dividing up the land of Ireland just as the controversies following Parnell's death had split the society. The hopeless political factionalism of the 1890s seemed to demonstrate an innate Irish inability to handle increased prosperity.

Yeats instead proposed the "subtler sources of national feeling" that lay somewhere outside politics and within the vaguely spiritual Irish past. Just as it sought to depoliticize a mass demonstration, his speech drained the object of that demonstration, England, of any specific political position. The Irish had once hated "the materialisms" of England, the economic suppression enforced by military garrisons and the defense of the landlord-tenant system, or the reluctance to provide adequate famine relief. Now, however, Yeats's Irish would hate materialism because it was abstractly "evil," not because it

was concretely British. The goal of independence remained similarly shrouded. "A day will come" for Ireland, Yeats promised:

> There is an old story that tells how sometimes when a ship is beaten by storm and almost upon the rocks, a mysterious figure appears and lays its hand upon the tiller. It is Mannanan ... the old god of the waters. So it is with nations, a flaming hand is laid suddenly upon the tiller.

In his citation of this speech, Ellmann notes its characteristically Yeatsian ambiguity. While waiting for the Messiah to take charge, just what, precisely, were Irish nationalists to do?[6]

The only answer the speech offered was to cultivate unity and noble hatred. Unity, in opposition to "Imperialism," also meant sympathy with the Boers in their war against the British. Such an identification had already become standard in Ireland, along with some confusion of sides. The Irish, within the political analogy, more nearly resembled the Afrikaners then under the domination of the Boers, but hatred of England clearly overruled. For Yeats a more serious political confusion grew out of his miscalculation of the Irish factional disputes. The Tone ceremonies failed to dampen the bitterness, and Irish hatred remained ignoble. Unity seemed as elusive as the spiritual values that were to resist materialism. Disappointed by his forays into politics, Yeats later spoke with bitterness and scorn of the entire decade, "the nine years of the Parnellite split, years of endless talk, endless rhetoric, and futile drifting; years which were taken out of the history of the nation and made nothing."[7] His ideals, like his love for Gonne, led him toward such programs of action as the Wolfe Tone centenary, yet those efforts, as with the Castle of Heroes, likewise proved a "vain attempt." Action ends in defeat and the comforting sanctuary of Coole Park. It is easy to be specious about the transformation of Gonne, as poetic muse, into Lady Gregory with her cups of hot soup and strawberries; the summers at Coole, however, allowed Yeats to write some of the greatest poetry of this period.

Of the personal influences on his art in the 1890s, the most bizarre and extravagant was MacGregor Mathers. Yeats's overly diligent and ambitious psychic experiments had finally led to his expulsion from Madame Blavatsky's Lodge in 1890. By that time, however, he had already joined the Golden Dawn, with its much greater emphasis on occult practice and exclusive, secret rituals, and under

Mathers' direction, began collecting evidence of an impending and bloody worldwide revolution. In a letter of 1896, Stuart Merrill, recently introduced to Yeats, described one of their conversations:

> Yeats, who has a very clear idea of social questions, and who sees them from a lofty level, favors a union of superior forces for revolutionary action. He envisages revolution after an impending European war, like us all. He has even collected the prophecies of various countries on this subject, and all are agreed that the war will be unleashed during these next years.[8]

The prospect of a bloody Armageddon did not dissuade those who foresaw a golden age rising from the ashes of Victorian England. The visionaries could easily imagine themselves surviving the slaughter and emerging into the millennium as the new cultural leaders.

Irish rhetoric on the subject of Armageddon was born in John Mitchel's *Jail Journal* (1864), a work Yeats found commendable for its scathing anti-British diatribe and historical subjectivity. Writing of war, revolution, and chaos as an almost Biblical cleansing of the earth, Mitchel called for nothing less than the complete destruction of British social and political institutions: "This destruction *is* creation: Death is Birth."[9] Yet Mitchel had a specific war in mind, against an actual enemy. Yeats, despite his "very clear idea of social questions," turned such historical frameworks into visions and myths that were far from clear. Excited by the rumors of war that followed President Cleveland's address to the American Congress on the 1895 Venezuelan crisis, he wrote:

> The war would fulfil the prophets and especially a prophetic vision I had long ago with the Mathers's, and so far be for the glory of God, but what a dusk of nations it would be!...Could you come and see me on Monday and have tea and perhaps divine for armageddon?[10]

Such divinations inevitably dissolved into the murk of God's glory, the dusk of nations, or Mannanan's flaming hand on the tiller. Edward Martyn had separately arrived at a similar utopian vision of the millennium in his notion of Agathopolis, with one important difference—he did not regard bloodshed as a necessary cleansing process, whereas Yeats understood, and to a large extent accepted, all the implications of Armageddon.

The gesture of innocently inviting someone to tea to discuss the holocaust did not appear grotesque to Yeats. The possibility that a spiritual ideal might actually succeed in shaping a whole world order had never seemed very great to him. And in any case, his customary posture of retreat and isolation from such massive social processes made his actual participation in and responsibility for them seem minor. Mathers' brand of magic did promise tremendous spiritual and visionary powers to the adept. Associating the practice of magic with the creation of his own literary symbols, Yeats later wrote: "I cannot now think symbols less than the greatest of all powers."[11] But as with Gonne, he preferred finally to possess the ideal in its latent, unrealized state. The magician could occupy himself with his secret rituals and detached powers and still have some effect on his society. One did not actively help spark an Armageddon, one tried passively to detect its coming. Irish nationalists could only wonder just what kind of war Yeats had in mind.

The circumstances of his entire personal life up to this time followed many of the patterns shaping his public experience during the 1890s: in his secluded and indefinite dreams, he could distinguish himself in ways the all too palpable external world refused to grant. Material deprivation and ill health faded away before memories of Sligo or hopes of becoming the artist who could afford to shun the crowd. It does not nearly suffice, however, to term him a dreamer who simply never understood the practical matters of politics or economics. Nowhere is this more apparent than in his numerous letters from this decade displaying intimate knowledge of all the details of the publishing, marketing, and profitability of his books. After meeting O'Leary in 1886 and Gonne in 1889, he could no longer remain wholly within the private dream. Theosophical groups, magicians' cults, the Castle of Heroes, literary societies, or Wolfe Tone addresses all served as devices for turning dream into substance.

Yet while they gave his ideals a more objective shape, these projects also kept the ideal sufficiently unsullied within the hands of an elect few. And they preserved the hero's compact wth failure. On Yeats's role as an Irish revolutionary, Ellmann writes that he "makes a cult of frustration, and courts defeat like a lover."[12] Ellmann's efficient combination of politics and magic ritual with love is deliberate, for love also shares with the enterprises of the 1890s the tendency to shrink from too great a commitment to success. In 1896 Yeats moved into an apartment with Mrs. Olivia Shakespear. After less than a year, and as if poised for the inevitable disaster, he became thoroughly upset over a

letter from Gonne, and the affair quickly dissolved. He chose finally to linger between real and ideal, not able to stay with the woman who brought love out of its ideal state in the imagination and into their real experience of a shared London flat.

By giving a more human shape to his symbol of the rose in *The Wind Among the Reeds*, Yeats manages to turn his quest for it away from the earlier mysticism and towards more recognizable human experience. The cost, to the poetry, is an increased awareness of the failure and despair that paralyze. For Edward Martyn's characters, by comparison, for Carden Tyrrell or Maeve, defeat and separation from the external world are total and signify their achievement of the ideal as spirit. For Yeats, defeat may be only temporary, allowing him to vacillate between the desired achievement of the ideal and the regretted loss of the real; neither is wholly rejected for the other. In his enterprises of the 1890s, this avoidance of commitment meant that he would involve himself in nationalist politics, but politics that did not necessitate an overly risky course of action or seek very explicit social changes. In his personal life it meant love for a woman who almost certainly would never return that love. His commitment to Gonne did not threaten to cancel out the ideal in the experience of the real, hence only gives the appearance of a definite choice. If love brings no results, the lover can continue to linger between sense and spirit. Art cannot do the same thing without severely limiting itself, however, and throughout the 1890s Yeats strives to create the persona who can heal that split and achieve unity.

The symbol of the rose, in the earlier poems, fails to mediate between eternal beauty and the human suffering of time and change. *The Countess Cathleen* seeks to unite real and ideal through the act of heroic social duty and responsibility, and the play asserts that such a resolution takes place. But Yeats remains too attracted to the character of Aleel as an alternative to and a retreat from social responsibility. The changes he made in the various drafts of *The Countess Cathleen* throughout the 1890s parallel the change from *The Rose* to the later group of poems, *The Wind Among the Reeds*. Aleel assumes an increasing importance in the play, and with him the force of his cataclysmic vision of despair also grows. In the poetry Yeats exchanges the passive ideal of the rose for the active process of the wind and thus forces his work towards the outcome inherent all along in the writing of this

decade, towards apocalypse and annihilation of experience. The irresolute wavering of the self between real and ideal may perhaps be
resolved by a force outside the self. In personal terms this fate casts up
for Yeats the vision of his own death; in social terms it is the vision of
Armageddon. [13]

The presence of MacGregor Mathers runs throughout *The
Wind Among the Reeds* in its apocalyptic yearnings. The poetry demands, for its means of expression, a specific foundation in the material world; magic and ritual, as represented by Mathers, sought to
remove the material. Feeling that his ideals could not be implemented
as real experience or social forces, Yeats found Mathers' brand of
mystical revolt one resolution of the melancholic and reckless despair
dominating these poems. The secret rituals, sacred texts, and magical
apparatus all facilitated visions into the ideal world; the difficulty lay in
communicating those glimpses. Art and magic, Yeats felt, had remained separate activities in his early career. The Castle of Heroes, for
instance, depended on magic ritual to open the "invisible gates" of
vision: "My rituals were not to be made deliberately, like a poem, but
all got by that method Mathers had explained to me, and with this hope
I plunged without a clue into a labyrinth of images." [14] The distinction
fails to hold for *The Wind Among the Reeds*, however. Its limitations lie in
precisely this confusion of deliberate poetry with visionary labyrinths.

Malcolm Brown discovers a similar confusion of categories in a
well-known 1892 letter to John O'Leary: "The mystical life is the centre
of all that I do and all that I think and all that I write. . . . I have always
considered myself a voice of what I believe to be a greater renaissance
— the revolt of the soul against the intellect — now beginning in the
world." [15] Yeats was responding to a complaint O'Leary had been making for some time, that mysticism and theosophy could only impede
poetic nationalism. His explanation of his position seems a
straightforward enough defense of the sanctity of art against the interference of practicality and utilitarianism. Except that O'Leary, who was
not likely ever to make such a criticism and had not in this case, was
concerned about Yeats's association with Mathers and the visions of
another kind of "renaissance," this one involving violent revolution.

It was the artistic theories of Arthur Symons, however, who
published *The Symbolist Movement in Literature* in 1899, that heavily
influenced the pervasive atmosphere, in *The Wind Among the Reeds*, of
dim suggestion and misty, evocative imagery, a Celtic note become
symbolic. A close friend of Yeats since the middle of the decade,
Symons brought Yeats's previous knowledge of mystics such as

Boehme, Swedenborg, and Blake into the modern setting of French symbolism. Symons claimed a vitality of essence for Yeats's long-awaited work,[16] but his opinions did not carry as much weight in Ireland as Yeats might have wished. The Irish papers found the poems, amidst their nationalist concerns, of less than apocalyptic importance. The *Freeman's Journal*, for instance, accorded it a polite notice in their "Literature" column along with reviews of such works as *Oliver Cromwell and His Times*, *A Lucky Dog* ("To wile away an idle hour this book will do as well as another"), and *Famous Ladies of the English Court* ("A handsome volume with 80 illustrations") (28 April 1899). The charge of philistinism clearly applied here; the hopeful belief in Ireland as soft wax no longer did.

Yeats had begun preparing the manuscript as early as 1893, but changes in style necessitated repeated revisions over the next years. To use symbols, as in *The Rose* poems, as a means of restoring a lost harmony meant discovering a proper poetic style, and Allen Grossman identifies five separate styles in this later work: the Ossianic style of manic dream; the trance style of reverie and magic; the aesthetic style of the Pre-Raphaelites; the style of personal transformation, as in the romances of William Morris; and the casual manner, the only style to survive the 1890s.[17] A similar diversity troubles the symbolic unity of the rose. In a note on one of these poems, Yeats offers a definition of the rose, "for many centuries a symbol of spiritual love and supreme beauty,"[18] that applies equally well to his earlier poetry. Although Frank Murphy accepts this as a serviceable guideline, he also identifies the following symbolic meanings of the rose as offered by both Yeats and his commentators: spiritual love, eternal beauty, woman's beauty, a compound of beauty and wisdom, Shelley's Intellectual Beauty (altered to sympathize with human suffering), physical love, Ireland, Maud Gonne, religion, the sun, the divine nature, the flower of the Virgin, Apuleius' flower *(The Golden Ass)*, the female impulse toward life (as opposed to the male impulse toward death), the female generative organs, and a key Rosicrucian symbol.[19] Murphy's exhaustive list suggests the dangers of such stylistic and symbolic range: the rose, like Fergus, has "grown nothing, being all."

Symbols were everywhere. The cover of the first edition, also a "handsome volume," contained an interwoven pattern suggesting the Book of Kells and a visual counterpart to the title. Yet in shifting from the static ideal of the rose to the more active and prophetic process of the wind, Yeats located a symbol that better expressed his specifically Irish experience in the later 1890s. As used in Ossian's poetry and the

romantic tradition, the wind suggested terror and alienation from nature. The narrator of "Mongan thinks of his Past Greatness" (p. 61) becomes a "hater of the wind," for it reminds him of his desire for his beloved. Once a hazel tree uniting earth and sky in the constellation of its branches, Mongan has now lost this unity. Horses trample the rushes, and the wind among the reeds gives no further spiritual inspiration. Throughout these poems it belongs to the spirits of the air, the most terrifying faeries in Celtic mythology. And it more effectively conveys Yeats's growing fear that Ireland, and Gonne, were moving in directions he could not follow.

The faeries remain as attractive in *The Wind Among the Reeds* as in earlier poems, but what previously inspired the poet with quiet longing now appears as a force that overpowers. They have become like Yeats's Leanhaun Shee, the faery mistress who causes mortals to "waste away." He wrote in 1888: "She is the Gaelic muse, for she gives inspiration to those she persecutes. The Gaelic poets die young, for she is restless."[20] The faeries no longer tempt human souls, they steal them. "The Hosting of the Sidhe" (p. 1) opens the volume with a compelling anapestic rhythm and the imagery of passion and sexual energy. The faery host sweeps past, carrying with it anyone who turns from his ordinary contentments to the lure of immortality and imaginative vision. Their domination of the twilight region "'twixt night and day," summer and winter, sweeps the poet into an almost violent separation from "the deed of his hand" and "the hope of his heart." As part of the autumn winds, they suggest decay and death, the grave on Clooth-na-bare and Maeve's cairn. Yet they replace the "mortal dream" with the Country of the Young, where Niam led Oisin. For the modern-day hero, it is one way out of Ireland.

Nature joins with the Sidhe, in "The Everlasting Voices" (p. 3), further to unsettle humankind. The world-weary poet directs their efforts to the "heavenly fold" and thereby raises a still more disquieting question: if the divine order falls victim to the lure of the voices, what results but a burning away of time in apocalyptic conflagration? And how ardently does the poet desire this? The third poem in the opening triad, "The Moods" (p. 4), unites both the terror of the apocalypse and the lure of the immortal into one answer that becomes further developed in subsequent poems. The phrase "fire-born moods" internalizes the Sidhe in the process of destruction. The real terror comes from within, from the imagination that formulates mood and gives shape to emotion; yet that terror holds the poet in its grasp with the hope that the world he burns away will be replaced by a better one.

Moods are revelations to the poet, Yeats argued, a manifestation of the transcendental, "invisible life" to which the poet belongs. As "a new ritual for the builders of peoples," these "imperishable moods" contain immense power. And, he added, so does the poet who wields them.[21]

Apocalypse, therefore, like Yeats's Second Coming, appears both terrifying and desirable within the ecstasy of vision. In these poems, however, the longing for destruction and rebirth far outweighs the fear of what will be lost. The visible world, in "Aedh tells of the Rose in his Heart" (p. 5), consists primarily of "things uncomely and broken," children that cry, carts that creak, ploughmen that splash heavily through the mud. These resist integration into the poet's vision, rather distract him from the image of the rose, his beloved. As "a wrong too great to be told," they are not fit material for poetry, and what matter if they burn away. The common things of the world, to which *The Rose* poems desired a commitment, here become mere nuisances. The mother who narrates "A Cradle Song" (p. 11) longs to remove herself and her baby to the faery world outside of sadness, change, and death. The cries of her child, like the sighing wind, express the separation of humankind, both from the natural order and the supernatural.

Aedh, as the Celtic god of death, predictably looks towards cataclysm in such poems as the one above and in "Aedh wishes his Beloved were Dead" (p. 59), which envisions his union with the beloved in death. He does not, however, represent one unique facet of the overall vision in these poems that is counterpointed by other poetic surrogates. Grossman finds that Aedh led Yeats "closest to the impulse to die and to destroy which represents [Yeats's] dominant fantasy both about the sexual relation and about the poetic act."[22] The narrator of "Mongan laments the Change that has come upon him and his Beloved" (p. 22) similarly longs for the end of the world. Apart from mortal life, seeing it as a "Path of Stones" and a "Wood of Thorns," he turns to apocalyptic sexual imagery in a vision of transformation. The cataclysmic boar that "lay in the darkness, grunting, and turning to his rest" combines both the horror of chaos and the hope of union with the beloved. In "Hanrahan laments because of his Wanderings" (p. 51), the figure of the peasant poet becomes yet another who seeks an apocalyptic resolution to his vague longings. Michael Robartes evokes the lurking threat of world destruction in all three poems bearing his name (pp. 24, 27, and 37). The lovers seek a brief interlude of peace before the impending "Horses of Disaster;" or their lovemaking reminds him of the passing of beauty, the "hours when all must fade like

dew;" or her evocation of the past, with its images of battles, death, suffering, and desolation, turns to a vague "longing for rest" in the moment when "change be dead/In a tumultuous song." In their fascination with the apocalypse, all of these narrative voices become finally indistinguishable and interchangeable. Like the "Boar without bristles," the "Horses of Disaster," or the "death-pale deer," they become symbols cut free of any poetic context more definite than the vague longing for destruction.

Not all the poems in *The Wind Among the Reeds* share in this mood of despair and chaos. "The Song of Wandering Aengus" (p. 15) recreates the visionary beauty of the "glimmering girl/With apple blossom in her hair" who lures the narrator outside the world of humankind and into a lifelong quest for her. Despite his tone of quiet melancholy, he sustains his hopeful optimism. A similar tone dominates "Into the Twilight" (p. 13), a poem that could well serve as a complete statement of the Celtic Note. Entitled "The Celtic Twilight" in its first printing in 1893, the lyric evokes all the standard motifs of the early 1890s poetry: timelessness, the replacement of mortal love and hope with the Country of the Young, the "mystical brotherhood" of nature, freedom from moral choice, gaiety mixed with sadness, eternal youth and beauty, "mother Eire," loneliness, and the visionary "gray twilight" just before dawn that muffles the world within a comforting, indefinite half-light.

In other poems the ballad form creates a rhythmical atmosphere of song gentler than the incantatory effects in the poems of apocalypse, and as narratives they further defuse the intense emotional stress of the visionary works. "The Host of the Air" (p. 7) combines both the sadness and gaiety of the faeries' piping, and also introduces to the volume the image repeatedly used in the love lyrics, that of the woman's "long dim hair" in which the lover seeks to veil himself. O'Driscoll's song and dream occasion the events of the poem, leave him open to the lure of the faeries separating him from Bridget, his bride. Their nature remains ambiguous, especially in this revision of an earlier version in which O'Driscoll returned home to find Bridget dead. "The Fiddler of Dooney" (p. 18) turns the ballad rhythms into an even more joyous lilt about the merriment of song. As one answer to the poem preceding it, "The Song of the Old Mother" (p. 17), the fiddler suggests that life need not consist solely of hard work, weariness, and old age. Yet even amidst his optimism, the fiddler thinks of the joy he will have, not in this world, but in heaven. The happiness that one can imagine remains more attractive than the kind that comes

from specific and limited experience. The ideal of love wins out in a further ballad, "The Cap and Bells" (p. 32), about the jester's courtship of the young queen. The veil of hair, however, becomes a shroud for his cap and bells; she accepts his heart and soul, but he himself is dead.

Yeats's more profound experience with love during these years, his actual affair with one woman and his continuous longing for a second, give these poems more immediacy than those of *The Rose*. Yet the same experience, its pain almost as intense as its joy, creates the wish for personal annihilation. His affair with Olivia Shakespear never escaped the passion in him that finally ended it. The poet in "Aedh laments the Loss of Love" (p. 21) addresses the image in his heart, the "old despair," that finally drove his "beautiful friend" away in sorrow. He remains obsessed with Gonne, with the "Pale brows, still hands and dim hair" of the woman who lures him outside of time and experience and into the deathlike dreams of eternity. "A Poet to his Beloved" (p. 29) associates the "White woman" with dreams, worn with passion and older than time itself; to her, he reverently dedicates his work, not as Aedh or Hanrahan, but here simply as the "Poet." Union with the beloved, as in "Michael Robartes remembers Forgotten Beauty" (p. 27), suggests to him not the fact of her living presence, but the timeless beauty she evokes: "And when you sigh from kiss to kiss/I hear white Beauty sighing, too,/For hours when all must fade like dew." Grossman notes the compulsion in this poetry "to turn away from the image of the real, or at least the historical, beloved in the direction of the profoundly subjective and timeless image of the woman of romance."[23] The image of the ideal shields the poet from the disappointment that experience of the real and finite will inevitably bring. Yet the melancholy sadness that compels him to seek the ideal within himself still holds part of him within the spell of real sighs.

As a gloss on this poetic dilemma, Grossman describes the European tradition of occult wisdom, which evolved out of such works as the Christian cabalas or the Upanishads and from such writers as Henry More and Jacob Boehme. In his association with Mathers and the theosophists, as in his work in the early 1890s with Edwin Ellis on the Blake edition, Yeats explored such a tradition and found it readily adaptable to his own work. Reality, the material world, is defined as the manifestation of its own origin within the ideal. The visionary experience of knowing the transcendent ideal is primarily a religious and subjective process, a dream- or trancelike understanding of reality as a temporal accident serving as a sign of eternal essence and divinity. On Yeats's adaptation of the Wisdom tradition to *The Wind Among the*

Reeds, Grossman notes that the "cognitive unattainability" of wisdom adds to its nature as a desirable ideal.[24] With no hope of attaining any reconciliation in the material world, Yeats then conceives of his own death and that of his beloved as a mystical state in which he can unite himself with the ideal. The inevitable losses and defeats of the ordinary world indicate to him the ideal quality of his love as an ecstatic state of completion that can only exist outside of material life and experience.

He further identifies his ideal with Ireland and with the unity of culture that, if the ideal could manifest itself in the real, would come from the aristocratic and peasant traditions of the past, as well as from the poets. If Gonne seemed spiritually attainable only through the transformation of the lovers in material death, then such a cultural ideal required for its realization a universal apocalypse. "The Secret Rose" (p. 48) summons the ideal much as did the earlier poem "To the Rose upon the Rood of Time." The poet wishes to join those who attained the rose and who now "dwell beyond the stir/And tumult of defeated dreams." The ancient heroes whose tales he evokes, Conchobar, Cuchulain, Caolte, Fergus, all abandoned their mortal dreams for that of the rose, in whose folds they have finally left defeat behind. Unlike the earlier invocation of the rose, however, this poem identifies its coming with "The hour of thy great wind." Previously a perfect harmony of the ideal and the real, the rose here demands of its followers an acceptance, even more so a welcoming, of the destruction of the world. As Yeats makes clear in "To my Heart, bidding it have no Fear" (p. 31), there can be no wavering. Ceremonial rituals and mysticism bring his conflicting emotions of fear and desire into harmony. Only by accepting the "flame and the flood" can he unite himself with the "proud, majestical multitude."

In his most famous of these poems of apocalypse, "The Valley of the Black Pig" (p. 35), Yeats speaks solely of the processes of social transformation. He takes the substance of his vision of Armageddon from the Irish peasant legends, but the immediate occasion for the poem, as he claimed in his *Autobiographies*, grew out of the teachings of MacGregor Mathers: "Was this prophecy of his, which would shortly be repeated by mediums and clairvoyants all over the world, an unconscious inference taken up into an imagination brooding upon war, or was it prevision?"[25] Whatever the answer, Yeats looks forward to the conflict. He identifies himself with the laboring peasants who, "Being weary of the world's empires, bow down to you/Master of the still stars and of the flaming door." Although Yeats maintains the passive role of the visionary who merely detects the approaching cataclysm, he also

longs for the day when he can pass through the "flaming door." The poem points the way towards a rebirth of society and toward new social ideals; but Yeats formulates the ideals and the processes of achieving them in ways that leave him little room to implement them actively. His lengthy and various prose explanations of this poem and its backgrounds only increase the vagueness of its vision.

A poem such as "The Valley of the Black Pig" shares with many other lyrics, "Into the Twilight," for example, the same tendency to evade a definite commitment and to cling instead to the moment between night and day, the expectant calm before the holocaust. Only rarely, as in "The Travail of Passion" (p. 52), does he overcome the paralysis of twilight. More often, the poet wavers between longing for the ideal that will burst forth and regret for the real that will perish. Unable to find a resolution within the self, he seeks one within the forces external to the self. Ellmann's analysis of Yeats's work in the 1890s points out many of the weaknesses in that indeterminate poetic strategy: "He would choose finally neither one state nor the other, neither dream nor act, but the crepuscular state between spirit and sense, where he was *not committed*. The twilight demanded no decision."[26] Yeats himself, in memoirs and letters that criticize his early work, provided many of the categories by which to judge it. Ellmann's language repeats the same concepts, in some cases the same phrases, and it largely confines itself to the guidelines Yeats himself chose. An early letter to Katharine Tynan in 1888 expressed his hope that he might someday write poetry of "insight and knowledge" and not of "longing and complaint." His earlier work, he admitted, "is almost all a flight into fairyland from the real world, and a summons to that flight. . . . the cry of the heart against necessity."[27] In a 1904 letter to George Russell, he complained of the same early tendencies, "an exaggeration of sentiment and sentimental beauty which I have come to think unmanly."[28] The *Autobiographies* repeat the repudiation of the "slight, sentimental sensuality" in his early work. Yeats assured his reader that he had "long abandoned" this temptation "to linger, or rather to pretend that we can linger, between spirit and sense."[29] Upon Yeats's final admission, Ellmann rests a great deal of his criticism of this period.

This early verse fails to attain its goal of ultimate wisdom and beauty, however, not only because of wavering commitments and melancholy sentimentality, but because of flaws inherent in the original concept of that wisdom. Faced with the despairing recognition that

complete happiness and peace lay beyond mortal experience, Yeats can only hope for a better life to follow his own, or his society's, transforming apocalypse. The retreat from life becomes a simultaneous embrace of death, an obliteration of personality. The "evasion" Ellmann speaks of thus serves to explain such works as *The Countess Cathleen* or *The Rose; The Wind Among the Reeds* has taken another, and more decisive, direction. Grossman identifies Yeats's use of the Wisdom tradition in relation to the concept of the Last Judgment, which, Grossman stresses, "means *death and cognitive success*" within that tradition. "The dead are the irrefutable speakers. The authority of true utterance and the condition of true identity are not found in life."[30] What changed for Yeats from *The Rose* to *The Wind Among the Reeds* was the tendency Grossman notes in the latter poems "which seems to demand nothing less than the exchange of life for art."[31] By avoiding such a sacrificial relationship to his art and by exploring the world outside as well as inside the self, Yeats directs his later work into the teeth of the world rather than away from it.

The Wind Among the Reeds, as Grossman suggests, pushes poetry about as far as it can go before it self-destructs. Over the course of the 1890s, the political meaning of Yeats's work thus undergoes a similar shift towards the elements of apocalypse. The irresolute wavering between real and ideal is akin to an emotional wavering between hope and despair. The loss of the real, or the failure to attain the ideal, occasions despair; the potential of the ideal to manifest itself within the real occasions hope. By the late 1890s Yeats's hope for what Ireland might become in the future had turned more toward feelings of despair that Ireland would never change, would only move progressively further from the ideal. Poetry at the beginning of that decade seemed to have a better chance of success within the political movements, a chance of resurrecting the ideals of Ireland's past and effectively using those ideals to influence political change. But with the limits of that influence becoming increasingly clearer, writers like Yeats soon felt themselves alienated from the politicians and programs. Failing to bring into line all the factions for the expected reunion at the Wolfe Tone Centennial, and turning more and more to the political eccentricities of Mathers' group, Yeats found that his ideals had even less currency than in the lost bargaining over the New Irish Library editorship. O'Leary had found new followers. Rumors were circulating in Dublin, confirmed by Yeats in late 1898, that Gonne had been involved in a love affair, even before he had met her, with the French journalist

and political extremist Lucien Millevoye. During several of these years Yeats suffered with health very near the breaking point. The poetry turned increasingly toward the emotions of despair.

Yet that tendency does not entirely cancel out hope. The poet of "The Valley of the Black Pig" stands before a worldwide cataclysm, but one that might clear the way for a better world to follow. Yeats recognizes the unlikelihood of effecting such an apocalypse, in fact avoids any definite personal commitment or responsibility by waiting passively within the poem. But by recording the vision he does give voice to a hope. Poetry may at last keep alive the ideal, the promise of redemption, that makes apocalypse worth the dangers. The poet's despair contains within it a greater faith in, or willingness to risk, eternal solutions, heroes who are more than literary and who act outside of the frustrating and ponderous restrictions of the political organizations. If poetry cannot create the hero itself, it can still hold out the ideals that might inspire and guide him to plunge his country through the "flaming door."

conclusion

The self-destructiveness of *The Wind Among the Reeds* necessitated a new direction in Yeats's career. The feelings of despair had produced too great a willingness to annihilate experience; the mystique of death had become too seductive as a way of resolving the intermediate state. Part of the process of change grew out of a better awareness of who his antagonists really were. The setback with the New Irish Library had been an isolated instance attributable to Duffy's idiosyncrasies; for the most part, when Yeats railed against Time and Fate and Change through the mists and twilights of the 1890s, his attacks met little solid resistance, leaving him increasingly entwined in his own impulse to destroy. In the first decade of the twentieth century, however, the national theatre gave him a more precise area of operations and made his opponents easier to identify: the Irish middle class, the "solid citizens," prudent, complacent, hostile to excellence and individuality, "the lowest class morally," O'Leary had said, "the class influenced by the lowest motives."[1]

In a slighting review of Duffy's *Young Ireland* in 1897, Yeats indicated the connections he saw between this class and art: "[O]ut of the ideas and emotions of the average man you can make no better thing than good rhetoric."[2] His earlier romantic attraction to Young Ireland, he explained in 1901, had given way to faith in the written "poetry of the coteries" and the unwritten "true poetry of the people," both kinds being symbolic, mysterious, and traditional. The middle class, by contrast, separated the two with its preference for "popular poetry."[3] From such early criticisms he now began to mount a more wideranging and virulent attack, for Ireland's entire future seemed to lie within grasping hands. In 1908 he warned that the country "was running the danger of surrendering her soul to the bourgeoisie. ... [who] had no past, no discipline, no good qualities. ... were, therefore,

essentially immoral."[4] The year before, the year of O'Leary's death, theatre riots had disrupted performances of *The Playboy of the Western World*, and by 1909 Synge himself was dead. In 1912 Sir Hugh Lane offered Dublin a valuable collection of paintings if the city would build a suitable gallery for them. The offer was rejected, and Yeats's involvement in the controversy over the next year further convinced him that in Ireland the artist faced nothing better than insolent bigotry and ignorance.

The romanticism and heroic idealism of the 1890s had come very quickly to seem totally anachronistic in the new century. In 1900 John Redmond finally managed to unite the warring political factions, and cultural nationalism gave way to a more pragmatic nationalism of compromise and gradual maneuvering, one affecting even the autonomy of art. The first serious clash between the new theatre and its audience took place in 1903 over the issue of Synge's *In the Shadow of the Glen*. Arthur Griffith, editor of the *United Irishman*, had initially supported Yeats and *The Countess Cathleen* because of the opportunity to oppose the influence of the Church on public affairs. Now, Griffith led the attack on Synge's play as an antinationalist slur on the Irish. Even more than the writing up to this time, because more public, the theatre was supposed to subordinate itself to nationalist ends.

Yeats's attacks on the middle class and on modern civilization, his prophecies of conflagration, or his attraction to the aristocratic Big House and the intellectual elite that should by right govern the society are all aspects of a world view dedicated to the ideals he felt would foster his art. But the language of the Literary Revival, its emphasis on the spiritual over the mundane, tends to obscure the particular political meanings embedded in the myths and ideals of the movement. William Irwin Thompson has analyzed the 1916 Easter Rising as an event that transformed into armed revolution the personal apotheosis inherent in those early myths.[5] As Conor Cruise O'Brien's influential essay suggests, Yeats's politics of the 1920s and 1930s likewise do not represent a mutant development of his earlier thinking. One outcome of the desire to annihilate history and experience, as in *The Wind Among the Reeds*, is the willingness to risk, or at least to entertain the possibility of, totalitarian solutions.

Yeats's interest in the politics of fascism dates from a visit to Italy in 1924 and from his attention to the ideas and policies of Kevin

Thoor Ballylee, County Galway, purchased by Yeats in 1917 and his summer habitat in the 1920s.

O'Higgins, "the one strong intellect in Irish public life," according to Yeats.[6] As Minister of Home Affairs, O'Higgins contributed more than any other official to crushing terrorist activities and imposing law and

order after the Civil War. His assassination in 1927 was but one more of the violent acts keeping the fear and memories of the war alive and seeming to underscore the need for a strong-man leader. The lawlessness, along with a general concern affecting all of Europe about failing national economies, led to the organization of the Irish Blueshirts in 1933 and to Yeats's overt connection with a fascist movement.

In regarding Yeats's support of the Blueshirts as a fairly typical response by the Protestant middle class, O'Brien concludes: "Yeats the man was as near to being a Fascist as his situation and the conditions of his own country permitted. . . . He turned his back on this movement when it began to fail, not before."[7] Communism, although largely an imaginary menace, also worried many intellectuals.[8] Yeats wrote to Olivia Shakespear in April 1933: "At the moment I am trying in association with [an] ex-cabinet minister, an eminent lawyer, and a philosopher, to work out a social theory which can be used against Communism in Ireland—what looks like emerging is Fascism modified by religion."[9] Although Yeats did not specify just what modifications religion would introduce, the events in Ireland immediately surrounding the date of this letter do suggest, not only a specific combination of "Fascism modified by religion," but also a particular social context in which to understand Yeats's brand of fascism.

As F. S. L. Lyons notes, W. T. Cosgrave's opposition party program in 1933 relied as much on Pope Pius XI's encyclical *Quadragesimo Anno*, with its emphasis on vocational organization and representation within the state, as on Mussolini's concept of the corporate state.[10] The more militant wing of this fascist-religious combination was represented by General O'Duffy and his Blueshirts. O'Duffy, a political colleague of Cosgrave's, was regarded as a threat by the Eamon de Valera government, and his proposed August 1933 demonstration did have some of the trappings of Mussolini's march on Rome. O'Duffy's organization lacked the size, strength, or determination for any coup attempts, however, and the demonstration was cancelled at the last minute. Yeats's letter suggests that his involvement took more of its shape from specifically Irish circumstances than from a close ideological sympathy with Mussolini or German National Socialism. And, as O'Duffy's aborted march demonstrated, Irish fascism never developed into anything very sinister or dangerous. But the attraction of fascism as an immediate and all-encompassing political solution, its emphasis on the hero-leader, and its opposition to radical social change all appealed to elements in Yeats's world view having definite beginnings in the 1890s.

The other side of his political theories and activities is the implication they had for his art. The poetry remains connected to the same ideology that led him towards fascism, and it is impossible to project a more admirable political posture into Yeats's thinking without radically altering the unquestioned brilliance of his achievements in literature. Government of the elite represented for Yeats a perfectly understandable defense of his autonomy as an artist and of the literary movement he had furthered. Believing this, he could more readily identify the poetic themes and aesthetic priorities enabling him to do his best work. He opposed materialism and commercialism, insisted on the need for art to resist the intrusion of any outside groups, and thus made the Literary Revival intellectually more respectable. The movement's exclusion of both the philistines and the propagandists resulted in neither a plunge into decadence nor an abnegation of all social responsibilities. The anti-clericalism likewise did not mean an indifference to moral values, but rather an opposition to the puritanical restrictions that could have crippled the artists. In his attention to the Irish peasantry as a spiritual background, Yeats revealed a rich source of genuine cultural energy. And finally, through his criticism of the world as he saw it and his evocation of an ideal world, Yeats kept alive the spiritual values of beauty and perfection. As long as these continued to attract even a few people, the possibility remained that the society was capable of change or, as Yeats hoped, a reversal of the changes he felt were rapidly decaying the better Ireland of the past.

Such ideals, shared for the most part by all the major writers of the 1890s, could best be expressed as symbol, heroic myth, or spiritual vision. And if the language of the Literary Revival obscured the specifics of politics, it cast a similar haze over economics. Sociological theories grew out of intuition and nostalgia, a vision of Ireland as a homogeneous country in which differences in politics, economics, religion, education, or culture seemed secondary to the mystique of unity. Literature could ignore the essentially commercial nature of the Big House in its ideal of an aristocracy too refined to worry itself with pence-counting. For the peasantry, as well, material concerns seemed to violate a heritage nourished on subsistence agriculture and simple needs. In representing poverty as a moral and spiritual boon, the writers could overlook famine, disease, market competition, landlord injustices, agricultural depressions, or the garrison conditions keeping the tenants under control. It was hoped that the people might seek the more enduring values of the past and avoid the shallow, materialistic gains now coming in large part at the expense of the landed gentry. In

rejecting the prosperity much of Ireland regarded as long overdue, the writers sought a more compelling model for their society. Yet the vagueness about economic programs was also determined by their unwillingness to answer that facet of the Irish question in terms the nation would accept.

The literary image of the hero thus functions in two opposing directions at once, as an expression both of hope and despair. As a message to the Irish tenants and middle class, as a strategy of containment, the hero demonstrates the futility of action that can bring no external rewards. While discouraging his society from changes too swift or radical, the hero further represents the hope, as an example for the landed class to emulate, that his superior leadership, values, and wisdom will be accepted. A literature functioning strictly at this public level, however, would have little value except as propaganda. In its primary and most powerful capacity, the image of the hero also expresses the writers' concept of their own experience and their resulting feelings of despair. Action brings no external rewards, the hero fails consistently in the world of action, there will be no more heroes. The image thus conveys the writers' accurate appraisal of their own position: Ireland was changing, and they, like O'Grady's aristocrats, were helpless to stop it.

The dream of the Irish Renaissance thus failed to unite with and transform the actual circumstances of Ireland. Seeking afterwards to explain this disparity, the writers frequently turned to reminiscences about their movement, Yeats in his *Autobiographies*, Lady Gregory in *Seventy Years*, Tynan in *Memories*, or Martyn in the "Paragraphs for the Perverse." The most successful and thorough account of the early Renaissance, however, is George Moore's epic masterpiece *Hail and Farewell!*, a "sacred book," Moore claimed,[11] one that would become "the turning-point in Ireland's destiny" (*Vale*, p. 361). Moore himself, as Siegfried or St. Paul or the son of Parnell, was to be Ireland's Messiah. He would liberate his country from priestcraft through a new gospel of "personality—personal love and personal religion, personal art" (*Vale*, p. 290), and Moore's own personality transfuses and unites the entire piece. Yet the dream still remained apart from the circumstances, for him and for Ireland, and by the end of his work he sees, more clearly than any other writer from the movement, why literature failed to reforge the sword that lay broken.

Like the Wagnerian vision of Siegfried's sword, which inspires

the writing of *Hail and Farewell!*, the opening overture also achieves an operatic sweep. Moore recalls an 1894 conversation with Edward Martyn that sent his thoughts ranging back over his Irish past and that suggested to him a novel "made of the life that lingered in Mayo till the end of the 'sixties: landlords, their retainers and serfs" (*Ave*, p. 17). Had he written such a book then, Moore thinks regretfully, it "would have been a great literary event" (*Ave*, p. 37). But he "was not the predestined hero whom Cathleen ni Houlihan had been waiting for" (*Ave*, p. 38) and so missed his chance. She is not through with Moore yet, however. As a child, he felt tormented by his parents' teasing prediction that he would have to marry an old beggar, Honor King. On a later visit to Ireland around 1880, he found the portrait of a beautiful woman in a rundown manor house and, fascinated, sought out the subject of the painting, then forty years older and caretaker to the house. In the form of Cathleen, the old woman finally claims him for Ireland.

His mystic summons to return gives way to detailed and mundane necessity, for he must dispose of his London flat and find a new one in Dublin. No matter; Moore feels driven by supernatural forces, and the language of the tribe must be purified. Then comes yet another dampening of his enthusiasm—Dublin barely notices his arrival. The ironic contrasts and abrupt shifts in tone or point of view create a protean focus controlling the entire work. Moore believes that "analogies can be discovered in all my boon companions. Could it be otherwise, since they were all collected for my instruction and distraction?" (*Ave*, p. 68). His artistic method feeds on such analogies, one character coming to resemble another just as the sky over Grafton Street blends into a landscape by Corot. Amidst constantly shifting outlines, the backdrop of real circumstances dissolves at will into more compelling reveries. Martyn appears "great in girth as an owl... Yeats lank as a rook, a-dream in black silhouette on the flowered wall-paper" (*Ave*, p. 41). T. P. Gill needs only to have his beard trimmed for his entire character to seem transformed. Another boon companion, George Russell, leads Moore in search of sacred ruins, and Moore rambles on at an exalted level. He must frequently interrupt his inspired discourse, however, to remove clothing because of the hot weather or to endure in silence the omnipresent Presbyterian ministers following the same route. But when Russell takes over the commentary, religious language gains full control, and this time, with even the ministers transformed, Moore becomes the disciple, Russell the prophet, all poised on the verge of a new age.

Despite his attraction to Russell, Moore occupies himself primarily with Edward Martyn, and *Hail and Farewell!* tells dear Edward's story as much as Moore's. Their journey to Bayreuth, in *Ave*, is yet another religious pilgrimage, one that includes sidetrips to view out-of-the-way artistic treasures and cathedrals but that finally seeks the inspiration of Siegfried. The full meaning of his identification with Wagner's hero only later becomes apparent to Moore. Here, he can still leave Martyn and the few remaining sights to join "Stella," the woman who will accompany him to Ireland in 1901. Out of place within Martyn's Catholic and aesthetic sensibilities, Stella will finally prove incompatible with Moore's own gospel as well.

The religious theme is fully developed in *Salve*. Initially outraged by clerical interference in the Irish Literary Theatre, Moore decides that Ireland must choose between Literature and Dogma. An "intellectual desert," Catholicism has not produced a book of merit since the Reformation, Moore claims, and to prove his point, he burdens friends and readers alike with lengthy analyses of Church history. Here, too, the attention to analogy does not waver. Moore's speculations on Catholicism lead into reminiscences about his youth and further occasions for anecdote, gossip, ideas interwoven with events blending into new reveries. If Catholicism so restricts literature and thought, however, what chance exists for a sacred book in Ireland? The idea overwhelms Moore like a sudden crisis of faith; his mission might be only a "bubble" after all.

The solution seems to lie in exile and sacrifice, in avoiding any circumstances that might compromise the dream. Stella, for instance, with her increasing demands on his time, must be abandoned, and her later death suggests to Moore that he has forever lost the possibility of love. He himself, musing on his sexual impotence, will instead choose chastity as one more form of the isolation that will preserve his mission. Ireland, as well, has rendered any further stay impossible. The sacred book, demanding the sacrifice of all externals for its completion, is inspired by Moore's climactic vision, his spiritual union with Siegfried and Parnell, his belief that he can reforge the shattered sword in the pages of *Hail and Farewell!*

Although the entire work has developed toward this climax, the concluding chapters suggest that Moore's sacred book now takes a new direction, into an awareness that he cannot find what has been lost or heal what has split apart. Recalling his landed class and its feudal past, he admits that "we often sundered wife and husband, sister from brother; and drove away a whole village to America if it

pleased us to grow beef and mutton for the English market" (*Vale*, p. 341). The disregard for so much of Ireland, the willingness to drive away those circumstances that did not fit the dream, the concern for the English market that drew literature as well as livestock — such attitudes once allowed Moore himself to stable his horse in a man's cabin: "But we shall never be able to do it again. . . . We are a disappearing class, our lands are being confiscated, and our houses are decaying or being pulled down to build cottages for the folk" (*Vale*, p. 32). His brother Maurice, as a different kind of landlord, represents the hope that Moore Hall will escape such a fate. But the process by which families are sundered, and George Moore's own participation in it, continues its course. His anti-Catholicism so alienates his brother that Maurice abandons the estate to the last stage in its decline.

Moore does not compromise, makes sacrifices that cost him dearly, remains true to his sacred book. But his own position, as he begins to see even before the vision of the sword, has isolated him too much. His portrayal of Russell comes to seem inadequate and lifeless, nor will Martyn ever achieve full expression in Moore's work. Imprisoned in dogma, he resists Moore's efforts to free him, for Catholicism is the essential core of his personality, and Catholicism is a story Moore cannot tell. Yet Martyn seems universal, more so than Moore himself, and so deserves the literary immortality Moore wishes to give him. The incompatibility of literature and dogma, so clear-cut in theory, here becomes hopelessly entangled in experience — to what should Moore remain faithful, his friend or his art? The demands of art appear even more self-serving when connected with Stella's death. Unable to put aside his feelings of guilt, Moore is finally left with himself as the author who did not save the things and people he knew best, and with *Hail and Farewell!* as the sacred book he hopes will save Ireland. What chance possibly remains for the work? In preaching the primacy of art over dogma, in seeking to diminish the influence of Catholicism over Ireland, has Moore finally created just one more limiting dogma? He cannot answer such questions, and *Hail and Farewell!* only dimly suggests the extent to which he consciously raises them. Yet the pages following his triumphant vision and concluding with his departure from Ireland focus primarily on what he has lost. On a gray, gloomy day, Moore leaves behind his Dublin friends, painfully and humbly aware of an extreme opposition between his "dreams" and his "circumstances."

The sacred book required such sacrifices for its completion as dream, as ideal example; but the sacrifice of those circumstances at the

same time rendered the dream incomplete. The fragments of the sword included Ireland as well, and that part, too imperfectly understood or accepted by the writers, resisted their attempts to forge a complete literary whole. It remains finally unclear whether Moore saw *Hail and Farewell!* as a sacred book different from his original conception. The work does, however, reveal an artistic movement separated from much of Ireland, incapable of uniting its literature with its society, even contributing to the same social decline it sought to reverse. Imprisoned by celibacy, Protestantism, agrarian ideals, the mythic past, class sympathies, or language, overly dogmatic in their adherence to art over Catholicism or nationalism, the writers had created a hero the Irish people would reject as alien. Literature and politics had tenuously joined forces at the beginning of the 1890s under the common banner of nationalism. But the writers advocated solutions that to much of the country seemed designed to maintain an older way of life in which one man could stable his horse in another's cabin. More clearly than any of his fellow writers, Moore recognized how such a life could appear natural before 1870 and hopelessly out of place in the 1890s.

The literary concerns of the 1890s nevertheless continued to occupy the writers of the twentieth century, and later works further refined the Parnell-hero myth, even as the split between artist and society widened. In Lady Gregory's play *The Deliverer* (1911) the hero first wins the adulation of the Israelites, but then they doubt and turn on him. In their desire to obey the Egyptians and throw him to the King's cats, they recall Parnell's reference, in his 1890 Manifesto, to "the English wolves now howling for my destruction,"[12] Seumas O'Kelly's *The Parnellite* was produced in 1917, and Lennox Robinson in *The Lost Leader* (1918) dramatized the legend of Parnell's return. Padraic Pearse, in *The Singer* (1912) and *The King* (1915), depicted Christ-figures who sacrificed themselves in the cause of heroic national redemption. Other Parnell-inspired plays include Lady Gregory's *The Image* (1909), Frank O'Connor's *Moses' Rock* (1938), and Padraic Colum's *The Challengers (Glendalough)* (1966). In the novel, too, writers took up themes related to the betrayed, failed hero. Sean O'Faolain's *Bird Alone* (1936) and Michael Farrell's *Thy Tears Might Cease* (1963) depict artist-rebels struggling against a repressive, mediocre society. In a novel as recent as Thomas Flanagan's *The Year of the French* (1979), the futility of Irish public life is examined within the rebellion of 1798. John Moore, one of

the leaders of the United Irishmen, must finally confront the hopelessness of his cause: "[T]he quiet, sun-drenched fields asserted the
inconsequentiality of his actions, of all action."[13] Within the pervasive
atmosphere of desperation, even language, as a recurrent theme in
Flanagan's work, must submit to the failure of all human effort.

If the literary hero continues to fail in the world of action, much
about him begins to change early in the century. With the landed
estates dying off, the new generation of writers took more of their
experience from the city and expressed it with a greater realism. They
also had sufficient distance from Celticism to avoid its excesses, the
political eccentricities, misty legends, and artistic quaintness. Synge
accords heroic status to beggars, tinkers, and tramps, but with a
peasant realism that directly confronts social restrictions and conventions. The values of his characters similarly change; in *The Playboy*,
Christy Mahon is finally and sardonically revealed as a hero built
primarily upon the power of deceiving words and naive Irish imagination. Stephen Dedalus, in both *Ulysses* and *A Portrait of the Artist as a
Young Man*, maintains much of the conventional aestheticism of the
1890s. With crippling persistence, the preferences of previous heroes
continue to shape his character, preferences for vision over experience,
heroic failure over practical success, art over life.

Joyce's work, however, completes the transformation of the
1890s hero into the humbled and suffering common man, most fully
realized in Leopold Bloom, heroic in his dignified, honorable, decent
humanity. Malcolm Brown recalls Bloom's decision that Parnell must
have been an ordinary man much like himself, and adds: "Bloom's
great discovery has run like spring sap through all the branches of
modern Irish literature."[14] Joyce had the benefit of Katharine O'Shea's
1914 biography of Parnell in gaining insight into the human side of the
Messiah, his sentimentality and foolishness. But Bloom, too, remains
to some extent a failed Messiah. In a world of betrayal and infidelity, he
finds himself with little control over either of the two women in his
family. His responses — masturbation, kisses on Molly's rump, and
plans to adopt a ready-made son named Stephen — do not promise
much tangible success. The men of action, on the other hand, Blazes
Boylan, Buck Mulligan, the Citizen, or Pvt. Carr, come off as an un-
pleasant bunch of heavies. No one can journey over into the Promised
Land when the entire city lies paralyzed; John Howard Parnell offers
little but a feeble shadow of his heroic brother.[15] As a spokesman for
moral and social responsibility, realistic and lower-middle class, suspicious of the eccentricities that the Literary Revival was prone to,

Bloom is better qualified as a commentator on Irish society than his predecessors from the 1890s; but he does keep some of the biases that go back to that decade. If we would understand Irish literature as history, we must know the prejudices and limitations of the writers as historians.

It is within that context that we can best define the principal failure of Irish literature as art in the 1890s. The authors responded to history by retreating from it, or by substituting for it myths of their own making, or by annihilating it altogether. The denial of history grew out of the same consciousness that denied human experience, and the literature of this decade ultimately voices such a denial. The cultivation of failure as a virtue, as a test of the ideal, followed from the assumption that the ideal was too good, too spiritually pure, to tolerate contact with material reality. Yeats remarked in 1929: "The one heroic sanction is that of the last battle of the Norse Gods, of a gay struggle without hope. Long ago I used to puzzle Maud Gonne by always avowing ultimate defeat as a test. Our literary movement would be worthless but for its defeat." The literary movement remained far from worthless, in part because it grew beyond its early limitations, in part because the defeat that Yeats cherished possessed an undeniable brilliance. Despite her puzzlement, Gonne felt attracted to Yeats and to the movement he helped foster. But the movement relied too greatly on the inner spirituality of the self; whatever her reasons, Gonne withheld the total acceptance of him that Yeats had asked for. In the same letter of 1929, he suggested the paradox at the heart of his failure to win her, and the failure of the Literary Revival to win Ireland: "Sexual desire dies because every touch consumes the Myth, and yet a Myth that cannot be so consumed becomes a spectre."[16] In its deliberate separation from the life of the ordinary world, the literature of the movement could allow itself the inclination to destroy if that would bring access to the ideal myth. Apart from the world to avoid its own consumption, however, the myth took on the deathlike elusiveness of a spectre. For all of their restlessness and yearning for the ecstatic union of sense and spirit, the writers ultimately lacked a clear and palpable concept of what they sought. When the fulfillment of desire remained always out of reach, therefore, the material world took on the character of a hostile barrier rather than becoming a manifestation of the ideal.

The politics of such literature lies in its willingness to sweep aside the barrier of the visible world and set in its place a myth of the poets' making. Ireland had given the poets their myths and visions, and when these did not materialize, they stood ready to replace the

imperfect reality before their eyes with a perfect Ireland of the imagination. Ireland, of course, refused to go away so quietly, and politics, too,
exacted its revenge. Hostility to art widened the distance the artists had
to cross to reach their society and eventually led, in 1929, to one of the
most extreme and viciously effective systems of literary censorship in
Western Europe. For their part, the writers depicted Ireland as a
country that consumes its own genius, and so they often chose to carry
on their love-hate relationship with it from vantage points outside.
Only the most well-known example, Joyce would eventually be followed by Moore, Russell, O'Casey, Gogarty, Beckett, O'Connor,
O'Faolain, Austin Clarke, Thomas Kinsella, Edna O'Brien, all at various times taking refuge in silence, exile, cunning. The Irish are their
own worst enemies, one hears, and are ever ready to turn on their
heroes. O'Leary thought otherwise about this "informer fallacy":
"Certainly all my experience is against this theory."[17] But the writers
had taken a different lesson from their country, an experience of Irish
betrayal, futility, corruption, and puritanism. They had cultivated the
mystique of the lost cause and disdained compromise. In their alienation from social processes, the writers would open themselves to the
same charge they leveled, with justification, at Ireland: the accusation
of paralysis.

notes

introduction

1. "The Felons of Our Land," *Cornhill Magazine* (May 1900), p. 634.

2. "Three Irish Poets," *Irish Homestead*, December 1897, in W. B. Yeats, *Uncollected Prose*, ed. John P. Frayne and Colton Johnson (London: Macmillan, 1975) II:70.

3. W. B. Yeats, "Ireland and the Arts," in *Essays and Introductions* (London: Macmillan, 1961), p. 210. The essay was first published in 1901.

4. James MacKillop, "Finn MacCool: The Hero and the Anti-Hero in Irish Folk Tradition," in *Views of the Irish Peasantry, 1800–1916*, ed. Daniel J. Casey and Robert E. Rhodes (Hamden, Conn.: Archon, 1977), pp. 86–106. See also Alf MacLochlainn, "Gael and Peasant—A Case of Mistaken Identity?" in Casey and Rhodes, pp. 17–36.

5. Letter, *Leader*, 1 September 1900, p. 13, in Frayne, II:237.

6. Editorial, *Leader*, 1 December 1900, p. 1.

Chapter 1— economics, religion, and society

1. These figures include the commonly accepted estimates of the population on the eve of the Famine and of the number of people who died as a result of it; see, for example, F. S. L. Lyons, *Ireland Since the Famine* (Glasgow: Fontana/Collins, 1973), p. 44.

2. Barbara Solow, *The Land Question and the Irish Economy, 1870–1903* (Cambridge: Harvard University Press, 1971), p. 55, cites figures from Parliamentary Papers (1881). Of the fifty thousand evictions, thirteen thousand families were subsequently readmitted to holdings on the insecure basis of "caretakers."

3. Raymond D. Crotty, *Irish Agricultural Production, Its Volume and Structure* (Cork: Cork University Press, 1966), p. 351, cites figures from the *Census Report 1841*, the Poor Law Commissioners' Return for 1845, and the *Census of Ireland for the Year 1851*.

4. Lyons, *Famine*, p. 47.

5. Ibid., p. 16.

6. Solow, *Land Question*, pp. 51–88. See p. 55 for eviction figures and p. 76 for rent increases and their relation to the rise in agricultural prices and to rent increases in England and Scotland.

7. F. S. L. Lyons, *Charles Stewart Parnell* (London: Collins, 1977), p. 83.

8. "A New Nation," in *The Writings of James Fintan Lalor* (Dublin: O'Donoghue, 1895), p. 29. The essay was first published in April 1847.

9. Letter, *Irish Felon*, June 1848, cited in Michael Davitt, *The Fall of Feudalism in Ireland* (London: Harper, 1904), p. 61.

10. Thomas Davis, *Prose Writings of Thomas Davis*, ed. T. W. Rolleston (London: Walter Scott [1889?]), pp. 44–75.

11. E. D. Steele, *Irish Land and British Politics* (Cambridge: Cambridge University Press, 1974), p. 3, cites figures from Parliamentary Papers (1876), and from J. Bateman, *The Great Landowners of Great Britain and Ireland*, 4th ed. (London, 1883; rpt. Leicester: Leicester University Press, 1971).

12. Crotty, *Irish Agricultural Production*, p. 351, cites figures from Parliamentary Papers (1902) .

13. S. H. Cousens, "The Regional Variations in Population Changes in Ireland, 1861–1881," *Economic History Review*, 2nd ser., 17 (2) (December 1964): 301–321.

14. Elizabeth R. Hooker, *Readjustments of Agricultural Tenure in Ireland* (Chapel Hill: University of North Carolina Press, 1938), p. 225, cites the Estates Commissioners' *Report* (1920–21).

15. Norman D. Palmer, *The Irish Land League Crisis* (New Haven: Yale University Press, 1940), p. 243, cites the *Preliminary Report...on Agriculture* (1881). The report by the Richmond Commission, Palmer claims, "agreed substantially with that of the Bessborough Commissioners" (p. 244).

16. Solow, *Land Question*, pp. 171–72. From £50 million in 1876, the value of crops and livestock fell to £40 million in 1881, and £32 million in 1886.

17. Lyons, *Famine*, p. 19.

18. Emmet Larkin, "The Devotional Revolution in Ireland, 1850–1875," *American Historical Review* 77 (3) (June 1972): 625–52, rpt. in Emmet Larkin, *The Historical Dimensions of Irish Catholicism* (New York: Arno, 1976).

19. Emmet Larkin, "Church, State, and Nation in Modern Ireland," *American Historical Review* 80 (5) (December 1975): 1244–76, rpt. in Larkin, *Irish Catholicism*. The citations in the text are from pp. 1245, 1253.

20. K. H. Connell, "Catholicism and Marriage in the Century After the Famine," in *Irish Peasant Society* (Oxford: Clarendon, 1968), p. 119, cites Gustav Sundbärg, *Aperçus statistiques internationaux* (Stockholm, 1908).

21. Patrick O'Farrell, *Ireland's English Question* (New York: Schocken, 1971), p. 224, discusses the Apostleship of Prayer movement.

22. Lyons, *Famine*, pp. 87–93, provides these figures on Irish education.

23. Ibid., pp. 18, 23.

24. Emmet Larkin, "Economic Growth, Capital Investment, and the Roman Catholic Church in Nineteenth-Century Ireland," *American Historical Review* 72 (3) (April 1967): 882, rpt. in Larkin, *Irish Catholicism*.

25. Lyons, *Famine*, p. 74

26. Ibid., p. 101.

27. Ibid., p. 277.

28. Ibid., p. 55 ff., analyzes these factors.

29. Sean O'Faolain, *The Irish* (Harmondsworth, Middlesex: Penguin, 1969), p. 148.

30. Paul Bew, *Land and the National Question in Ireland, 1858–82* (Atlantic Highlands, N.J.: Humanities Press, 1979), p. 221.

31. Ibid., pp. 30–32.

Chapter 2— **politics transformed**

Parnellism and the Landed Gentry

1. John O'Leary, *Recollections of Fenians and Fenianism* (London: Downey, 1896) II:160.

2. Michael Davitt, *The Fall of Feudalism in Ireland* (London: Harper, 1904), p. 239.

3. Conor Cruise O'Brien, *Parnell and His Party, 1880–90* (Oxford: Clarendon, 1957), pp. 14–18.

4. Barbara Solow, *The Land Question and the Irish Economy, 1870–1903* (Cambridge: Harvard University Press, 1971), p. 55, cites eviction figures from Parliamentary Papers (1881). The figures on agrarian outrages are given in R. Barry O'Brien, *The Life of Charles Stewart Parnell, 1846–1891* (New York: Harper, 1898) I:247, n. 1.

5. *Mr. Parnell's Speeches, Letters, and Public Utterances* (Dublin: Webb, 1889), p. 47.

6. A. S. Sullivan, *New Ireland* (London: Washbourne [1877?]), pp. 457–58.

7. William O'Brien, *Recollections* (London: Macmillan, 1905), pp. 291–92. O'Brien is not to be confused with the Young Irelander, William Smith O'Brien.

8. Davitt, *Fall of Feudalism*, p. 317.

9. See the *Report of Special Commission*, VII, Evidence of Michael Davitt, p. 6, cited in P. S. O'Hegarty, *A History of Ireland Under the Union, 1801 to 1922* (London: Methuen, 1952), pp. 483–84.

10. Davitt, *Fall of Feudalism*, p. 137, quotes Parnell's speech of 15 November 1878, in Tralee, from the *Freeman's Journal*, 16 November 1878. Davitt's lengthy quotation from the speech bears out his assessment of it.

11. Solow, *Land Question*, p. 176.

12. Elizabeth R. Hooker, *Readjustments of Agricultural Tenure in Ireland* (Chapel Hill: University of North Carolina Press, 1938), p. 225, cites the Estates Commissioners' *Report* (1920–21).

13. Davitt, *Fall of Feudalism*, p. 309.

14. F. S. L. Lyons, *The Fall of Parnell, 1890–91* (London: Routledge and Kegan Paul, 1960), p. 12.

15. Letter to Katharine O'Shea, 13 October 1881, in her *Charles Stewart Parnell* (New York: Doran, 1914) I:194.

16. Davitt, *Fall of Feudalism*, p. 349.

17. F. S. L. Lyons, *Charles Stewart Parnell* (London: Collins, 1977), p. 237.

18. Robert F. Foster, *Charles Stewart Parnell* (Atlantic Highlands, N.J.: Humanities Press, 1976), p. 308.

19. *Mr. Parnell's Speeches*, p. 200.

20. O'Leary, *Fenians and Fenianism*, I:38.

21. Lyons, *Parnell*, p. 623.

22. Ibid., p. 468.

23. Ibid., p. 613.

24. "A Defence of Mr. Parnell's Leadership of the Irish People," *Freeman's Journal*, 3 January 1890.

25. Letter, *Irish Times*, 1 December 1890.

26. *Freeman's Journal*, 29 July 1891.

27. *Freeman's Journal*, 23 December 1890.

28. Lyons, *Parnell*, p. 537.

29. Ibid, p. 614.

30. F. S. L. Lyons, *The Irish Parliamentary Party, 1890–1910* (London: Faber and Faber, 1951), p. 37.

31. *Daily Express*, 8 October 1891. The remarks in the *Express* carried particular weight since the paper had strongly opposed Parnell's conduct in the preceding months.

32. *Daily Telegraph*, 14 October 1891, rpt. *Irish Times*, 16 October 1891.

33. "The Chronicle," *United Ireland*, 5 December 1891.

34. Herbert Howarth, *The Irish Writers 1880–1940* (London: Rockliff, 1958), pp. 1–31, provides a major discussion of "literary messianism" and its relations to Parnell.

35. *Freeman's Journal*, 13 October 1891.

36. John Sweetman, "The National Movement," *New Ireland Review* (January 1895), p. 699.

37. Hooker, *Agricultural Tenure*, p. 225, cites the Estates Commissioners' *Report* (1920–21) for figures on the Land Bills; p. 222 cites "Agricultural Holdings" (1870) and *Agricultural Statistics for Ireland* (1906) for land tenure figures.

38. Standish James O'Grady, *The Crisis in Ireland* (Dublin: Ponsonby, 1882), p. 51. I am indebted to Malcolm Brown, *The Politics of Irish Literature* (London: George Allen and Unwin, 1972), pp. 296–300, 373–74, for drawing attention to O'Grady's work.

39. Standish James O'Grady, "Irish Conservatism and Its Outlooks," in *Selected Essays and Passages* (Dublin: Talbot, 1917), p. 167.

40. O'Grady, *Crisis in Ireland*, p. 49.

41. Standish James O'Grady, "Ireland and the Hour," in *Toryism and the Tory Democracy* (London: Chapman and Hall, 1886), p. 281.

42. Oliver MacDonagh, *The Nineteenth Century Novel and Irish Social History* (Dublin: National University of Ireland, 1970), p. 5.

43. Sir Samuel Ferguson, "A Dialogue Between the Head and Heart of an Irish Protestant," *Dublin University Magazine* (November 1833), p. 591.

44. O'Grady, "The Great Enchantment," in *Selected Essays*, p. 181.

45. O'Grady, "Irish Conservatism and Its Outlooks," p. 169.

46. F. S. L. Lyons, *Ireland Since the Famine* (Glasgow: Fontana/Collins, 1973), pp. 216–17.

47. Standish James O'Grady, *The Story of Ireland* (London: Methuen, 1894), p. 210.

48. Ibid., p. 211.

49. William O'Brien, *The Parnell of Real Life* (London: T. Fisher Unwin, 1926), p. 125.

50. Lyons, *Parnell*, p. 613.

51. Ibid, p. 616.

52. "Placing Parnell: Terence de Vere White Talks to F. S. L. Lyons," *Irish Times*, 16 June 1977.

Chapter 3— celticism and the vision of unity

1. Matthew Arnold, *On the Study of Celtic Literature* (London: Smith and Elder, 1867), p. 101. Further references to this work appear in the text.

2. John Kelleher, "Matthew Arnold and the Celtic Revival," in *Perspectives of Criticism*, ed. Harry Levin (Cambridge: Harvard University Press, 1950), p.197. Kelleher's essay, pp. 197–221, is a major work on the Celtic Revival and its relation to Irish literature and society.

3. W. B. Yeats, "The Celtic Element in Literature," in *Essays and Introductions* (London: Macmillan, 1961), pp. 178–88.

4. In Sir Charles Gavan Duffy, *Young Ireland* (New York: Appleton, 1881), p. 299.

5. John O'Leary, *Recollections of Fenians and Fenianism* (London: Downey, 1896) I:3.

6. Ernest Boyd, *Ireland's Literary Renaissance* (London: Grant Richards, 1923), p. 27.

7. *Daily Express*, 28 October 1899.

8. Vivian Mercier, "From Religious Revival to Literary Revival: Irish Protestantism in the Nineteenth Century," IASAIL Conference, Maynooth, 10 July 1979.

9. W. P. Ryan, *The Irish Literary Revival* (London: privately printed, 1894), p. 34.

10. W. B. Yeats, "The Trembling of the Veil," in *Autobiographies* (London: Macmillan, 1955), p. 199. "The Trembling of the Veil" was first published in 1922.

11. "Prospects of the Irish National Literary Movement," *United Ireland*, 19 December 1896. The essay was delivered as a lecture to the National Literary Society, Dublin.

12. W. B. Yeats, "The Literary Movement in Ireland," in *Ideals in Ireland*, ed. Lady Augusta Gregory (London: At the Unicorn, 1901), p. 90.

13. Unpublished manuscript, in Richard Ellmann, *Yeats: The Man and the Masks* (New York: Macmillan, 1948), p. 113. The quotation is from a speech delivered in New York in 1904.

14. Yeats, "The Trembling of the Veil," p. 362.

15. "The Poetry of William Allingham," *Irish Fireside*, 30 October 1886, pp. 261–62, cited in Phillip L. Marcus, *Yeats and the Beginning of the Irish Renaissance* (Ithaca, N.Y.: Cornell University Press, 1970), p. 2.

16. D. P. Moran, "The Future of the Irish Nation," *New Ireland Review* (February 1899), p. 353.

17. *Leader*, 1 September 1900, p. 12

18. *An Claidheamh Soluis*, 1 July 1899, p. 249.

19. *Daily Express*, 23 February 1899.

20. Dominic Daly, *The Young Douglas Hyde* (Totowa, N.J.: Rowman and Littlefield, 1974), p. 173.

21. Ibid., p. 166.

22. Ibid., p. 163.

23. Ibid., p. 146.

24. Douglas Hyde, *Love Songs of Connacht* (Dublin: Gill, 1893), pp. v–vi.

25. All the citations in this paragraph are from Hyde, *Love Songs*, p. 3. Further references to this work appear in the text.

26. "Old Gaelic Love Songs," *Bookman*, October 1893, in *Uncollected Prose*, ed. John P. Frayne (London: Macmillan, 1970) I:295.

27. Review of Hyde's *The Story of Early Gaelic Literature* (1895), *Bookman*, June 1895, in Frayne, I:359.

28. Letter to Horace Reynolds, *Dublin Magazine* 13 (1938):29.

29. Boyd, *Ireland's Literary Renaissance*, p. 89.

30. Letter, *United Ireland*, 17 December 1892, in Frayne, I:255.

31. W. B. Yeats, "Ireland and the Arts," in *Essays and Introductions*, p. 208. The essay was first published in 1901.

32. Colin Meir, *The Ballads and Songs of W. B. Yeats* (London: Macmillan, 1974), p. 47.

33. Allen R. Grossman, *Poetic Knowledge in the Early Yeats* (Charlottesville: University Press of Virginia, 1969), pp. xiii–xiv.

34. Marcus, *Yeats*, pp. 1–34, provides a broad, influential analysis of the concept of Celticism in 1890s Ireland.

35. "The Publication of Irish Books," *United Ireland*, 14 May 1892, in Frayne, I.223.

36. "The Literary Movement of the Present Day," *United Ireland*, 25 January 1896.

37. *United Ireland*, 3 May 1894.

38. Yeats, *Autobiographies*, pp. 101–02. The "Reveries" were first published in 1916.

39. Letter to Katharine Tynan, 25 March 1895, *The Letters of W. B. Yeats*, ed. Allan Wade (London: Rupert Hart-Davis, 1954), p. 254.

40. Robert Blake, "The Publisher in Ireland," *New Ireland Review* (October 1897), p. 112.

41. Letter to Katharine Tynan, 7 April 1895, Wade, p. 255.

42. Sir Charles Gavan Duffy, "What Irishmen May Do For Irish Literature," in Sir Charles Gavan Duffy, George Sigerson, and Douglas Hyde, *The Revival of Irish Literature* (London: T. Fisher Unwin, 1894), p. 17.

43. Sir Charles Gavan Duffy, "Books for the Irish People," in Duffy et al., *The Revival of Irish Literature*, pp. 47–48. The essay was delivered to the Irish Literary Society of London in June 1893.

44. Letter, *United Ireland*, 1 September 1894, in Frayne, I:340.

45. See also Marcus, *Yeats*, pp. 61–129, for an extensive discussion of the beginnings of the Literary Revival, including Yeats's various literary controversies.

46. Duffy et al., *The Revival of Irish Literature*, p. 159.

47. W. B. Yeats, "The Literary Movement in Ireland," p. 101. Further references to this work appear in the text.

48. John Eglinton et al., *Literary Ideals in Ireland* (London: T. Fisher Unwin, 1899), p. 13. Further references to this work appear in the text.

49. "A Bundle of Poets," *Speaker*, 22 July 1893, in Frayne, I:276–79.

50. *United Irishman*, 31 May 1902.

51. "John Eglinton," *United Irishman*, 9 November 1901, in *Uncollected Prose*, ed. John P. Frayne and Colton Johnson (London: Macmillan, 1975) II:260.

52. "Our Ideals," *Daily Express*, 4 March 1899.

53. "Literature and Politics," *United Ireland*, 16 December 1893.

Chapter 4— SOMERVILLE AND ROSS

1. Edith Somerville and Martin Ross, *Wheel-Tracks* (London: Longmans and Green, 1923), p. 218. Somerville continued to include Martin's name in the authorship of her work after the death of her partner.

2. Edith Somerville and Martin Ross, *Irish Memories* (London: Longmans and Green, 1917), p. 238.

3. Ibid., p. 28.

4. Ibid., p. 90.

5. Ibid., p. 4.

6. Ibid., p. 27.

7. Ibid., p. 4.

8. Ibid., p. 37.

9. Ibid., p. 34.

10. Letter to Stephen Gwynn, *Wheel-Tracks*, p. 219.

11. Somerville and Ross, *Irish Memories*, p. 91.

12. Ibid., p. 145.

13. Somerville and Ross, *Wheel-Tracks*, p. 67.

14. Somerville and Ross, *Irish Memories*, p. 143.

15. Ibid., p. 133.

16. Somerville and Ross, *Wheel-Tracks*, pp. 230–34.

17. *Through Connemara in a Governess Cart* (1893) was serialized in the *Lady's Pictorial* in 1891 and *In the Vine Country* (1893) in 1892.

18. Somerville and Ross, *Wheel-Tracks*, p. 84.

19. Edith Somerville and Martin Ross, *The Real Charlotte* (London: Ward and Downey, 1894) I:134. Further references to this work appear in the text.

20. Somerville and Ross, *Irish Memories*, p. 229.

21. Ibid., p. 88.

22. Ibid., p. 131.

Chapter 5— GEORGE MOORE

1. Joseph Hone, *The Life of George Moore* (New York: Macmillan, 1936), pp. 185–86.

2. George Moore, *Ave*, Vol. I of *Hail and Farewell!* (London: Heinemann, 1911), p. 292.

3. Ibid., p. 43.

4. Ibid., pp. 94–95.

5. Ibid., p. 2.

6. Letter to John Eglinton, Hone, p. 383.

7. George Moore, *Salve*, Vol. II of *Hail and Farewell!* (London: Heinemann, 1912), p. 21.

8. George Moore, *Vale*, Vol. III of *Hail and Farewell!* (London: Heinemann, 1914), p. 25.

9. George Moore, *Confessions of a Young Man* (London: Swan Sonnenschein, 1888), p. 11.

10. Col. Maurice Moore, *An Irish Gentleman, George Henry Moore* (London: T. Werner Laurie, 1913), p. xx.

11. Hone, *George Moore*, p. 71.

12. Malcolm Brown, *George Moore* (Seattle: University of Washington Press, 1955), p. 15. I rely on Brown's work, the most significant critical study of Moore to date, for my general view of Moore's early career.

13. Moore, *Confessions*, p. 187.

14. Helmut Gerber, ed., *George Moore in Transition* (Detroit: Wayne State University Press, 1968), p. 111.

15. Aside from the novels, other Paterian works include the *Confessions* and two volumes of impressionistic criticism, *Impressions and Opinions* (1891) and *Modern Painting* (1893).

16. George Moore, *Vain Fortune* (London: Henry, 1891), pp. 198–99.

17. Hone, *George Moore*, p. 150.

18. Ibid., p. 167.

19. Moore, *Confessions*, p. 340. The importance Moore accorded to the *Confessions* as an autobiographical work is indicated by the extent of his continued work on the book; he revised it for editions in 1889, 1904, 1917, and 1918.

20. Geraint Goodwin, *Conversations with George Moore* (London: E. Benn, 1929), pp. 114, 115.

21. Moore, *Confessions*, pp. 160–61.

22. George Moore, *Parnell and His Island* (London: Swan Sonnenschein, 1887), p. 233. Further references to this work appear in the text. Moore translated and revised the book from his earlier French edition *Terre D'Irlande* (1887).

23. Brown, *George Moore*, p. 102.

24. Moore, *Confessions*, p. 150.

25. Hone, *George Moore*, p. 85.

26. Brown, *George Moore*, p. 17.

27. George Moore, *A Drama in Muslin* (London: Vizetelly, 1886),p. 95. Further references to this work are given in the text. The novel was rewritten and published as *Muslin* in 1915. For a discussion of the extensive revisions, see Peter Ure, "George Moore as Historian of Conscience," in *Imagined Worlds*, ed. Maynard Mack and Ian Gregor (London: Methuen, 1968), pp. 257–76, rpt. in *The Man of Wax*, ed. Douglas Hughes (New York: New York University Press, 1971), pp. 87–112. Ure concludes that the original version "would have done better if it had been left alone" (p. 104 of Hughes).

28. Moore, *Confessions*, p. 192.

29. Ibid., pp. 114–15.

30. Brown, *George Moore*, p. 98.

31. Moore, *Ave*, p. 1.

32. Moore, *Salve*, p. 2.

33. Moore, *Ave*, p. 292.

34. Moore, *Vale*, p. 165.

35. Letter to Edouard Dujardin, Hone, p. 245.

36. Moore, *Confessions*, pp. 209–210.

37. Letter to Clara Lanza, Hone, p. 161.

38. Letter to Lena Milman, November 1893, Gerber, p. 80.

39. See Janet Dunleavy, *George Moore* (Lewisburg: Bucknell University Press, 1973), pp. 101–108, for an extensive discussion of the Irish details. Dunleavy concludes that there is a split vision in the novel, one combining observed details from the present and remembered details from the past, and she provides one of the rare discussions of *Esther Waters* as an "Irish" novel. For the non-Irish position, see Brian Nicholas' influential and controversial essay, "The Case of *Esther Waters*," in *The Moral and the Story*, ed. Ian Gregor and Brian Nicholas (London: Faber and Faber, 1962), pp. 98–122, rpt. in Hughes, *The Man of Wax*, pp. 151–83. Nicholas writes that "the melodramatic conception of virtue.... has involved Moore in a full-scale portrait of a woman with whose ideals he has nothing in common, who is to him essentially indifferent" (p. 178 of Hughes).

40. Moore, *Ave*, p. 306.

41. Ure, "George Moore," p. 99, regards Woodview as "plainly Moore Hall transplanted to the Sussex downs."

42. Moore, *Vale*, p. 25.

43. George Moore, *Esther Waters* (London: Walter Scott, 1894), p. 31. Further references to this work are given in the text. *Passages from the Life of a Workgirl*, an early version of chapters XX–XXIII, XXV–XXVII, and XXIX, was serialized in eleven installments in the *Pall Mall Gazette*, 2–4, 6–7, and 9–14 October 1893. Moore issued revised editions in 1899 and 1920 and a uniform edition in 1932. His dramatization of a portion of the novel appeared as *Esther Waters* in 1913. Royal Gettmann, "George Moore's Revisions of *The Lake, The Wild Goose*, and *Esther Waters*," *PMLA* 59 (2) (June 1944): 540–55, discusses the revisions of the novel. In summary, Gettmann finds that scarcely twenty pages remain unaltered, yet "In narrative method, theme, and purpose the novel remains unchanged. ... the work of a competent craftsman patching surface details" (p. 555). He claims that the style becomes smoother and more colloquial and that the novel is presented more from Esther's point of view. Many of the stilted or redundant or simply pompous passages have been removed; some exposition is recast into dialogue; and many of the short, choppy sentences are combined into longer ones.

44. Dunleavy, *George Moore*, pp. 108–109.

45. Letter to Lena Milman, Summer 1895, Gerber, p. 110.

46. Moore, *Confessions*, p. 38.

47. In later editions Moore omitted the second group of sentences as perhaps too mechanical a literary device.

48. Brown, *George Moore*, p. 133.

Chapter 6— εδwarδ martyn

1. Denis Gwynn, *Edward Martyn and the Irish Revival* (London: Cape, 1930), p. 150, cites a reviewer from the *Irish Truth*.

2. Ernest Boyd, *Ireland's Literary Renaissance* (London: Grant Richards, 1923), p. 304; among the three, Boyd includes *The Bending of the Bough* for Martyn's original conception of the play.

3. Edward Martyn, *Morgante the Lesser* (London: Swan Sonnenschein, 1890), p. 291. Further references to this work appear in the text.

4. W. B. Yeats, "Dramatis Personae," in *Autobiographies* (London: Macmillan, 1955), p. 386.

5. Sister Marie-Thérèse Courtney, *Edward Martyn and the Irish Theatre* (New York: Vantage, 1956), gives Martyn's grandfather's name as John Smythe and the dowry as £20,000. The information in the text is from Gwynn, and I rely on his biographical account here because of his access to Martyn's personal papers, since lost.

6. Courtney offers this version of Martyn's years at Oxford; Gwynn, on the other hand, maintains that those years were relatively happy ones for Martyn. But given Martyn's status as a member of a distinctly minority religion, his unsuccessful attempt to earn a degree, and his later satiric blasts at Oxford and Cambridge, Courtney's view seems the more probable one.

7. Yeats, "Dramatis Personae," p. 401.

8. George Moore, *Salve*, Vol. II of *Hail and Farewell!* (London: Heinemann, 1912), p. 211.

9. Gwynn, *Edward Martyn*, p. 56.

10. Yeats, "Dramatis Personae," p. 386.

11. George Moore, *Ave*, Vol. I. of *Hail and Farewell!* (London: Heinemann, 1911), p. 235.

12. Arthur Symons, "A Causerie:—From a Castle in Ireland," *Savoy* (October 1896), p. 93.

13. Ibid., p. 95.

14. Yeats, "Dramatis Personae," p. 386.

15. W. B. Yeats, "Autobiography—First Draft," in *Memoirs*, ed. Denis Donoghue (London: Macmillan, 1972), p. 119. Donoghue notes that this sentence is from a typescript version of "Dramatis Personae" located in the Morris Library, Southern Illinois University, Carbondale, Illinois.

16. "Catholic Church Music in Dublin," *Leader*, 6 October 1900, p. 88.

17. Gwynn, *Edward Martyn*, p. 254.

18. Ibid., p. 211.

19. "Some Thoughts at the Galway Feis," *Leader*, 8 September 1900, pp. 24–25.

20. "Unmusical Dublin and the Dublin Orchestra," *Leader*, 6 December 1902, pp. 238–39.

21. Gwynn, *Edward Martyn*, p. 246, cites an article from *An Claidheamh Soluis*.

22. Ibid., p. 164, cites the Preface to "Paragraphs for the Perverse," Martyn's unpublished memoirs that have subsequently been lost.

23. Ibid., p. 144, cites an unpublished essay.

24. Jan Setterquist, *Edward Martyn*, Vol. II of *Ibsen and the Beginning of Anglo-Irish Drama* (Sweden, 1960; rpt. New York: Oriole, 1973), discusses the textual similarities of Martyn's plays to those of Ibsen.

25. Gwynn, *Edward Martyn*, pp. 158, 161, cites an unpublished essay.

26. Edward Martyn, *The Tale of a Town and An Enchanted Sea* (London: T. Fisher Unwin, 1902), p. 156. According to Gwynn, Martyn had in his collection a painting by George Russell entitled "The Enchanted Sea."

27. Courtney, *Edward Martyn*, p. 147.

28. Edward Martyn, *The Heather Field and Maeve* (London: Duckworth, 1899), p. 17. Further references to these two plays are given in the text.

29. Yeats, "Dramatis Personae," p. 417.

30. Ibid., p. 418.

31. Ibid., p. 426.

32. Moore, *Ave*, p. 165.

33. In Martyn's use of "The O'Heynes," the definite article prefixing the surname is a Gaelic convention designating the chieftain of a clan.

34. Yeats, "Autobiography—First Draft," p. 118.

35. Moore, *Ave*, p. 73.

Chapter 7— GEORGE RUSSELL

1. Letter to Yeats, 3 April 1897, *Letters from AE*, ed. Alan Denson (London: Abelard-Schuman, 1961), p. 19.

2. Letter to Yeats, April 1899, Denson, p. 31.

3. "Irish National Literature, III," *Bookman*, September 1895, in *Uncollected Prose*, ed. John P. Frayne (London: Macmillan, 1970) I:380.

4. Letter to Russell, 22 January 1898, *The Letters of W. B. Yeats*, ed. Allan Wade (London: Rupert Hart-Davis, 1954), p. 295.

5. Letter to Yeats, 1 February 1898, Denson, p. 25.

6. Letter to Synge, Christmas 1897, Denson, p. 23.

7. George Moore, *Ave*, Vol. I of *Hail and Farewell!* (London: Heinemann, 1911), p. 159.

8. George Russell, *The Candle of Vision* (London: Macmillan, 1918), p.11.

9. John Eglinton, *A Memoir of AE* (London: Macmillan, 1937), p. 24.

10. Russell, *The Candle of Vision*, p. 98.

11. Letter to Carrie Rea, Autumn 1886, Denson, p. 4.

12. Russell, *The Candle of Vision*, p. 2.

13. Henry Summerfield, *That Myriad-Minded Man* (Gerrards Cross, Buckinghamshire: Colin Smythe, 1975), p. 59. I rely on Summerfield's work for the biographical information throughout this chapter.

14. Denson, *Letters from AE*, pp. 17–18.

15. Russell, *The Candle of Vision*, pp. 99–101.

16. Wade, *Letters*, p. 266.

17. Letter to Yeats, June 1897, *Letters to W. B. Yeats*, ed. Richard Finneran, George Mills Harper, and William M. Murphy (New York: Columbia University Press, 1977) I:32.

18. George Russell, *Ideals in Ireland* (Dublin: n.p., [1897?]), p. 5.

19. Ibid., p.7.

20. "Politics and Character," *Daily Express*, 25 February 1899.

21. George Russell, *Homeward Songs by the Way* (Dublin: Whaley, 1894). Further references to this work appear in the text.

22. George Russell, *The Earth Breath and Other Poems* (London: John Lane, 1897), p. 51. Further references to this work appear in the text.

23. Russell, *The Candle of Vision*, p. 15.

24. George Russell, *Imaginations and Reveries* (Dublin: Maunsel, 1915), p. 115.

25. Russell, *The Candle of Vision*, p. 61.

26. Letter to Yeats, 3 April 1897, Denson, p. 21.

27. Letter to Dowden, 13 August 1894, Denson, p. 12.

28. Letter to Yeats, 3 April 1897, Denson, p. 19.

29. Letter to John O'Leary, July 1892, Wade, p. 211.

30. George Moore, *Salve*, Vol. II of *Hail and Farewell!* (London: Heinemann, 1912), p. 64.

31. "The Poetry of A.E.," *Daily Express*, 3 September 1898, in *Uncollected Prose*, ed. John P. Frayne and Colton Johnson (London: Macmillan, 1975) II:123.

Chapter 8— W. B. YEATS

Prose Works and *The Countess Cathleen*

1. George Moore, *Vale*, Vol. III of *Hail and Farewell!* (London: Heinemann, 1914), p. 206.

2. Richard Ellmann, *Yeats: The Man and the Masks* (New York: Macmillan, 1948), p. 290.

3. Alex Zwerdling, *Yeats and the Heroic Ideal* (New York: New York University Press, 1965), p. 9.

4. Letter to John O'Leary, November 1888, *The Letters of W. B. Yeats*, ed. Allan Wade (London: Rupert Hart-Davis, 1954), p. 94.

5. Review, *Bookman*, April 1894, in *Uncollected Prose*, ed. John P. Frayne (London: Macmillan, 1970) I:324.

6. W. B. Yeats, *The Tables of the Law. The Adoration of the Magi* (London: R. Clay, 1897). The story was first published in the *Savoy* in November 1896. Further references to this work appear in the text.

7. W. B. Yeats, *The Secret Rose* (London: Lawrence and Bullen, 1897). Dates of first publication appear in parentheses for individual stories.

8. *The Vision of MacConglinne*, ed. Kuno Meyer. Yeats reviewed Meyer's version in *Bookman*, February 1893, in Frayne, I:261–63.

9. Letter to Katharine Tynan, February 1889, Wade, pp. 112–13.

10. R. Barry O'Brien, *The Life of Charles Stewart Parnell, 1846–1891* (New York: Harper, 1898) II:218.

11. W. B. Yeats, *The Trembling of the Veil* (London: T. Werner Laurie, 1922), p. 192.

12. W. B. Yeats, "Journal," in *Memoirs*, ed. Denis Donoghue (New York: Macmillan, 1972), p. 163.

13. W. B. Yeats, *Estrangement* (Dublin: Cuala Press, 1926), p. 26.

14. W. B. Yeats, *The Poems of W. B. Yeats* (London: Macmillan, 1949) II:189. These lines first appeared in 1932.

15. Letter to John O'Leary, Ellmann, p. 100, unpublished letter in the National Library of Ireland.

16. *United Ireland*, 10 October 1891, in *The Variorum Edition of the Poems of W. B. Yeats*, ed. Peter Allt and Russell Alspach (New York: Macmillan, 1957), p. 737.

17. W. B. Yeats, *Ideas of Good and Evil* (London: Bullen, 1903), pp. 306–307.

18. *Samhain* (October 1901), p. 9.

19. Yeats, "Journal," p. 225.

20. George Moore, *Ave*, Vol. I of *Hail and Farewell!* (London: Heinemann, 1911), pp. 348–49.

21. Donald T. Torchiana, *W. B. Yeats and Georgian Ireland* (Evanston: Northwestern University Press, 1966). Torchiana gives close attention to the Gregory family as models for Yeats's ideas.

22. Moore, *Vale*, p. 161.

23. "A Reckless Century. Irish Rakes and Duellists," *United Ireland*, 12 September 1891, in Frayne, I:201–202.

24. Peter Ure, *Yeats the Playwright* (New York: Barnes and Noble, 1963), p. 24.

25. Yeats, "Autobiography—First Draft," in Donoghue, p. 63.

26. F. Hugh O'Donnell, *The Stage Irishman of the Pseudo-Celtic Drama* (London: Long, 1904), p. 33.

27. W. B. Yeats, "Dramatis Personae," in *Autobiographies* (London: Macmillan, 1955), p. 416.

28. Letter, *Freeman's Journal*, 10 May 1899.

29. Letter, *Morning Leader*, May 1899, Wade, p. 319.

30. W. B. Yeats, *The Countess Cathleen*, in *Poems* (London: T. Fisher Unwin, 1901), p. 16. Further references to this work appear in the text. An 1899 reprinting appeared almost simultaneously with the first performance and received various changes for purposes of the production. The text in *Poems* (1901), the third version, represents the most accurate version of the 1899 performance. A new version appeared in 1912, and a fifth and final one in *Poems* (1919). See Ure, *Yeats the Playwright*, pp. 9–30, and David Clark, "Vision and Revision: Yeats's *The Countess Cathleen*," in *The World of W. B. Yeats*, ed. Robin Skelton and Ann Saddlemyer (Seattle: University of Washington Press, 1965), pp. 140–58, for detailed analyses of the various revisions.

31. Yeats, "Autobiography—First Draft," p. 47.

Chapter 9— **W. B. yeats**

The Rose and *The Wind Among the Reeds*

1. W. B. Yeats, *Poems* (London: T. Fisher Unwin, 1895). Further references to this work appear in the text.

2. "The Poetry of Sir Samuel Ferguson — II," *Dublin University Review*, November 1886, in *Uncollected Prose*, ed. John P. Frayne (London: Macmillan, 1970) I:90.

3. W. B. Yeats, "The Trembling of the Veil," in *Autobiographies* (London: Macmillan, 1955), p. 254.

4. Frayne, I:104.

5. Richard Ellmann, *Yeats: The Man and the Masks* (New York: Macmillan, 1948), p. 111, cites the 1898 Centennial Association of Great Britain and France, *Report of Speeches at the Inaugural Banquet ... 13th April, 1898* (Dublin: Bernard Doyle, 1898), pp. 8–10.

6. Ellmann, *Yeats*, p. 112.

7. Programme for F. Norreys Connell's play *The Piper*, 20–22 February 1908, in Donald T. Torchiana, *W. B. Yeats and Georgian Ireland* (Evanston: Northwestern University Press, 1966), p. 63.

8. Ellmann, *Yeats*, p. 97, cites Marjorie Louise Henry, *Stuart Merrill* (Paris: Librairie Ancienne Honoré Champion, 1927), p. 109.

9. John Mitchel, *Jail Journal* (Dublin: Corrigan, 1864), p. 54.

10. Letter to Florence Farr, December 1895, *The Letters of W. B. Yeats*, ed. Allan Wade (London: Rupert Hart-Davis, 1954), pp. 259–60.

11. W. B. Yeats, "Magic," in *Essays and Introductions* (London: Macmillan, 1961), p. 49.

12. Ellmann, *Yeats*, p. 82.

13. In his analysis of Yeats's poetic vision from this period, Allen Grossman, *Poetic Knowledge in the Early Yeats* (Charlottesville: University Press of Virginia, 1969), p. xiii, uses other social terms and perspectives to conclude that "Yeats possessed a genius for culture in the constructive sense. ... The new culture which Yeats 'half-planned' in his early years was in a sense the modern poetic culture of the English-speaking world." By contrast, I am concerned here primarily with Yeats's relationship to a specifically Irish culture, a context for which his genius was not as well suited nor his half-plans always constructive.

14. Yeats, "The Trembling of the Veil," p. 315.

15. Wade, *Letters*, p. 211. Malcolm Brown, *The Politics of Irish Literature* (London: George Allen and Unwin, 1972), pp. 364–66, discusses this letter.

16. "Mr. Yeats as a Lyric Poet," *Saturday Review* (6 May 1899), pp. 553–54. Grossman, p. xxiii, takes this review as the "groundwork or conceptual prolegomenon for the study of *The Wind among the Reeds*."

17. Grossman, *Poetic Knowledge*, pp. 14–17.

18. W. B. Yeats, "Aedh Pleads with the Elemental Powers," *The Wind Among the Reeds* (London: Elkin Mathews, 1899), p. 74. Further references to this work appear in the text. As with *The Rose* poems, titles of individual poems are here capitalized as they appear in *The Variorum Edition of the Poems of W. B. Yeats*, ed. Peter Allt and Russell Alspach (New York: Macmillan, 1957).

19. Frank H. Murphy, *Yeats's Early Poetry* (Baton Rouge: Louisiana State University Press, 1975), p. 33–34.

20. W. B. Yeats, *Fairy and Folk Tales of the Irish Peasantry* (London: Walter Scott, 1888), p. 81.

21. "Irish National Literature II," *Bookman*, August 1895, in Frayne, I:366–73.

22. Grossman, *Poetic Knowledge*, p. 114.

23. Ibid., p. 19.

24. Ibid., p. 34.

25. Yeats, "The Trembling of the Veil," p. 336.

26. Ellmann, *Yeats*, p. 80.

27. Wade, *Letters*, p. 63.

28. Ibid., p. 434.

29. Yeats, "The Trembling of the Veil," p. 326.

30. Grossman, *Poetic Knowledge*, pp. 202–203.

31. Ibid., p. xiv.

conclusion

1. John O'Leary, *Recollections of Fenians and Fenianism* (London: Downey, 1896) I:31.

2. *Bookman*, January 1897, in *Uncollected Prose*, ed. John P. Frayne and Colton Johnson (London: Macmillan, 1975) II:34.

3. W. B. Yeats, "What is 'Popular Poetry'?" in *Essays and Introductions* (London: Macmillan, 1961), pp. 3–12.

4. *Irish Times*, 11 February 1908. The *Times* reported on Yeats's address to the National Literary Society.

5. William Irwin Thompson, *The Imagination of an Insurrection* (New York: Oxford University Press, 1967).

6. Letter to Olivia Shakespear, 1927, *The Letters of W. B. Yeats*, ed. Allan Wade (London: Rupert Hart-Davis, 1954), p.727.

7. Conor Cruise O'Brien "Passion and Cunning: An Essay on the Politics of W. B. Yeats," in *In Excited Reverie*, ed. A. Norman Jeffares and K. G. W. Cross (London: Macmillan, 1965), p. 258.

8. See F. S. L. Lyons, *Ireland Since the Famine* (Glasgow: Fontana/Collins, 1973), p. 523.

9. Wade, *Letters*, p. 808.

10. Lyons, *Famine*, p. 523.

11. George Moore, *Vale*, Vol. III of *Hail and Farewell!* (London: Heinemann, 1914), p. 291. Other volumes from the trilogy are *Ave* (1911) and *Salve* (1912), likewise published by Heinemann. Further references to *Hail and Farewell!* appear in the text.

12. Lyons, *Famine*, p. 504.

13. Thomas Flanagan, *The Year of the French* (New York: Holt, Rinehart, and Winston, 1979), p. 245.

14. Malcolm Brown, *The Politics of Irish Literature* (London: George Allen and Unwin, 1972), p. 389.

15. See Herbert Howarth, *The Irish Writers 1880–1940* (London: Rockliff, 1958), pp. 245–308, for a discussion of Joyce's use of Parnell.

16. *W. B. Yeats and T. Sturge Moore: Their Correspondence 1901–1937*, ed. Ursula Bridge (London: Routledge and Kegan Paul, 1953), p. 154.

17. O'Leary, *Fenians*, I:21.

selecteᗞ BIBLIOGRaphy

newspapeRs anᗞ jouRnals

An Claidheamh Soluis
Daily Express
Freeman's Journal
Irish Times
Leader
New Ireland Review
United Ireland
United Irishman

histoRy anᗞ society

Bew, Paul. *Land and the National Question in Ireland, 1858–82*. Atlantic High-
    lands, N.J.: Humanities Press, 1979.
Carty, James, ed. *Ireland from the Great Famine to the Treaty (1851–1921)*. Dublin:
    C. J. Fallon, 1951.
Clark, Samuel. *Social Origins of the Irish Land War*. Princeton: Princeton Univer-
    sity Press, 1979.
Crotty, Raymond D. *Irish Agricultural Production, Its Volume and Structure*. Cork:
    Cork University Press, 1966.
Cullen, L. M. *An Economic History of Ireland Since 1660*. London: Batsford, 1972.
Curtis, L. P., Jr. *Coercion and Conciliation in Ireland, 1880–1892: A Study in
    Conservative Unionism*. Princeton: Princeton University Press, 1963.
Davis, Thomas. *Prose Writings of Thomas Davis*. Ed. T. W. Rolleston. London:
    Walter Scott, [1889?].
Davitt, Michael. *The Fall of Feudalism in Ireland: or, The Story of the Land League
    Revolution*. London: Harper, 1904.

Donnelly, James S., Jr. *Landlord and Tenant in Nineteenth-Century Ireland*. Dublin: Gill and Macmillan, 1973.

Edwards, R. Dudley, and T. Desmond Williams, eds. *The Great Famine: Studies in Irish History, 1845–52*. Dublin, 1956; rpt. New York: New York University Press, 1957.

Ferguson, Sir Samuel. "A Dialogue Between the Head and Heart of an Irish Protestant." *Dublin University Magazine* 2 (11) (November 1833): 586–93.

Foster, Robert F. *Charles Stewart Parnell: The Man and His Family*. Atlantic Highlands, N.J.: Humanities Press, 1976.

Hooker, Elizabeth R. *Readjustments of Agricultural Tenure in Ireland*. Chapel Hill: University of North Carolina Press, 1938.

Larkin, Emmet. *The Historical Dimensions of Irish Catholicism*. New York: Arno, 1976.

———. *The Roman Catholic Church and the Creation of the Modern Irish Free State, 1878–1886*. Philadelphia: American Philosophical Society, 1975.

———. *The Roman Catholic Church in Ireland and the Fall of Parnell, 1888–1891*. Chapel Hill: University of North Carolina Press, 1979.

Lyons, F. S. L. *Charles Stewart Parnell*. London: Collins, 1977.

———. *Culture and Anarchy in Ireland, 1890–1939*. Oxford: Clarendon, 1979.

———. *The Fall of Parnell, 1890–91*. London: Routledge and Kegan Paul, 1960.

———. *Ireland Since the Famine*. Rev. ed. Glasgow: Fontana/Collins, 1973.

———. *The Irish Parliamentary Party, 1890–1910*. London: Faber and Faber, 1951.

Mansergh, Nicholas. *The Irish Question, 1840–1921: A Commentary on Anglo-Irish Relations and on Social and Political Forces in Ireland in the Age of Reform and Revolution*. 3rd ed. London: George Allen and Unwin, 1975.

Mitchel, John. *Jail Journal*. Dublin: Corrigan, 1864.

Moran, D. P. *The Philosophy of Irish Ireland*. 1905; Dublin: Duffy, 1907.

O'Brien, Conor Cruise. *Parnell and His Party, 1880–90*. Oxford: Clarendon, 1957.

O'Day, Alan. *The English Face of Irish Nationalism: Parnellite Involvement in British Politics 1880–86*. Dublin: Gill and Macmillan, 1977.

O'Faolain, Sean. *The Irish*. Rev. ed. Harmondsworth, Middlesex: Penguin, 1969.

O'Farrell, Patrick. *England and Ireland Since 1800*. London: Oxford University Press, 1975.

———. *Ireland's English Question: Anglo-Irish Relations 1534–1970*. New York: Schocken, 1971.

O'Grady, Standish James. *The Crisis in Ireland*. Dublin: Ponsonby, 1882.

———. *Selected Essays and Passages*. Dublin: Talbot, 1917.

———. *The Story of Ireland*. London: Methuen, 1894.

———. *Toryism and the Tory Democracy*. London: Chapman and Hall, 1886.

O'Hegarty, P. S. *A History of Ireland Under the Union, 1801 to 1922*. London: Methuen, 1952.

O'Leary, John. *Recollections of Fenians and Fenianism.* 2 vols. London: Downey, 1896.

O'Shea, Katharine. *Charles Stewart Parnell: His Love Story and Political Life.* 2 vols. New York: Doran, 1914.

Palmer, Norman D. *The Irish Land League Crisis.* New Haven: Yale University Press, 1940.

Paul-Dubois, L. *Contemporary Ireland.* Trans. T. M. Kettle. Dublin: Maunsel, 1908.

Pomfret, John. *The Struggle for Land in Ireland, 1800–1923.* Princeton: Princeton University Press, 1930.

Solow, Barbara L. *The Land Question and the Irish Economy, 1870–1903.* Cambridge: Harvard University Press, 1971.

Steele, E. D. *Irish Land and British Politics: Tenant-Right and Nationality, 1865–1870.* Cambridge: Cambridge University Press, 1974.

Strauss, Erich. *Irish Nationalism and British Democracy.* London: Methuen, 1951.

White, Terence de Vere. *The Anglo-Irish.* London: Gollancz, 1972.

lIteRaRy hIstoRy

Boyd, Ernest. *Ireland's Literary Renaissance.* Rev. ed. London: Grant Richards, 1923.

Brown, Malcolm. *The Politics of Irish Literature: From Thomas Davis to W. B. Yeats.* London: George Allen and Unwin, 1972.

Casey, Daniel J. and Robert E. Rhodes, eds. *Views of the Irish Peasantry, 1800–1916.* Hamden, Conn.: Archon, 1977.

Costello, Peter. *The Heart Grown Brutal. The Irish Revolution in Literature from Parnell to the Death of Yeats, 1891–1939.* Dublin: Gill and Macmillan, 1977.

Daly, Dominic. *The Young Douglas Hyde: The Dawn of the Irish Revolution and Renaissance, 1874–1893.* Totowa, N.J.: Rowman and Littlefield, 1974.

Deane, Seamus. "The Literary Myths of the Revival: A Case for their Abandonment." In *Myth and Reality in Irish Literature.* Ed. Joseph Ronsley. Waterloo, Ontario: Wilfrid Laurier University Press, 1977, pp. 317–29.

Duffy, Sir Charles Gavan, George Sigerson, and Douglas Hyde. *The Revival of Irish Literature.* London: T. Fisher Unwin, 1894.

Dunleavy, Gareth. *Douglas Hyde.* Lewisburg, Penn.: Bucknell University Press, 1974.

Eglinton, John et al. *Literary Ideals in Ireland.* London: T. Fisher Unwin, 1899.

Eglinton, John. *Two Essays on the Remnant.* Dublin: Whaley, 1894.

Fallis, Richard. *The Irish Renaissance.* Syracuse: Syracuse University Press, 1977.

Gregory, Lady Augusta. *Seventy Years: Being the Autobiography of Lady Gregory.* New York: Macmillan, 1974.

———, ed. *Ideals in Ireland.* London: At the Unicorn, 1901.

Howarth, Herbert. *The Irish Writers 1880–1940: Literature Under Parnell's Star.* London: Rockliff, 1958.

Hyde, Douglas. *Love Songs of Connacht.* Dublin: Gill, 1893.

Kelleher, John. "Matthew Arnold and the Celtic Revival." In *Perspectives of Criticism.* Ed. Harry Levin. Cambridge: Harvard University Press, 1950, pp. 197–221.

Loftus, Richard J. *Nationalism in Modern Anglo-Irish Poetry.* Madison: University of Wisconsin Press, 1964.

MacDonagh, Oliver. *The Nineteenth Century Novel and Irish Social History: Some Aspects.* Dublin: National University of Ireland, 1970.

Mercier, Vivian. "From Religious Revival to Literary Revival: Irish Protestantism in the Nineteenth Century." IASAIL Conference, Maynooth. 10 July 1979.

O'Connor, Frank. *The Backward Look: A Survey of Irish Literature.* London: Macmillan, 1967.

O'Driscoll, Robert, ed. *Theatre and Nationalism in Twentieth-Century Ireland.* Toronto: University of Toronto Press, 1971.

Ryan, W.P. *The Irish Literary Revival: Its History, Pioneers and Possibilities.* London: privately printed, 1894.

Taft, Maria H. "The Influence of Parnell on Irish Imaginative Literature." Diss., Trinity College, Dublin, 1971.

Thompson, William Irwin. *The Imagination of an Insurrection: Dublin, Easter 1916. A Study of an Ideological Movement.* New York: Oxford University Press, 1967.

Tynan, Katharine. *The Middle Years.* London: Constable, 1916.

Worth, Katharine. *The Irish Drama of Europe from Yeats to Beckett.* Atlantic Highlands, N.J.: Humanities Press, 1978.

SOMERVILLE AND ROSS

Collis, Maurice. *Somerville and Ross.* London: Faber and Faber, 1968.

Cronin, John. *Somerville and Ross.* Lewisburg: Bucknell University Press, 1972.

Flanagan, Thomas. "The Big House of Ross-Drishane." *Kenyon Review* 28 (1) (January 1966):54–78.

McMahon, Séan. "John Bull's Other Island: A Consideration of *The Real Charlotte* by Somerville and Ross." *Éire-Ireland* 3(4) (Winter 1968): 119–35.

Powell, Violet. *The Irish Cousins: The Books and Background of Somerville and Ross.* London: Heinemann, 1970.

Somerville, Edith, and Martin Ross. *The Big House of Inver*. London: Heinemann, 1925.

———. *Further Experiences of an Irish R.M.* London: Longmans and Green, 1908.

———. *In Mr. Knox's Country*. London: Longmans and Green, 1915.

———. *Irish Memories*. London: Longmans and Green, 1917.

———. *The Real Charlotte*. London: Ward and Downey, 1894.

———. *Some Experiences of an Irish R.M.* London: Longmans and Green, 1899.

———. *Stray-Aways*. London: Longmans and Green, 1920.

———. *Wheel-Tracks*. London: Longmans and Green, 1923.

GEORGE MOORE

Brown, Malcolm. *George Moore: A Reconsideration*. Seattle: University of Washington Press, 1955.

Cave, Richard. *A Study of the Novels of George Moore*. New York: Barnes and Noble, 1978.

Dunleavy, Janet E. *George Moore: The Artist's Vision, The Storyteller's Art*. Lewisburg: Bucknell University Press, 1973.

Farrow, Anthony. *George Moore*. Boston: Twayne, 1978.

Gerber, Helmut, ed. *George Moore in Transition: Letters to T. Fisher Unwin and Lena Milman, 1894–1910*. Detroit: Wayne State University Press, 1968.

Gilbert, Elliot L. "In the Flesh: *Esther Waters* and the Passion for Yes," *Novel* 12 (1) (Fall 1978):48–65.

Hone, Joseph. *The Life of George Moore*. New York: Macmillan, 1936.

Hughes, Douglas A., ed. *The Man of Wax: Critical Essays on George Moore*. New York: New York University Press, 1971.

Moore, George. *Confessions of a Young Man*. London: Swan Sonnenschein, 1888.

———. *A Drama in Muslin*. London: Vizetelly, 1886.

———. *Esther Waters*. London: Walter Scott, 1894.

———. *Evelyn Innes*. London: T. Fisher Unwin, 1898.

———. *Hail and Farewell!* Vol. I: *Ave*. London: Heinemann, 1911. Vol. II: *Salve*. London: Heinemann, 1912. Vol. III: *Vale*. London: Heinemann, 1914.

———. *Parnell and His Island*. London: Swan Sonnenschein, 1887.

———. *The Untilled Field*. London: T. Fisher Unwin, 1903.

———. *Vain Fortune*. London: Henry, 1891.

Owens, Graham, ed. *George Moore's Mind and Art*. Edinburgh: Oliver and Boyd, 1968.

eÒWARÒ MARtyn

Courtney, Sister Marie-Thérèse. *Edward Martyn and the Irish Theatre*. New York: Vantage, 1956.

Gwynn, Denis. *Edward Martyn and the Irish Revival*. London: Cape, 1930.

Martyn, Edward. *The Heather Field and Maeve*. London: Duckworth, 1899.

———. *Morgante the Lesser: His Notorious Life and Wonderful Deeds*. London: Swan Sonnenschein, 1890.

———. *The Tale of a Town and An Enchanted Sea*. London: T. Fisher Unwin, 1902.

GEORGE RUSSELL

Davis, Robert B. *George William Russell ("AE")*. Boston: Twayne, 1977.

Denson, Alan, ed. *Letters from AE*. London: Abelard-Schuman, 1961.

Kain, Richard, and James H. O'Brien. *George Russell (A.E.)*. Lewisburg: Bucknell University Press, 1976.

Russell, George. *The Candle of Vision*. London: Macmillan, 1918.

———. *The Earth Breath and Other Poems*. London: John Lane, 1897.

———. *The Future of Ireland and the Awakening of the Fires*. Dublin: n.p., 1897.

———. *Homeward Songs by the Way*. Dublin: Whaley, 1894.

———. *Ideals in Ireland: Priest or Hero?* Dublin: n.p., [1897?].

———. *Imaginations and Reveries*. Dublin: Maunsel, 1915.

———. *Letters from AE*. Ed. Alan Denson. London: Abelard-Schuman, 1961.

Summerfield, Henry. *That Myriad-Minded Man: A Biography of George William Russell "A.E." 1867–1935*. Gerrards Cross, Buckinghamshire: Colin Smythe, 1975.

W. B. yeats

Ellmann, Richard. *Yeats: The Man and the Masks*. New York: Macmillan, 1948.

Flannery, James. *W. B. Yeats and the Idea of a Theatre: The Early Abbey Theatre in Theory and Practice*. New Haven: Yale University Press, 1976.

Flannery, Mary. *Yeats and Magic: The Earlier Works*. Gerrards Cross, Buckinghamshire: Colin Smythe, 1977.

Grossman, Allen R. *Poetic Knowledge in the Early Yeats: A Study of "The Wind Among the Reeds."* Charlottesville: University Press of Virginia, 1969.

Harper, George Mills, ed. *Yeats and the Occult*. [Toronto?]: Macmillan, 1975.

Harris, Daniel. *Yeats: Coole Park and Ballylea*. Baltimore: Johns Hopkins University Press, 1974.

Hone, Joseph. *W. B. Yeats, 1865–1939*. London: Macmillan, 1942.

Jeffares, A. Norman. *W. B. Yeats: Man and Poet*. New Haven: Yale University Press, 1949.

Lynch, David. *Yeats: The Poetics of the Self*. Chicago: University of Chicago Press, 1979.

Marcus, Phillip L. *Yeats and the Beginning of the Irish Renaissance*. Ithaca: Cornell University Press, 1970.

Meir, Colin. *The Ballads and Songs of W. B. Yeats: The Anglo-Irish Heritage in Subject and Style*. London: Macmillan, 1974.

Murphy, Frank H. *Yeats's Early Poetry: The Quest for Reconciliation*. Baton Rouge: Louisiana State University Press, 1975.

Nathan, Leonard. *The Tragic Drama of William Butler Yeats: Figures in a Dance*. New York: Columbia University Press, 1965.

O'Brien, Conor Cruise. "Passion and Cunning: An Essay on the Politics of W. B. Yeats." In *In Excited Reverie: A Centenary Tribute to William Butler Yeats, 1865–1939*. Ed. A. Norman Jeffares and K. G. W. Cross. London: Macmillan, 1965, pp. 207–278.

O'Driscoll, Robert. *Symbolism and Some Implications of the Symbolic Approach: W. B. Yeats During the Eighteen-Nineties*. New Yeats Papers, 9. Dublin: Dolmen, 1975.

———, and Lorna Reynolds, eds. *Yeats Studies: An International Journal*. Shannon: Irish University Press, 1971.

Sidnell, Michael, George Mayhew, and David R. Clark. *Druid Craft: The Writing of "The Shadowy Waters."* Amherst: University of Massachusetts Press, 1971.

Skelton, Robin, and Ann Saddlemyer. *The World of W. B. Yeats*. Rev. ed. Seattle: University of Washington Press, 1967.

Smith, Peter H. "'Grown to Heaven Like a Tree': The Scenery of *The Countess Cathleen*." *Éire-Ireland* 14(3) (Fall 1979):65–82.

Torchiana, Donald T. *W. B. Yeats and Georgian Ireland*. Evanston: Northwestern University Press, 1966.

Ure, Peter. *Yeats the Playwright: A Commentary on Character and Design in the Major Plays*. New York: Barnes and Noble, 1963.

Whitaker, Thomas. *Swan and Shadow: Yeats's Dialogue with History*. Chapel Hill: University of North Carolina Press, 1964.

Yeats, W. B. *Autobiographies*. London: Macmillan, 1955.

———. *The Celtic Twilight: Men and Women, Dhouls and Faeries*. London: Lawrence and Bullen, 1893.

———. *Ideas of Good and Evil*. London: Bullen, 1903.

———. *John Sherman and Dhoya*. London: T. Fisher Unwin, 1891.

———. *The Letters of W. B. Yeats*. Ed. Allan Wade. London: Rupert Hart-Davis, 1954.

————. *Literatim Transcription of the Manuscripts of William Butler Yeats's The Speckled Bird*. Ed. William O'Donnell. Delmar, N.Y.: Scholars' Facsimiles and Reprints, 1976.

————. *Memoirs: Autobiography — First Draft, Journal*. Ed. Denis Donoghue. London: Macmillan, 1972.

————. *Poems*. London: T. Fisher Unwin, 1895.

————. *Poems*. London: T. Fisher Unwin, 1901.

————. *The Secret Rose*. London: Lawrence and Bullen, 1897.

————. *The Tables of the Law. The Adoration of the Magi*. London: R. Clay, 1897.

————. *Uncollected Prose*. Vol. I. Ed. John P. Frayne. London: Macmillan, 1970.

————. *Uncollected Prose*. Vol. II. Ed. John P. Frayne and Colton Johnson. London: Macmillan, 1975.

————. *The Variorum Edition of the Plays of W. B. Yeats*. Ed. Russell Alspach. New York: Macmillan, 1966.

————. *The Variorum Edition of the Poems of W. B. Yeats*. Ed. Peter Allt and Russell Alspach. New York: Macmillan, 1957.

————. *The Wind Among the Reeds*. London: Elkin Mathews, 1899.

Zwerdling, Alex. *Yeats and the Heroic Ideal*. New York: New York University Press, 1965.

index

shadowy heroes

was composed in 10-point VIP Palatino and leaded two points
with display type in hand-set Libra,
by Utica Typesetting Company, Inc.;
printed on 50-pound Warren acid-free Antique Cream paper,
Smyth-sewn and bound over boards in Columbia Bayside Linen,
by Maple-Vail Book Manufacturing Group, Inc.;
and published by

SYRACUSE UNIVERSITY PRESS
Syracuse, New York 13210